RAPTOR'S
PREY

11/29/03

RAPTOR'S PREY

Vietnam 1966-1967

G.K. STESIAK

Checkmate Productions
Howell, MI

25 percent of this book's net profits will be donated to the Michigan Vietnam Monuments Maintenance Fund.

Published by Checkmate Productions
366 N. Hughes Road
Howell, MI 48843

Publisher's Cataloging-in-Publication Data
Stesiak, G. K.
    Raptor's prey : Vietnam 1966-1967 / G. K. Stesiak — Howell, MI:
Checkmate Productions, 2001.
        p. ; cm.

        ISBN 0-9708740-0-6
    1. Stesiak, G.K. 2. Vietnamese Conflict, 1961-1975—Personal narratives. 3.
United States—Armed Forces—Medical personnel—Biography. I. Title. II.
Vietnam 1966-1967.

DS559.5 .S74   2002   2001087714
959.704/309/2   —dc21   CIP

06 05 04 03 02 • 6 5 4 3 2

Project Coordination by Jenkins Group, Inc. • www.bookpublishing.com
Cover design by Eric Norton

Printed in the United States of America

For my son, Kenneth Gerald . . .

It is not the span of time a man lives that will afford him the luxury of being remembered. Time on this earth is secondary to how a person lives his life; for those he touched, helped and loved will never forget him.

There was a time when you and I were known as "me and my arrow." I will never forget that, my son.

Although the pain never really goes away, it is a little easier to cope when I reflect on the fond memories of the time we spent together, from 6:25 A.M. on April 13, 1968 until 1:55 P.M. on April 3, 1990.

Sleep well, my son. Rest in peace . . . I still love you.

"The Bow"

Dad (Gerald Kenneth)

CONTENTS

Prologue   ix

Acknowledgments   xi

Chapter 1   TWO WEEKS TO GO   1

Chapter 2   HOW IT ALL BEGAN   10

Chapter 3   ARRIVING AT FORT CAMPBELL   29

Chapter 4   MOVEMENT TO VIETNAM   41

Chapter 5   ARRIVING IN VIETNAM   61

Chapter 6   BAPTISM OF FIRE   83

Chapter 7   INTRODUCTION TO THE BOONIES   104

Chapter 8   TAKING THE PLACE OF A DEAD MAN   123

Chapter 9   AN ENCOUNTER WITH THE NVA   137

Chapter 10   COMMUNICATING WITH CHARLIE   166

Chapter 11   HOA KHAN CHILDREN'S
             HOSPITAL—DA NANG   171

Chapter 12   HILL 358   186

Chapter 13   SURROUNDED BY CHARLIE   211

Chapter 14   CEASE FIRE TRUCE   222

Chapter 15   ENOUGH IS ENOUGH   231

Chapter 16   ATROCITIES   236

Chapter 17   MINEFIELD   249

Chapter 18   THE ULTIMATE EDUCATION   256

Chapter 19   A REPRIEVE   263

Chapter 20   THE LAST CASUALTY   281

Chapter 21   GOING HOME   294

Epilogue   *311*

PROLOGUE

T HE SIMPLE INTENT of this book is to portray what it was like to find oneself on the front lines of the Vietnam War as a United States paratrooper.

Although this book is a writing of fiction, it is based upon my time spent serving our country in the U.S. Airborne Army. Any similarity to real names and real persons, whether they served in Vietnam or not, is purely coincidental and is not meant to injure, slander or defame anyone. In fact, my actual medical platoon sergeant was a soldier's soldier. He lead by example and displayed courage and true leadership. Thanks to all true combat leaders in every war who exemplified true leadership while under fire—there were many.

This project was undertaken to fulfill a promise I made while in the army; a promise to my fellow medics to one day write about what it was like to be an airborne infantry medic in Vietnam. Many in my outfit knew I kept daily notes of our activities and encounters with the enemy. They offered encouragement and informed me of events I would have otherwise never been aware of. Most, if not all, knew I wanted to write a book of our experiences in the preparation of war and in war itself. I apologize for taking so long to write this story.

The time lines covered in this book, the army units, and the names of the search and destroy operations are real, which date from July 1964 through April 1967, and are a matter of military record.

FACT

The vast majority of those who went to Vietnam were there in various support roles, supporting those of us out on the line and in the line of fire. All who went to Vietnam though had a job to do. My job just happened to be that of a medic, an airborne infantry medic. My role in the war would lead me into combat, placing me on the edge of mankind's primordial past. Years ago men in battle threw stones at one another in an effort to do great bodily harm to their enemy. In the jungles of Vietnam, we too threw objects at one another, but our stones traveled at supersonic speed; they're called bullets.

There were 2.1 million people who went to Vietnam during the span of the Vietnam War. Of this number, less than 6,000 young men were airborne infantry medics. This story is about one of those "grunt" airborne infantry medics, Harry Spencer.

Although I am not a spokesman for any veteran, it is my belief that what separates the Vietnam Veteran from veterans of other wars is that when we came back we dared to pose a simple question—Why? The rest is history.

As a result of questioning our government, society has learned—support for its returning troops is paramount to ensure the veteran his or her rightful place upon return from serving their country. And like all veterans of previous wars, the Vietnam Veteran followed our nation's call to arms—nothing more, nothing less. In God and country we did trust.

The objective of this book is not meant to condemn our government or the military. It is a portrayal and dramatization of what any combat vet may have been subjected to in his training, and then his experiences in war. The book is written from a personal observation viewpoint.

So, sit back and take a trip with our leading character Harry Spencer. And remember as you read this book: War never is what you thought it would be.

ACKNOWLEDGMENTS

WITHOUT THE SUPPORT and expertise of the following people, this book would have never been published. Thanks to Nikki Stahl, production coordinator at The Jenkins Group, who pulled all the details together and who kept the project on target; Kelli Leader, for the cover design, also of The Jenkins Group; Keith King of Keith King & Associates for the many hours he spent promoting this book; Jack Devine and R. Michael Sand for their efforts in reaching out to the veterans community to support this book; Professor James Thomas for his guidance and encouragement while I wrote the manuscript; and Amy Sand, the first person to see the writing, and who edited the first three drafts for me. A special thank you to the copy editor, Pat Staten, who made my words and story come alive, and to Mareesa Orth, the proof editor who put the finishing touches on the writing. All of you encouraged and supported my efforts to write a story, which simply had to be told.

G.K. Stesiak

RAPTOR'S PREY

Chapter 1

TWO WEEKS TO GO

A S I SIT HERE contemplating what to write next in my diary, I think to myself, how in the world did I get myself in this predicament? What could I have done differently to not end up in a crack U.S. Army Airborne infantry outfit? My mind flashes back to when I first arrived here at Fort Campbell, Kentucky, the home of the 101st Airborne Division. It was late November of 1964 when a bus loaded with airborne candidates arrived here. It was then that I noticed a huge sign hanging over the base's intake compound that read:

A Rendezvous with Destiny.

At that time I was just eighteen. Given my background and lack of education, I did not understand the word "rendezvous." The second most striking things to register were simultaneous: the smell of coal used to heat the barracks and the smell of diesel fuel in the air. Queer as the environment was to me, the smell of coal in the air gave me the warm fuzzies. Growing up in Detroit in a working class neighborhood, one of the first scents in my life was the smell of coal burning to heat homes. Because of my ignorance in not knowing what that sign meant when I first arrived, I developed a thirst for knowledge, which would eventually cause me to document a journey I instinctively knew would one day be of some historical significance. Significant in that someone, somewhere has got to know what it feels like to not be in control of your life—life growing up with parents who were ill-prepared to raise seven kids, and life in the U.S. Airborne Army in the mid 1960s.

The daily routine for the past six months has begun with 5 A.M. reveille. Despite the fact I have finished with official training, which is supposed to prepare me for all this bullshit, the way they continue to treat us makes me feel as if I were still in boot camp or worse yet, the infamous jump school at Fort Benning, Georgia. Like every day previous to this one, it starts out with a scream from the dark:

"First call, you dogs of war! Up and at 'em. Now!" bellows the Platoon Sergeant, "Let's go . . . let's go, on your feet."

Startled, new guys in the platoon jump like Pavlov's dogs at the command, trying in vain to please the monsters who mysteriously appeared. "You," screams the sergeant or sergeants. Whoever looks up or says, "Yes, Sergeant," is rewarded by the next command, "Get down and give me twenty (pushups)."

At this point in my life I have been in the service nearly two years. At nineteen years of age, I am street-smart and airborne-wise. I smile to myself in amusement and disdain of the deployment of such insane tactics. I suspect, however, such tactics are designed to get us to respond in a positive manner in a combat situation. Obedience without questioning may save your life and the life of your buddy. I further suspect the psychology will serve some of us well in combat, but to others, such tactics may serve to be overbearing to the point of injury or death.

If you're the poor bastard who gets caught moving too slowly at first call, or for whatever reason the sergeant decides you need some punishment for doing or not doing, he will put you on display as an example to the others. And as you're doing the pushups, you will be ridiculed unmercifully by him. If he does not like the speed of your pushups, or your posture while doing them, or the volume at which you shout out the count, you are in hot water. There is no way you can win, and you can never please him. I further suspect we are being whipped into a frenzy for the sole purpose of unleashing our building anger upon the enemy. But we all cope, though in a ubiquitous manner as a result of our training. The chant and beat has been drilled into our heads: *Here we go—All the way—Airborne—All the way—Every day.* This simple refrain is designed to push us in difficult times and situations for the remainder of our lives, be it in Vietnam or further down the road.

We have thirty minutes from the time lights go on at 0430 hours until we stand in formation for reveille at 0500 hours—thirty minutes to straighten our bunk areas, shit, shower and shave (for those of us who need to shave) and "break starch." Following the usual formalities of a head count and general statements by the first sergeant, who is the head non-commissioned officer of our company, we begin our first two-mile run of the day.

At this moment in time I hold the rank of Specialist Fourth Class, or, as we called it, a "Spec 4" and I am also the senior member of the medical platoon. Those who have been in the service longer than I outrank me, but no one has been in my platoon longer. This feeling, for whatever it's worth, gives me a sense of power and confidence. Newly transferred guys have arrived because the brass wants us to be at full combat strength. (There are ten guys to a squad, four squads to a platoon, four platoons to a company, and four companies to a battalion.)

Because I am a medic, I am assigned to Headquarters Company; the remaining companies are titled A, B, and C or, the military way of saying it, Alpha, Bravo, and Charlie Companies. The battalion is known as the 1st of the 501st, of the 101st Airborne Division—the famous Screaming Eagles. The 1/501st is also known by its nickname, the Geronimos—yes, named after the Indian chief, Geronimo. Without knowing it, I have made my way into one of the most decorated fighting machines in U.S. Army history.

A few months earlier, sensing I was on the cutting edge of war, I purchased a diary. It is against regulations to keep a diary on the frontlines, but I felt compelled to do so. The guys in the platoon at first kidded me some about this, but when they realized I was serious, their words encouraged me: "If you're going to keep a record of this shit, then tell it like it really is. Tell it straight. Tell it true. And you better put my fucking name in it, too." Then we laughed.

With just two weeks to go until our departure, I read everything I can about Vietnam. I even read over and above what they are teaching us. Yes, I am scared, but I know I have to go. It is, after all, the *honorable* thing to do. My father did it; all my friends' fathers are veterans of World War II. I had been brought up watching *Victory At Sea* and other war pictures every Sunday morning. In effect, I had been born and programmed to go to war.

My thoughts are interrupted. Steve Best, a fellow medic, sticks an old issue of a military newspaper, *The Stars and Stripes*, in my face. He smiles satirically, points to an article and says, "Look at this man; more medics being knocked off in 'Nam. Boy, aren't we going to have fun?"

I don't smile; I just grab the paper from him and notice it's dated January 1966. It turns out to be an article describing a November battle in the Ia Drang Valley located in the Central Highlands of South Vietnam. The writer spared no details. It is explicit. In an attempt to prove to the world that they, the North Vietnamese Army, could meet us head on and beat us, threw everything they had at the U.S. Army's 1st Air Calvary Division. Within two weeks, 2,000 American, South Vietnamese, and North Vietnamese soldiers died. Reports indicated that bodies were piled on top of bodies in the rush to have them removed by Vietnam's jeep—the Huey helicopter. As I scanned the article, I got the impression we got our asses kicked. From the Army's point of view we won—because more of the enemy died than did Americans.

As I continue to read the details of the battle, my mind flashes to the summer of 1965. Our sister brigade was shipping out to Vietnam. As they drove by our battalion area in what we called "cattle trucks," I waved goodbye to many faces I had come to know. They were all hyped, yelling and hooting like a bunch of bloodthirsty combat veterans. But deep down I was sad and felt like running away, but where would I run? Where could I go? As the last of them passed by us, I turned to go back inside my barracks and thought, God be with you guys. Some of you, maybe even most of you, will not be coming back. Goodbye, my fellow troopers, goodbye. Once back in my barracks, I lay on my bunk and listened to the planes taking off one by one. It seemed to last an hour before the dreaded silence of reality set in. They're gone. They're actually gone. Holy shit. Who's next?

A few months later, I read a news article about some of those very troops in *The Stars and Stripes*. It said that a North Vietnamese

Army regiment ambushed a company-size patrol of 120 men. (A regiment is considerably larger in strength than a company of U.S. Infantry Paratroopers.) Given the fact men are spread out about five yards from one another, it would have required at least a 1,000-man force to ambush a company-size patrol. Their confidence to take on my fellow paratroopers served to undermine my confidence in who I thought we were and that for which we stood.

According to the reporter, the enemy's plan was pulled off with precision and was almost flawless in its execution. However, the North Vietnamese underestimated the amount of fight we had in us. I'm sure the enemy felt once the young, inexperienced company commander realized he was outnumbered, he would simply surrender. So, with ammunition running low, casualties mounting and the paratroopers outnumbered seven to one, it came down to hand-to-hand combat. Street fighters taught to be paratroopers—fighting people born in the jungle to be jungle fighters.

But rather than surrendering, I know what was echoing in that company commander's head. He had the same training all paratroopers had—the cadence, the rhythm of boots hitting the pavement in unison, the chant: *Here we go—Airborne—All the way.* So instead of surrendering the young captain called an air strike on his own position. To you, my captain, wherever you are, *Airborne, Sir. WETSU! (We Eat This Shit Up.)*

Up until this battle no one would have guessed American soldiers had what it took to win such a battle, especially with the overwhelming odds. In fact, we only heard about such heroic measures from stories of the previous "real wars"—"the big ones." However, one thing grows increasingly clear to me: Real heroes lie six feet under. *Anyone who says he is a hero has never seen combat. Heroes die once and don't tell; cowards live to tell. Those who may have performed heroic deeds are the first to admit that they are not heroes.*

Ninety percent of the men in the company, which was being overrun, were either killed or injured. Those who died made the ultimate sacrifice. They allowed themselves to be put in such a position because their country wanted them there. Ours is not to question why; ours is simply to do and to die. I sat mesmerized by what I was recalling, and I also prayed not to be put in such a position but, if need be, it would be.

After all, going to war is the natural thing to do. Soldiers of other wars are proud of what they did for God and country. Besides, if I didn't go, what would my parents think? What would my friends and relatives say? My gut tells me war is wrong, but all my teachings mandate that I have to go. Hell, if John Wayne portrayed it, Aldo Ray acted it, and Audie Murphy went through it, so can I. Right?

As I continue to mull over the news article, my platoon sergeant, Alvin Flock, a thirty-three-year-old black guy, enters our barracks. He and I never got along from the get-go. Flock carries himself with cock assuredness. He possesses a demeanor that exudes dominance and strength. He stands approximately 5'8" and weighs about 180 pounds. His body is ripped with muscle, which he meticulously maintains by working out at the gym five days a week. To say this guy is in love with himself would be an understatement. The men in the platoon fear and respect him; however, I don't think much of him. He is intoxicated with the power he holds over us. He reminds me of my father, and that doesn't sit well with me. I hate my father for he, too, carried the proverbial big stick and wasn't at all shy about using it. Standing at the bay entrance, hand on hips, Flock scans the room and sees me sitting here, then barks, "What's up with you, trooper? You bored? Get down and give me twenty! Now!" I get up from my bunk, not with the speed of a new guy, but with the begrudging acceptance of a seasoned veteran.

Once I finish doing the pushups, I jump to my feet so as not to show any sign of strain. I look him in the eyes, letting my stare say what my lips cannot. If I do, it will likely lead to a Dishonorable Discharge. A "DD" from the military is analogous to a death sentence. I could never vote, own property, or get a job in any form of civil service. It would be a cloud over my head for the rest of my life. No, I won't go off. He knows it. In fact, he reminds us every time any one of us begins to display an attitude of belligerence.

Because of my past, I'm pretty much at home here. My parents inadvertently helped prepare me for all of this bullshit. They were the sergeants in their home and personified physical and mental cruelty. All I have to do is realize that I am under the same form of constraint. Actually, it is a little easier to take here in the army. The army is more consistent. They don't keep you guessing when they will hammer you.

There are rules, regulations, policies, and witnesses. I cannot say the same regarding my upbringing. Compared to those who came from a loving family and cannot adjust to the nonsense, it's a cakewalk for me—most of the time.

Done hazing me, Flock announces his reason for storming into our barracks. Normally he stays out of our direct barracks area, but he has a detail for a few of us (and of course, me) to go to—a burial detail. A guy from Bells, Tennessee was killed in action. Word has it he was a medic, and medics will serve as honor guards burying him.

The next day, five of us medics chosen by Flock are driven to Bells, a small town not far from Fort Campbell. As we congregate outside the funeral home, we can't help but notice a number of good-looking, charming Southern beauties. The Southern belles are sending out all sorts of estrogen signals. I think it is strange—making a pass at a funeral—but after all, I'm just nineteen years old. So all five of us ruggedly handsome U.S. Paratroopers with body-builder physiques return their signals through every pore of our bodies. We're confident in our uniforms; paratroopers wear decidedly different looking uniforms than the standard army uniform.

Still, we have a solemn duty to perform. We have to bury one of our own, even if he wasn't a paratrooper. He was an infantry medic. We put aside our horny feelings and bury our fallen brother with honors—as sharp and professional as one would expect from a military funeral. The staccato precision of our movements brings us praise from the officer in charge of the detail.

However, there is one minor glitch. As we fold the flag, the young widow cries out with total abandon, speaking towards the coffin. "Johnnie! Johnnie, our baby will come to know you! I promise."

All of us shot a fleeting glance toward Johnnie White, a fellow medic. His eyes show shock and fear. He, too, has a wife and a small child. It seems as if he is playing out his own funeral, and he is rattled. Christ, we all know the life expectancy of a medic in combat is very short. In medical school we were taught if the enemy ambushes us, they would first assign shooters to take out the radio operator—to cut communication. Then they'll go after the machine-gunner—to kill firepower. And if that doesn't work, once the firefight begins, they will kill the first person moving who responds to the cry of "medic." That will effectively kill the only source of life support. They will kill one of us—the medics!

Once the formalities end, those lovely not-too-subtle Southern belles spring into action. A tall blond with flowing hair, a flawless smile, and green eyes hands a note to a fellow medic, Larry Gasberich. The note contains their names and phone numbers in bold handwriting. It is then that the good looking blond flashes a seductive smile while spinning on her heels, and states, "Now, ya'll come back and see us some time, ya'll hear?" As she turns, our eyes meet. She then makes a gesture with her eyebrows that I have never seen before, but I certainly knew what it means. Her fluid stride mesmerizes me as she struts away like a filly in heat. As she walks away we all look at each other and simultaneously shout a paratrooper's response to a stimulating encounter—"Airborne!"

On the way back to Fort Campbell, we begin making plans for a three-day pass this upcoming weekend to take those girls up on their invitation. However, the problem is transportation. Gasberich has a XKE V-12 Jaguar, a two-seater convertible. Obviously, Larry comes from a wealthy background, but he tries to fit in with the rest of us. After a discussion, it comes down to the three of us—Larry Palm, Larry Gasberich, and me will make the trip back to Bells. The other guys beg off. No money, no suitable clothes, no transportation.

The night before our Friday morning departure, I decide not to go. It would be too cramped for the three of us in his Jaguar. Instead, I decide to take the Greyhound bus back to Detroit to say goodbye to family and friends prior to shipping out to Vietnam. I really don't think I will make it back from 'Nam, so I want to spend some time with my siblings. I have a six-year-old brother and a four-year-old sister, whom I adore. I want them to see me one more time . . . just in case.

While at home, I live and laugh with friends in total abandon. By blind luck, one of my friend's parents is throwing a graduation party for a younger kid. There I meet up with my long-time love, Beatrice Davis—a girl I want to think will one day become my wife. She is going to University of Michigan and is in her second year. Bea stands five feet and weighs about one hundred pounds. I met her in the ninth grade. She is a bundle of energy and inherited the genes of her

Japanese mother. Coupled with genes from an English/German father, she is striking. From that first look in band class, I knew that someday she would become my wife. I know most of those present at the party. The older ones exchange their experiences since graduation. They run down the list of who's where, who's in jail, who's in college.

As the evening wears on, a guy I have known for years, John Yard—a stocky, red-faced Kentucky boy—asks me, "Harry, do you think you'll make it?" His tone is solemn and serious.

I respond honestly, "I don't know, man. I could get lucky. I hope I'll do just fine, but there are no guarantees."

"Man, oh, man," he shakes his head. "Harry, how did you get yourself into this shit?"

I take the opportunity to cleanse my soul, like a young boy in a confessional booth. I have to tell someone. Up until now no one besides Bea knows what I have been through and why. Bea and I communicated via letters at least monthly and kept each other current on our lives.

Chapter 2

HOW IT ALL BEGAN

THREE WEEKS PRIOR to graduation, I pulled a stupid, stupid stunt. I left work one Friday night, in May of 1964. I worked as a cashier at Wrigley's Supermarket, and a friend of mine, Jim Palmeriski, picked me up to go to Daly's Burgers Drive In. When I got in his car, I was thinking how happy I was that I had finished another forty-hour workweek. I had gotten paid, had $53 in my pocket, and was anxious to check out those beautiful chicks, driving their daddys' beautiful cars.

Out of nowhere, my friend Jim pulled out a gun, stuck it in my ribs and growled, "OK, you fuck, give me your money." I recoiled in shock.

"What the hell are you doing, Jim? Get that shit away from me!" I told him, half demanding and half scared.

He smiled and said, "Pretty real looking, huh?" Laughing, he slapped me on the back of the head. "Here, take a look," he said and handed me the gun. Grasping the gun, I was impressed by how real it looked and felt.

As he drove, we made small talk about cars and girls and what we would be doing after graduation. It was an unusually warm May night; our windows were down, and he was driving his dad's '63 Pontiac Bonneville; all was right by the world.

Then we spotted a hitchhiker, some greaseball-looking dude. For whatever reason, when I saw this guy I told Jim to pick him up. As we drove on with the greaseball in the back seat, out of the blue I turned and pointed the pistol at him and yelled, "Hey, greaseball, how much money you got?" I didn't really mean a damn thing I said. I was just trying to scare the shit out of him.

He muttered, "Ah, not much man, just some change." All the time I was smiling because I had no intentions on going through with the charade. After all, I had fifty-three bucks in my pocket.

So this guy's demeanor suddenly goes from "I'm bad," to "Here, Sir, all I've got is a quarter."

A quarter, I thought, a lousy fucking quarter. The guy then hands me the money and begs Jim to stop the car, like right now, saying, "If you let me out right here I won't tell anyone; just let me out now."

Jim slowed the car and pulled over to the curb. With the car still in motion, I decided to let the guy in on the prank. I turned to face him in the back of the car, but he was so shook up that he jumped out just as I flipped his quarter back. Well, Jim panicked, floored the car, and off we went. Oh well, we thought, what a pussy. He didn't even stick around long enough for us to tell him we were just pulling his leg. What an asshole.

John is laughing his head off. "Harry," he snorts, "tell me you're making this up? This is too funny, man! You've got to be kidding me."

My eyes grow wide. Here I am, confessing something I am deeply ashamed of, and this asshole's laughing at me. "Wait, wait," I said, "there's more."

Once I got back to my parents' home that night around midnight, I took in some TV before going to bed. I was chilled, kicked back and watching the "Tonight Show" with Steve Allen, when I heard this pounding at the front and rear doors almost simultaneously. A voice boomed from the front door, "Detroit Police—open this door now!" At the same time, I heard the back door being broken down. Holy shit, I thought to myself, what's going on?

My mother slept on a foldout sofa bed in the living room, right next to the front door. She jumped up and opened the door as I headed her way in a defensive stride. The cop pushed her aside and came straight toward me. "Are you Harold Spencer?" he asked in a harsh tone.

Scared, I answered, "Yes, why?"

"Why," he shouted, "you're under arrest, you piece of shit."

"What for?" I demanded.

"What for?" pleaded my mother.

"For armed robbery," stated the cop as he manhandled me into submission.

Holy shit! Holy shit! This has got to be a big mistake, I thought.

My heart was racing. The cops grabbed me from behind and pulled my arms backwards with such force I thought I would fall over on my face. At that point, I started to get pissed.

"Ma," I said, "Ma, it is a joke! I'll straighten it out when I get to the police station. Don't worry!" I yelled as the cops led me away. "It was just a joke, Ma."

The cuffs were cutting off the circulation to my hands. While walking to the police car I asked as politely as I could, "Do you guys think you can loosen these cuffs?"

The reply was a barrage of insults all meant to humiliate, embarrass, and scare the living shit out of me. "Shut up you little punk. You're going to jail for at least fifteen years. Get used to it."

As I learned at home, no matter what I said, I was not going to win. So I shut up. The cops kept asking me questions, but I remained silent. I figured, when I get to the police station, I'll simply tell them the whole story and everything will be just fine.

When I got there, I saw Jim Palmeriski and his father sitting on a bench, but Jim wasn't handcuffed. The cops marched me right up to the desk sergeant, who stood up, walked around his desk, put his face into mine, and with a dead serious tone asked, "OK punk, where did you get the brilliant idea to hold somebody up?" I said nothing.

"My name, young man, is Sosnowski, Sergeant Sosnowski. What's yours?"

I bargained, "If you'll just loosen these cuffs, I'll tell you."

Smack. He hit me right across the face. "I'm going to ask you one more time, punk; where did you come up with the brilliant idea to hold someone up?"

I twitched with pain from the cuffs. Unfortunately, the sergeant saw that as a sign of aggression. Smack! He hit me again.

"OK, OK," I said. "I watch TV a lot."

Just then, Jim's father interjected. "For God's sake, his hands are turning purple, loosen his cuffs, will ya?"

The cops capitulated; my cuffs were taken off, and I was thrown into a cell. To make a long story short, I went to court and was given the choice: jail or service? Well, guess what? I *volunteered* to go into the service! However, to expunge my record, I must serve my country and come out with an honorable discharge. That was fine by me. At the time I had no intentions of going to college. Yeah, I could have gotten a job in one of the many factories that dotted the Detroit metro area, but what the hell, it was a ticket out of my parents' home—by my observations, not a bad trade-off.

Two weeks after graduation, on July 1 1964, I entered the world of the U.S. Army. Basic training took place at Fort Knox, Kentucky. After sizing up the other recruits, I realized I had a mental edge. While still in civilian clothes, we stepped off the bus while the sergeants eyed us individually. I didn't know any better, so when I noticed a sergeant giving me the eye, I gave it right back to him. Mistake number one.

"You!" screamed the sergeant, "Baby boy, front and center. Get your scrawny white ass right here, right now," he said, pointing to the ground by his feet.

That was my indoctrination to the world of the U.S. Army. And it got a lot worse, but suffice it to say, not as bad as jump school.

Just before we graduated from advance infantry training in Fort Gordon, Georgia, a couple of close friends—we called ourselves the Three Musketeers—and I got together to see the town. While in the town of Augusta I decided, since it was my birthday, to get a paratrooper's tattoo. Well, I should have known better, but I went ahead anyway. I mean, how tough can jump school be? Right?

As the guy was gouging my left arm, I heard him state rather casually, "I hear that fifty percent of all who go to jump school washout."

I looked at him in shock and gulped. It was then I remembered the airborne recruiter's admonition. "Most who go to jump school won't cut it." I squirmed on the stool and thought, well, here's another fine mess you've gotten yourself into, Spencer, you dumb shit!

At that, the tattoo artist reared back in his stool, shook his head and asked, "Do you want me to try and change it before I go any further?"

Now my fucking pride was on the line.

I gulped again and took a deep breath. With false bravado I managed to say to the guy, "Just do it." I'll handle the consequences one way or another. It can't possibly be that tough to complete jump school. In the meantime, Terry and Louie, my two buddies, were cracking up.

After they stopped laughing, Louie managed to say, "Harry, you stupid son of a bitch! Have him change it."

I thought, laugh at me, will you? I'll show you, you . . . I turned my head to look away from Terry and Louie and told the tattoo guy once again, with stronger yet false bravado, "Just finish the goddamn tattoo!"

However, inside I was dying. My heart was racing, and I found it difficult to breathe just sitting there. I tried to suppress the thoughts running through my head but couldn't. What the fuck have I done now? And then somewhere deep down within me a little voice from within asks, "What the hell are you doing, Spencer? Stop this nonsense!" But I did not heed even my own inner alarm bell.

JUMP SCHOOL: NOVEMBER 1964

As the bus pulled into Fort Benning, we were on higher ground than the majority of the compound. That allowed for a quick view of the rows and rows of barracks laid out before us. In the foreground lay an airstrip. I saw a plane taking off, which appeared to be at the same elevation as our bus. I thought, wow, this is too cool. And then we heard it . . . the beat of boots hitting the ground in unison and the chant, "*Here we go—All the way—Every day—Airborne—Wine—Women—No good—Blood—Guts—So good—Airborne . . . .*" The chants seemed to be coming from all directions. The sight of the T-shirted jump school students inspired me. Man, I thought, they look impressive. I was totally geeked.

As our bus pulled up to our barracks, we were met by a group of sergeants who ran up to the bus as it slowed and began beating on its sides. "Let's go you sorry-ass bastards. Let's go, let's go."

We filed out of the bus to more shouts, more screams, and conflicting directions. "Fall in. Move! Move! Move! Nobody ever walks around here . . . ever. You (directed at whoever was dumb enough to look around), you," his voice grew louder, more demanding, "I'm talking to you, soldier," His hand smacked me on the back. I instinctively turned, part of me wanting to scream—you talking to me? And part of me was full of dread that I had done something wrong.

"Yes, you, motherfucker, get down and give me twenty."

I dropped to the ground like I had been hit by a bullet, knocking off twenty with no effort whatsoever, and then joined the forming platoon. As I dropped my duffel bag next to me, I felt the area where my tattoo was; it felt warm and wet. A trickle of blood was slowly making its way down my arm. Ooooh, shit. I had bandaged it, but it was soaking through the gauze dressing. Fortunately, I had a long-sleeve dress khaki shirt on. November in Georgia is cold, even for a Yankee.

After the command, "Atten-Hut!" the biggest sergeant I had seen in the army staged himself directly in front of us. His uniform fit him like a glove. He must have been 6'5" tall—Jesus, was he a big guy. And then he began, "You boys are the sorriest, puniest bunch of punks I have ever seen. You've got a lot of fucking nerve to think you're good enough to be here, let alone thinking you can become a United States Army Paratrooper! In the next three weeks at least fifty percent of you will not make it through the training." I gulped on that one. "You'll come to realize you're simply not good enough. But, we need people to *not* pass this test of mind and body. We want those of you who flunk out to go back to the regular army and tell them how crazy our demands are. And when you crawl out of here on your yellow belly, I am going to kick your ass and I guarantee you'll get the worst possible assignment in this man's army. *But*, not before we use up your energies here first. We need cowards who can't cut the mustard to pull KP, dig ditches, and clean latrines. Real men don't have time for that bullshit."

As he droned on, my stomach felt as if someone had stabbed me. I felt weak and had hot flashes. No, hang on, Spencer, I told myself. Hold on; don't panic. While growing up, my father would administer similar scare tactics, but Christ, I never felt this before. I struggled against the signals my body sent to my brain.

"Now," the sergeant continued, "if anyone wants out, say so now. I can respect a man who knows his limits."

Jesus Christ, I had to tell somebody. I was sicker than a dog. Something was terribly wrong. No, I didn't want to give up, but I was sick. I gulped back, trying to contain the fluids within. Suddenly several guys raised their hands out of the same fear I felt; I'm sure of that. Fortunately, that helped. I stood my ground. I waved the storm within.

Minutes later I was among a new bunch of guys at the barracks. None of them were familiar looking to me. Many had obviously been in the service longer than I. I was an E-2, just one paygrade above the E-1 entry level. The others in my platoon were PFC's, E-3 and up in rank, and older than me by an average of two years. My new name was number 644. That number was taped to my helmet and stenciled across the back of my fatigue shirts. There were 854 men who would go through everything that I would in the next three weeks. Then I remembered the big, tough-looking sergeant who greeted us when he stated, "At least fifty percent of you will not make it through jump school." As I made my way to my bunk, I thought about Louie and Terry. I was without my fellow musketeers for the first time in four months. I was without my support group—on my own.

A typical day began at 4 A.M. with the ubiquitous barking of the Sergeants. God, I thought, don't they ever sleep? We had ten minutes to shit, shower, and shave. We did not have to clean anything else— that would be done while we were out in the training fields by those who couldn't cut it. The same sergeant's words come back to me, "And before we release you to the worst possible assignment in the army, we are going to use your energies up here first. We need people to . . ." Yeah, I thought, but not me buddy!

After a couple of days of heavy exercise and training, I realized my tattoo would not heal over. I concocted a sick call story to go see a medic at the battalion aid station. I told a sergeant I had a terrible headache that needed attention. Instinctively I knew I had to keep my tattoo a secret from everyone for fear they might blow the whistle on me. Once at the aid station for a quick exam, I confided in a medic about my bleeding tattoo. Fortunately and without comment, he dressed the wound and gave me some extra gauze and ointment to protect it and help it heal. His only admonition was for me to keep the sergeants from seeing it. "They're sure to break you if they catch wind you have it," he said. I was grateful for the only display of humanity I have seen since being in the army. As I thanked him profusely, I prayed the sergeants wouldn't ask me to take off my bandage, which was plainly visible because we exercised and ran in T-shirts only.

The pace was incredible. The drill instructor's (DI's) were constantly barking and constantly monitoring our every move. It was tantamount to passive euthanasia of the former self. They were remaking us, reprogramming us. Our minds were being altered. We were going through a mental transformation without knowing it. The effects will be permanent,—to the positive for some, to the negative for others.

After number call, as opposed to roll call, we ran for about thirty minutes. Each stride had the same cadence and chant: *"Airborne— All the way—Every day."* More words were introduced at this stage of the game, *"If and when I'm called to die, I'll die proud and here is why,"* and we repeated, *"Airborne—All the way—Every day. We are the toughest on this Earth—Because we're tough, we'll die first— Airborne—All the way!"* Our songs grew louder and longer the more we ran.

The DIs got off on having us run past regular army personnel on the base. As we passed by them during our morning run, we would respond to their cadence calls a lot louder. Thirty some guys running in tight formation and in perfect unison of mind and body was an impressive sight and sound. Every man's boot was hitting the pavement in perfect synchronization, every man's clap of the hands hitting together to form a beat or tempo. As we ran past those who were not paratroopers during our three-to-five-mile runs, we took subtle notice of their responses to our presence. We were, so to speak, strutting our stuff. Those who saw and heard us knew we were the chosen ones— the first to go to combat should the situation warrant it.

Once we completed the run, we'd line up at the mess hall. More than 300 to 400 guys lined up in single file, five feet apart, on a winding, twisting sidewalk, at the position of parade rest. The other 300 to 400 guys would eat at a different mess hall. Speaking was prohibited. Every time the guy in front of you moved, you came to the position of attention, stepped smartly forward, stopped when he stopped, and went back to the position of parade rest—precision personified even in the chow line.

If one of us fidgeted once too often, one of the sergeants would shout, "Number 644, get down and give me twenty," or, whatever number he arbitrarily picked. He kept a clipboard and recorded various infractions to keep a tally of those who screwed up too often. Too many goof-ups and the cadres pressed in, like raptors stalking their prey. In an effort to weed us out, to make us quit jump school, they would attempt to devour us—not just physically, but mentally as well.

Guys were quickly cracking under the pressure. A soldier who was calling it quits would typically put his hands in the air, shrug his shoulders, lower his head, and state, "sergeant, I want out, I've had enough. I can't take it anymore. I quit."

The nearby sergeant would then call everyone's attention to the man and make a spectacle of him. "Boy, what did you say? You want to quit? You can't take it anymore? Say it one more time for all of us to hear."

The man had to publicly announce to all within earshot his intentions to quit. Once said, the guy was quickly led away by three or more sergeants who pushed and pulled at him for further humiliation—a lesson for those of us still remaining.

Every time we'd see someone crack it served to strengthen those of us that remained. My confidence, however, was checked every time I thought about my bandaged arm. I was scared stiff they'd find out. One week into jump school, I still managed to hide the tattoo from the guys in my barracks. I took showers with the bandage still on. Of course there was the casual question every now and then, "Hey, man, what did you do to your arm?" I just gave them some cock and bull story, and, for the most part, they bought it. But how long could I keep it a secret?

I knew I would need some help, so I purposely befriended a couple of guys in my platoon. I felt confident enough to confide in them—I needed some form of insurance. I wanted them to shield me from the sergeants who always seemed to be walking among the rows of men when we were at the fitness field for daily calisthenics. They agreed to help me. I felt I had chosen them wisely. I took comfort in their concerns for my secret. However, they were paying a high price to help me. Every time a sergeant got close enough to examine my bandage, one of the two would cough uncontrollably or spit or laugh —anything to distract the sergeant. Man, after one week of jump school, how much longer could I get away with this? Between them, my new friends had performed some 2,000 pushups to cover for me. And then in the beginning of the second week my luck ran out.

Two days into the second week, while stripping off our fatigue shirts and getting ready for P.T. (physical training), a Sergeant grabbed me by my left arm, the one with the bandage. It had healed some and wasn't too tender until someone grabbed it, like the sergeant just did. Zap—pain.

"And what do we have here, 644?" he asked.

Oh, shit! This is it. I've had it. Damn. Now what? I involuntarily jerked from his grasp.

"Nothing," I said as I turned away from him, "Just a cut I got in Advanced Infantry Training at Fort Gordon." I was hoping the command for the first exercise would begin.

"Well, let's just see how injured you are," he mocked as he pulled tenderly at the bandage. A minute later he exclaimed, "Oh, my, what have we here?" His face was beaming with excitement. At first he was having a hard time comprehending what the tattoo was with the amount of ointment and the scab over it. He continued to study it and finally realized what it was.

Then, as if he'd heard the best joke of his life, he said, "My, oh, my, looky what we have here!" He called out to the others. "Sergeants Bloom and Lang, come over here. You won't *believe* what I found." The fucker was jubilant. In fact, he was beside himself, that cocksucker!

When the other two joined him, they all cracked up. One yelled at the top of his lungs, "Gentlemen, we have a United States Paratrooper among us. It says so right here." He slammed his fist into my arm with such force a tingle ran all the way down my forearm, like he hit a nerve.

That's it, I thought, it's time to do or die. I'd played this scenario out in my head a hundred times, if not more. I'd seen at least a couple hundred guys give up before me, and said to myself, not me guys. You can do anything you want, but I'm not quitting. How could I? I'd have live down the fact I have a paratrooper tattoo but wasn't a paratrooper! No, I won't quit. My tattoo was dripping blood from the DI's blow, but I ignored the blood, flicking it off my hand as it trickled down my arm.

I felt about as confident as a one-legged, clawless cat on thin ice as he continued: "Well, Mr. Paratrooper. May I call you Mr. Paratrooper, 644?"

I knew he wasn't looking for an answer. I simply put myself at his mercy.

"Son, how old are you?" he asked with what appeared to be a genuine tone. My genes made me look fourteen to fifteen years old at that time.

I answered, proudly, "Eighteen, Sergeant. Why?"

He broke out into laughter again, saying with glee in his eyes, "Cause you can count on living at least fifty more years knowing you never is or was a U.S. Paratrooper, you stupid piece of shit. What the fuck were you thinking?" Then he barked, "Follow me, Mr. Paratrooper."

There were about 300 guys in formation, standing there waiting for the fitness instructor to begin the session. The instructor stood on an elevated platform for all to see and wore a microphone neatly tucked around his neck for all to hear his commands during exercise. He had obviously seen this scenario before; he waited for the sergeant to lead me up to him. The sergeant stopped me a few feet away from the platform and continued on without me. The fitness instructor cupped his microphone, smiled, and nodded to the sergeant, who marched me up to the platform. The instructor stood erect—hands on his hips, feet shoulder width apart, looking like a lean mean fighting machine —and turned his attention to the assembled men and began, "Gentlemen, we have a real treat for you this morning." Looking down at me, he motioned for me to jump up onto the platform. I complied. He continued: "Gentlemen, say hello to our very own Mr. Paratrooper." He waved his hand for them to respond in unison. "Our Mr. Paratrooper here is going to demonstrate the correct way to do pushups this morning." I stood next to him, and you must know what I felt like—the proverbial lamb.

When the command was given to assume the position, I dropped to the ground, landing in position perfectly—my arms outstretched, tattoo still bleeding, palms flat on the platforms surface. The only other point of contact with the wooden platform were the toes of my boots. And I waited in that position while he went into some bullshit spiel about the virtues of being mentally and physically strong. As he droned on, I waited. One minute passed, and the first warning flag went off in my head. My body was sending out early signals of what would come soon. Two minutes, I didn't flinch. He turned his attention to me, still speaking to the men in formation. I was listening to him intently; he had my fate in his hands. I made eye contact with the crowd for a second. All eyes were glued to me. Some of the guys had a sad look; others smirked.

"And now, our Mr. Paratrooper, is going to show us how to properly execute just twenty-five pushups. Count out loud, Mr. Paratrooper, by the numbers. Begin."

More warning signs from my body. I tried to put mind over matter. I began shouting out the count, "One.Two.Three.Four."

"Stop," he interjected. "Did you men hear him in the back row?" I knew no one would say a word. It could be any one of them next. They all stood silent. The army was about to teach them and me a lesson.

"Mr. Paratrooper," he cynically stated, "I don't think they heard you back there. Let's try that again, only this time try yelling a little louder please."

Nice game plan, I thought. I'm the bull; he's the matador. He's bleeding off my strength.

"Begin, Mr. Paratrooper." One. Two. Three. Four. "Hold it! Did I see your ass sag on that last pushup, Mr. Paratrooper?"

"No, Sergeant," I responded.

"Oh, OK. I'm sorry. Let's start over again, shall we?"

I began to tremble. I've been in this position for about five minutes.

He was sapping my energy quicker than I had ever felt it dissipate before. "*One! Two! Three! Four! Five!*" Screaming for all I was worth was a trick too, and it was working.

"Very good, Mr. Paratrooper, continue," he said and turned his attention to the men in formation again, extolling the virtues of upper body strength. Another minute passed as he continued with his dissertation, and I continued to pump out the pushups.

"And now, gentlemen, take our Mr. Paratrooper here and observe."

He began the chant. He started the rhythm by stomping his boots on the platform and invited the guys to play the role of the person doing the prompt—as if they were the sergeants and I was the responding platoon. "I want to be an Airborne Ranger," they all sang in unison, and I repeated, screaming with everything I had in me, "I want to be an Airborne Ranger."

My body began to betray me. I was losing muscle control. My legs shook almost beyond control. It felt like a knife was sticking in my arms and the small of my back and my chest. I gasped for air then fell flat on my face with a loud thud.

All fell quiet. The 300 men present were mesmerized by the show. The instructor leaned down and asked if me I wanted to quit. I was so out of breath I couldn't muster a response other than to shake my head in the negative.

"What," he yelled into the microphone, "did I hear you say you can't take it any more, and that you want out?" There are rules to this game, and we had some 300 witnesses.

Urging me to say the words, he tried again, "Just say you want out, Mr. Paratrooper, and your pain and humiliation are history. Ah, huh." He stood up and said, "That's it; I heard you say it."

My anger overcame me. I jumped to my feet, gasping for air, staggering a little when a hamstring cramp ripped at me with the force of a lightning bolt. I jerked involuntarily and shrieked in pain with total hysteria, "*No! I won't quit. No. I don't quit. You can do anything you want, but I will not quit. Do you hear me now, Sergeant?*"

From that day on, I was known as "Mister Paratrooper." Everyone called me that. Even while standing in the chow line, the sergeants would playfully bellow, "Where is our Mister

Paratrooper?" Then, "Oh, there you are. Drop down and give me twenty." In every class we attended, the instructor, even though he might never have seen me prior to the class, started out saying, "I hear there is an honest-to-God paratrooper among us. Are you here, Mister Paratrooper?" It was amusing to most of the guys, but I wasn't amused. I knew what they were doing and why. It was an insult for someone like me to come before them and proclaim himself a paratrooper prior to having earned that right; they all wanted me to quit.

I ended each day more exhausted than the last. For the first time in my life I was awakened by muscle cramps. I thought I was having a heart attack. The cramps ran down my arms to my elbow and radiated from the shoulder to the chest. I was scared shitless—my mind may be able to endure the bullshit, but my body was betraying me. But I wouldn't quit.

When the guys in my barracks first learned of the news, they wanted me out. But because of my dogged determination to make it, they looked after me. They made comments like, "Are you OK, Harry?" and "Hang in there, bud; you're going to make it." Sometimes they'd say, "You know, for a baby face, you're one tough hombre. Hang tough dude. You'll be just fine. Airborne." Their words meant more to me than they'll ever know.

And yet all around me, one by one, other men were folding, giving up. We could tell just by the lack of bodies showing up for each morning's call and run. Rumors circulated among us that more than 350 had quit since day one of jump school. From an initial 854, we estimated we were down to about 500. Five hundred had made it through two long weeks of seventeen-hour days of torture. I was going to make it. The more men that quit, the stronger I felt.

WEEK 3—JUMP WEEK

As I strapped on my parachute harness in the hanger just off the runway, I thought, this is it. The long road I have traveled in just five months has led me to this point. Can I do it? Sure I can. But that thought didn't reassure me as it should have. Hundreds of us gathered and began to file out, on command, in a single line. Dozens of C119 cargo planes were lined up before us—"flying boxcars," as they were called. And then a thought occurred to me: It's strange the sergeants are not harassing us today. Instead, as we filed past them to our designated aircraft, they checked each one of us over to ensure we were "chuted up" properly.

As I approached a sergeant, he began to pull and tuck at my parachute harness to look for improper rigging. He spun me around to check the parachute deployment bag, and pulled and tucked again. When he finished checking me over, he slapped me on top of my helmet as a sign of saying, "You're good to go." I turned slightly to see him wink at me with an approving smile and say, "Good luck, Mister Paratrooper." Wow, I thought, he really does care. How strange. "Next," he shouted, and I moved toward the plane which was beginning to fire up its engines.

The roar was deafening as the plane began its thunderous journey down the runway, gaining speed for lift-off. The noise was so terrific that you could actually feel your internal organs vibrate. My heart beat with excitement and anticipation. It was great, but I was still scared shitless. We were in the air for ten minutes before the first of seven commands began. The commands were given in sign language because the engines were so loud you could not even hear a person yelling, even if they were just five feet away from you. We knew the commands like a newborn knows a nipple. Anticipation grew. The first command, *"Get ready."* We were all tense, ready to spring from our seated positions. *"Stand up." "Hook up."* We grabbed the wire that ran the length of the plane and hooked our static lines to it. The hook in turn was connected to a strap that was connected to our deployment bag.

"Check static lines." We immediately pulled our hooks toward the guy standing directly behind us who performed a double check and determined if we'd hooked it up correctly. A slap on the helmet from the guy behind us meant all was OK. The guy behind me was so excited that he slapped me with such force I thought I'd get a stiff neck. Asshole! I threw him a look that said, "Cool it, will ya?" He smiled, shrugged his shoulders as if to say sorry, and pointed toward the jump master.

"Check equipment." We looked ourselves over again. We checked and double-checked all the connections we could see and touch. Then we turned 180 degrees so our buddy could look over the spaghetti-like

static line to determine, one more time, that it was in its proper configuration, while also looking over the bag-like device that housed our parachute. Again, I knew the slap on the helmet was coming. This time I flinched in anticipation of being smacked too hard, but instead of slapping me, the guy stuck his finger in my ear. I recoiled at the sensation, turned slightly to see him flip me the bird with a smile, then give me a thumbs-up sign. Fucking idiot.

Meanwhile, the sergeants were walking up and down the center of the aircraft, double and triple checking everyone's equipment. The mere sight of them poring over us reassured me they really didn't plan on killing me.

"*Stand in the door.*" We pushed forward. They did not want any room between us. I pressed up against the man to my front; the guy behind me pushed up against my rear. We were poised. Green Light. Go! Go! Go!

As I neared the door, I nearly tripped, but a sergeant steadied me and pushed forward. Go! Go! I was out the door before I knew what hit me. Once you jump out the door, you'll free fall for about twenty-five feet and your chute should open, but it'll take another one hundred feet for the chute to fully deploy. *One thousand one*—my eyes were shut from the shear terror of the event. *One thousand two. One thousand three.* No deployment of my parachute yet. Eyes still shut. *One thou . . .* Swoosh! The chute deployed overhead. My rapid decent stopped with such force that the straps, which ran from my front to rear, via my groin, cut into my balls! Oooccchhh. Damn, that hurts.

My senses were overwhelmed. I looked up, as trained, to determine if I had a good chute. It was fine. I kicked and struggled to get the strap off my balls, reaching down over the reserve chute and pulling. Aaahhh. Better. I then looked around to see the most fascinating sight I had ever seen. The plane was moving away like a ship at sea. The guys all around me were hooting and hollering in total ecstasy. "Airborne," someone screamed. We all screamed back, "Airborne." "All the way," someone else screamed. "All the way," was returned.

There must have been three to four hundred of us in the air. I spotted a tree line in an attempt to gauge how quickly I was descending. God, what a sensation. It was terrific. I was overjoyed with my accomplishment. I felt free. Totally free from all bounds, all restrictions. Some of the men were already hitting the ground; some were still above me, and some were too damn close to me. "Slip right," I yelled at a guy who was drifting too close for comfort. If he got too close, he could spill the air from my chute. He pulled hard on his risers to comply. I looked down again, and it didn't appear that I was descending—that is, until I got to treetop level. Boy, was I coming down fast! Then the training came back to my mind. "Knees slightly bent, legs together, three point contact—feet, hips and shoulders." Splat. I was down.

I struggled to get to my feet, but I was immediately pulled backward onto my back, like an overturned turtle. The ground wind was causing my chute to stay filled with air. However, my training instinctively took over. I reached up and unsnapped the two buckles that were directly connected to the parachute, and presto, my chute blew away, and I was no longer being dragged across the ground. Wow. I did it! I really did it. I smiled to myself from ear to ear, but my euphoria was interrupted by the barking of sergeants who were stationed all over the drop zone.

"Get that chute, soldier," a sergeant yelled, pointing downwind to my collapsed parachute.

"Sure, sure, Sarge." I took off running after it, all the while dodging the others who were landing all around me. When I got to my chute, I stuffed it into my bag along with my harness and off I went, running in the direction the sergeants pointed.

After your first jump, it was a ritual to call home and share your experience with friends or family. Only one phone call was allowed and was limited to only five minutes. Dozens of guys were lined up along a bank of public phone booths. Some called their girlfriends, some called brothers, and some, like myself, simply called home. My mother answered the operator's question, "I have a collect call for anyone from Harold Spencer. Will you accept the charges?" Of course she will. "Mom," I blurted out, "Mom, I did it, I made my first jump."

She shouted to anyone in earshot, "Harold made his first jump today! And he's alright!" We exchanged pleasantries and I told her that I was fine, my health was fine, and then my father took the phone from her. His voice was as condescending as ever when he said, "Hello, Harold, now listen. I'm glad you're OK and everything is working out for you, but look, son, I cannot afford to have you calling home every time you think you have some earth-shattering news to tell us." My high was nose-diving. I gulped in disbelief. Nothing had changed. He was still a fucking asshole. I had only called home three times in the five months I'd been in the service.

"Yeah, OK, Dad. I'm sorry to waste your time," I responded.

"No problem. Anything else you want to say?" he asked.

"No, Dad, nothing else."

"Well then, take care of yourself, son. Goodbye."

"Goodbye, Dad."

Four jumps later, I found myself standing in formation with all who sustained the rigors of jump school.

At graduation exercises we were praised by the respective speakers and, once again, kicked in the ass. On the parade field, I saw my two fellow musketeers, Louie and Terry for the first time since I got off the bus three long weeks ago. We smiled at each other and nodded our heads, acknowledging our triumph. Meanwhile, the training battalion commander was espousing the virtues of being airborne.

Early on in jump week we submitted our choice of units. Based on my last phone call home, my first choice was the 173rd Airborne Brigade located in Okinawa, Japan. My second choice was the 101st Airborne Division. Before I opened the envelope containing my orders, I resigned myself to simply follow orders. Then I read the top line, "101st Airborne Division, Fort Campbell."

Guys all around me were excited, far more excited than I was. "I got it," exclaimed one guy. "Me, too," said another. "Yeah, baby. I'm going to the 173rd," shouted another. The word among us was that the 173rd was the place to go. Another nickname for the 173rd was "The Rock." They were the bad boys most likely to go to war first. Their mascot was the patron saint of warriors, Saint Michael. I shook my head at the paradox—a saint of warriors. Crazy, it's all so absolutely crazy!

I pushed that thought out my head. It was dangerous to think that way. As I ran to my barracks, I let my mind drift to the 101st, the Screaming Eagles. I created visions of bird-like men swooping down on the enemy with machine guns blazing. It was not that bad—the 101st was rated second only to the 173rd. I could live with that.

Within hours of graduation, buses pulled into our compound. Each bus was marked with its destination. I found mine and began to scan the crowd, looking for Louie and Terry. Try as I might, I couldn't spot them. I finally gave up and thought to myself, All for One . . . and, One for All, but not with the same bravado I had once felt. Good luck, my fellow musketeers, good luck.

Waving goodbye to familiar faces, I saw the two guys who helped protect me from the sergeants who eventually discovered my tattoo. We made eye contact and smiled at one another. One of them called out as he waved. "So long, Mr. Paratrooper! Live up to that name, you've earned it," and then he dropped his head. Although he still smiled, he was shaking his head in disbelief that I had made it through jump school. "Good luck to you guys, too, and thanks," I said. "I couldn't have done it without you." I then stepped into the bus.

A strange feeling came over me as I walked down the bus aisle. Some of these guys would not live to see their ETS (an acronym for Estimated Time of Separation, which means you're out of the army).

As our bus headed out in a caravan of three, the training battalion colonel's last statement stuck in my head, "Gentlemen, all of you standing before me today have yet to learn what it is to become a paratrooper. As you stand here proud of your accomplishments, you are only airborne qualified. When you get to your assigned units, you will have just begun the journey to become a United States Paratrooper. Good luck, men. God speed." That thought gave way to sleep. I slept so hard, and so sound, that I didn't wake up until we pulled into Fort Campbell, Kentucky ten hours later.

Chapter 3

ARRIVING AT FORT CAMPBELL

TIMELINE: DECEMBER 1964

ONCE IN THE intake compound at Fort Campbell, my records were screened and processed. After that was completed, I expected to be assigned to the company of record. But, for some unexplained reason, three other guys and I were pulled aside and given the option of going to medical school. The other guys were Rocky Southern, Johnnie White and Fred Torrent. Medical school! Bullshit, I thought. I'm tired of the rigors of training.

Then the sergeant started his pitch. "Look, guys, I can tell you're not happy to hear this, but I'm telling you, your records indicate you are mentally a cut above the requirements of an infantryman. Medics are respected by infantrymen, and your physical living conditions will be a little more accommodating as well."

I interrupted, "Sarge, do I have a choice in this matter?"

"Of course you do."

"Then convince me," I said, "over and above what you just told us."

"Well," he searched for the right words, "Fort Sam (Houston) is located almost in the heart of San Antonio." He looked at us for some kind of positive response. "It's an open post," meaning anyone at anytime for any reason can drive on to the base.

"So," I said, "What else?"

He paused, "Look guys, how can I say this without appearing stupid?" He stammered, "You are already airborne: you'll be wearing the patch on your shoulders showing you're a paratrooper with the 101st Airborne; I'll even have orders cut to make you guys PFCs."

We were E-2s at the time, no stripes, nothing showing rank, thereby, signifying we were new guys.

"What else, Sarge? Come on," I urged.

"Well," he continued, "Fort Sam is a basic (boot camp) training post for *women*, WACS. Get it? There'll be more horny pussy down there than you can shake a stick at."

"Women!" we all shouted simultaneously. "Pussy!" we screamed as if we were asking a question.

Rocky had a big hungry smile plastered all over his face. "I'm in. Where do I sign?"

The sergeant continued, "I'm telling you guys, the women will be all over you. They love paratroopers, especially paratroopers with," he pointed to his sleeve, "rank."

That's it. I was hooked. "Where do I sign?" I asked.

"Me, too," chimed Johnnie and Freddie simultaneously.

I was eighteen, good looking, proud, bad, and hadn't been on leave in *five months*. I got a hard-on just thinking about those WACS and Fort Sam. Hell, anybody would want to become a medic with enticement like pussy; subsequently we were scheduled to go to medical school in six weeks.

The first two weeks at Fort Campbell were preparation for the "Cherry Blast." I learned the significance of this term all too well. On the day of our "Cherry Blast," we were suited up with our combat gear in a hangar not far from where the planes taxied and stopped. In jump school we had not had all this gear strapped to our bodies outside of the parachute itself. Here I had my first-aid kit, rifle, pistol, sleeping bag, poncho, rain garb, extra clothes, and two canteens filled with water—all of this on top of the main parachute on my back as well as my reserve chute on my stomach. Holy shit, I could barely walk. I actually thought this was a joke until I saw everyone else had the same cumbersome load. Man, I thought, this is crazy. How in the hell am I going to jump out and away from the plane's fuselage without being thrown back against the side of the aircraft?

Of course there was no answer. But my expression must have said it all because all the guys around me chided me with comments like, "What's the matter, Cherry? Didn't they tell you about this shit in jump school?" They knew damned well they hadn't. I was hunched over in pain as we began the laborious task of walking out to the planes. The bag hanging under my reserve that contained the majority of my gear did not allow me to take strides any longer than about twelve inches. My rifle was inside a bag-like device designed to pad it and stop it from cutting into me or my parachute. The rifle bag was strapped over my shoulder and was difficult to keep in place. The guy behind me called out, "Hey, Cherry, you've got some silk hanging out of your deployment bag." That was the bag that actually contained the parachute. I turned around to make eye contact with him to see him pulling some of my chute out of the bag. I recoiled in shock!

In jump school you were taught to trust your buddy, that your buddy would look out for you and you for him. I screamed at the guy in both anger and fear, jerking away from him out of instinct, but my moves were slow. In fact, I almost tripped over the weight I was wearing.

I screamed in horror. "You cock-sucking son of a bitch! Don't you ever touch me again." I stared at him as if I would kill him if he tried that shit again.

He just smiled, put his hands up in the air in surrender and said, "Chill out, Cherry, that little pull isn't going to hurt you, man. Relax, man."

"Relax, shit," I snapped, "Don't ever do that shit again. Do you understand me?" I pointed at him to emphasize my words.

A squad leader walked over to me and stuffed the silk back into my deployment bag. He did it with such force I nearly fell on my face. "You'll be just fine, Cherry!" he said.

Oh, great, I thought. Isn't that comforting. I spit at the ground in disgust. "Fuck it," I muttered. If that's how they want to play, cool. Let's get it on. I turned one more time to the guy who pulled on my chute and said, "If I die, you bastard, I'll kill you!"

With that, everyone began jeering me. "Cherry's gonna die." "He's got a Mae West for sure!" (a partial chute opening) They were having fun all right, at my fucking expense. Although part of me knew that I was going through a ritual and I really shouldn't be alarmed, the other part of me thought, these guys are absolute animals. And then I thought of what the Sergeant said while talking me into becoming a medic. "Medics are a cut above the infantryman." Yeah, right, I thought. A very thin cut.

The aircraft was different than those in jump school. It was about three times bigger. The C119 "flying boxcar" holds about twenty-four guys; this aircraft, a C124, looked to hold nearly one hundred men. We were airborne for about thirty minutes when the commands began: "Get ready!" "Stand up!" "Hook up!" "Check static lines!"

Then we waited, and waited, and waited. I have no idea why. I looked at the jump master. He had on a headset with a microphone. I assumed he was in contact with the pilot. He stuck his head out of the open door of the aircraft. It was mid-December, very cold outside, maybe thirty-five degrees. His cheeks rippled as the wind rushed by his face. He nodded his head to whomever he was speaking to through the headset, turned to us, and, with his arm raised over his head, gave a thumbs-up sign. I wondered what the hell is that.

Suddenly the aircraft pointed its nose upward at a sixty-degree angle of attack, and I felt as if my weight increased by 300 pounds. My knees buckled under the strain. The guy behind me steadied me, screaming, "Hold on, Cherry." The seasoned troopers laughed at my inability to stand as steady as they were. Up, up . . . still climbing. My insides shook from both the cold and my nerves. Someone screamed, "Cherries, you're all going to die." Goddamn, I thought, these guys are really crazy. They are really crazy. The cadence stirred from deep within. The beat, the rhythm . . . *Airborne—All the way.* If that's what it takes, you tough guys, fine, OK, let's go.

Without a warning the plane leveled off. Wow, what a relief. All I had to do now was get myself off the plane's ceiling. Then we waited, and waited, and waited. Then finally another command was given, "Check equipment." Again I looked over my straps and buckles and touched all critical connections, the guy behind me tapped me on the helmet. We were the last two in what was called a Chalk—a line of men designated to go out together on the aircraft's first pass at the drop zone. As I turned, I saw him pull on my silk, exposing it. OK, asshole, if that's the way you want to play it. He then turned his back to me so I could look his backside over for proper connections. Seeing that his static line was all neatly laid out in spaghetti fashion on his deployment bag, I pulled the small string that held it in place. The static line fell to floor, all twenty-five feet of it. There, I thought to myself. How you like them apples, you piece of shit? I was shocked at my audacity. He looked down at the static line lying at his feet. Then it suddenly hit me—the guy was Jim Waters! Waters was the chest-beating mad man who had berated me when I first stepped into the barracks two weeks ago. Shit. If I had a choice of foe it would not have been him. Oh, well, too late now. Then that voice from within breaks my thought: "Don't punk on him, Harry; stand your ground. You have every right to do that."

All the other guys were smiling, anticipating how Waters would handle the ripping of his static line. One screamed, "Looks like you met your match, Waters. The Cherry doesn't scare so easy." Our eyes met like the eyes of two combating wolves, then Waters smiled, casting his gaze to the sky, and screamed, "God, you haven't got a hair on your ass if you don't strike me dead!" Then he screamed, "Airborne! Airborne! Motherfuckers, Airborne!" I shook my head at that one, thinking maybe I was really dreaming.

The last command was given, *"Stand in the door!"* The chalk tightened up. We pushed forward. There was absolutely no space; twenty-four guys poised on both sides of the plane were squeezed together like sardines in a can. Waters gathered his static line, leaned forward against me so his face was very near my neck and screamed, "Cherry, I'll be right behind you, and I'm going to wrap this static line around your fucking neck as we go out the door! You got that, motherfucker?"

After hearing him talk to God like he just did, I believed him! "Go! Go! Go!" Jesus Christ, the line moved incredibly fast compared to jump school. We were damned near running, but we were so burdened with gear that I could only move my feet six to eight inches with each step before my knees hit the equipment bag that dangled just under my reserve chute. My legs grew weak. My stomach turned inside out. As I moved toward the door, I leaned on the guy in front of me to keep from falling on my face. Waters, in turn, kept pushing me.

As I leaped out the door of the aircraft, my last thought was, onto you, my Lord, I commit myself; help me if you would! Swoosh. *One thousand one.* I was free falling, waiting for the chute to open. *One thousand two.* My eyes were open. I was looking at the ground as my body twisted from the aircraft's prop blast and the force of being thrown from an aircraft moving 130 mph. My body rotated; I was headed toward the ground head-first, my feet pointed skyward at the aircraft. I spotted Waters coming at me face-first. The aircraft was floating away. My body was horizontal with my back toward the ground. *One thousand three.* The static line tightened and flipped me around with my back to the plane. Swoosh. Pop. The chute deployed. All fell quiet. It was an incredibly rapid transition from the loud chaos I had just left.

As we drifted toward earth, guys around me were maneuvering their chutes to keep away from each other. Waters screamed, "How ya doing, Cherry?" I didn't answer. I was still intoxicated by the jump. It was only my sixth jump: five in jump school and this one, my "Cherry Blast." And it was over. Wow, what a thrill! What a rush!

Most of the guys slowly accepted me. I hoped in the ensuing months to gain the respect of all my fellow medics. The military was very seniority-minded. It was called "Time in Grade." Even if you were only a private first class, a one striper, if you had been in the service and in the outfit itself for some time, you would command respect from your fellow paratroopers.

However, the mental and physical training never stopped. It was as if we were still in boot camp. We were conditioned to respond in a military manner. We knew we were the nation's first line of defense. Though we hated what we were subjected to day after day, most of us secretly wished to go to war. That is what we lived for and what we trained for—war.

Occasionally, we'd go on IRF (Immediate Reactionary Force). The entire battalion was locked down and confined to barracks, all of our gear preloaded into various aircraft, and we waited for the call by the commander-in-chief, the President of the United States. If there were an uprising anywhere in the U.S. or the Western Hemisphere, we, upon notification, would be airborne within the hour. All five hundred or so men in the 1st/501st of the 101st Airborne Division would go to war together. We were a team. And on this team there was no room for slackers. Ergo, second place in combat is not an option.

———≫≪———

One of my former high school friends interrupts, "You really have been through some tough stuff, Harry! I don't think I could have done it."

"Yeah," I respond, letting his perspective sink in, "but there's so much more I could tell you. Obviously though, time is running out. I've got to go now."

However, Bea wants me to stay longer. "Harry, you've got to tell them about your time at West Point; that is too funny of a story to leave out. Besides, I'm proud to say my boyfriend trained West Point Cadets, even though you know full well I'm against the war."

I look at her and her face says it all. She is scared; she knows we will be saying goodbye very shortly, and she wants me to stay. She has a great poker face, but I can see right through her. She is fighting back a storm within. So I oblige them for a few more minutes. Part of me wants out of the party because I feel like a freak on display. Those gathered have distinctively differing viewpoints than I. I am growing uncomfortable, but something genuine is in Bea's tone. Always wanting to please her, right from the moment I met her, I continue.

———≫≪———

West Point grads postured themselves differently than officers who were commissioned via Officer's Candidate School or college ROTC. West Point graduates were simply more arrogant. They looked upon themselves as the elite of the officer's corps. But now they had me to deal with. I would make them pay the price for their arrogance, and I could hardly wait to have at them.

My particular responsibility was to indoctrinate the pleebs by running them through an infiltration course. In preparation for the pleebs, Steve Best, a fellow paratrooper from New York, and a few others built the obstacle course from the ground up, although building it proved to be hard labor for all of us.

The first obstacle was what the army called a "tank ditch"—which was nothing more than a large hole in the ground, too deep and too wide for a tank to get through or over. Sounds good to me, I thought. "Let's get the backhoe here," I said.

Infantry company platoon Sergeant James Lims, a tough looking, tough-talking yet fair man with freckles and reddish short hair, who was from Texas, just smiled at me while pointing to a stack of shovels, and said, "*Y'all* are the backhoe."

"Excuse me, Sarge," I said as I gulped. "How big did you say the ditch has to be?"

"Fifteen feet long, ten feet wide, and six feet deep."

We looked at each other in disbelief. Sergeant Lims barked, "Now, troops, let's move."

We dug and dug for ten hours a day; eight of us dug our way to hell for five days. Boy, what an obstacle that hole in the ground turned out to be. We took pride in it, even if it was simply a hole in the ground.

Next came the construction of a double-picketed barbed-wire fence. We knew, based on what Sergeant Lims had told us, the pleebs would have to crawl from the tank ditch to the fence. So we gathered stones, all kinds of stones, the bigger and sharper, the better, and placed them in the pleebs' path. I thought, yeah, let's make this as difficult as possible on those pricks. I salivated at the vision of the pleebs bleeding at the elbows and knees while I pushed them along. Yeah, that'll work.

Once completed, the course consisted of six obstacles. First, there was a small hill that lead to the tank ditch, which the pleebs would be expected to hurdle. And if they did not clear the ditch, they would simply splatter themselves on to the bottom of it and have to scramble to get out. We laughed at that thought. The tank ditch from the top of the mound of earth turned out to be a nine-foot drop. Second, there was the tortuous crawl through a carefully laid bed of hand-picked rock, which contained the sharpest edges imaginable. Third, there was the double-picketed barbed-wire fence. Fourth, there was another crawl, this time through thick sand, approximately seventy-five feet in length. Fifth, there was the "over-the-hill-wall," which they'd have to pull themselves up and over via a rope. And, lastly, there was another wall, just low enough for the pleebs to jump and pull themselves over. That was it.

We could hardly wait. The anticipation grew on the morning of the first day as the first group of pleebs was heard marching toward us. We heard them singing regular army chants to the cadence of their march.

My assignment was to put them through the double-picketed barbed-wire fence obstacle. I had memorized my spiel: "Men, this obstacle is the infamous double-picketed barbed-wire fence. It is the most effective barrier you will encounter, or construct, to stop or slow your infiltration of the enemy, or to stop and slow the enemy from getting to you. However, in the interest of survival and understanding this obstacle's strength, as well as its inherent weakness, we are gathered here to educate you firsthand." I was on a high. I was in charge. I would now be the bastard dolling out the hazing instead of the one receiving it. Yeah, baby!

After a brief tour of each obstacle, where each one of us gave our respective lectures, unbeknownst to us, Sergeant Lims said, "And now, gentlemen, a demonstration by one of the army's finest." He pointed toward me, "A United States Paratrooper."

You have got to be kidding me, I thought. This is a joke. Right? I was wearing my best fatigues, and my jump boots were spit-shined to perfection. If I hadn't been in front of the pleebs, I would have told Lims to kiss my ass. Shit. Why me? It's always fucking me!

Lims knew I was upset. He followed me over the mound of dirt that led to the tank ditch. "Look, son," he said, "we have to show them we not only expect them to go through this course, but that we can go through it faster and better than any one of them."

"Yeah, Sarge, sure," I responded. "Christ, you could have told me. I would have practiced. I would have worn some working fatigues. I've got my best pair of jump boots on. Give me a break, Sarge."

"Harry, I'm counting on my best man to make all of us look good. Are you airborne, son?"

"All the fucking way, Sarge," I retorted.

He smiled, and with a nod of his head and a wink of the eye, said, "That a boy. All the way." He gave me a thumbs-up, then walked back towards the pleebs. "I'll blow this whistle when I want you to start; you've got two minutes, trooper," he said loud enough for all to hear.

The whistle blew. I jumped up and ran at the mound of earth, intending to clear the ditch with a flying leap. Ohhh, shit! I'm not going to make it. Splat! My mid-section hit the edge on the far side of the ditch, and I slid ever so gracefully down it. I couldn't breathe. I had knocked the fucking wind out of myself. Once at the bottom of the ditch, I rolled up on all fours, gasping for air. I felt faint.

Lims ran to the ditch's edge, his eyes wide in bewilderment at what he just saw. "You all right, son?" he asked.

I glanced up and nodded my head, feeling like an absolute fool. Seconds later, fighting off the pain, I got to my feet and jumped for the top of the ditch, pulling for all I was worth to get out of that stupid ass ditch.

Despite the pain, my mind raced, thinking of what was yet to come. I knew I had to crawl to the next obstacle, my double-picketed barbed-wire fence. Those cruel stones we laid would be staring me dead in the face. Never did I think I would be the one to go through them. If I had known, I certainly would not have been so tough on myself. Shit!

Still fighting back the pain from deep within, I somehow managed to pull myself out of the ditch while Lims carried on with his narrative. "Gentlemen, you must dig in to the surface, making contact with your elbows, knees, and the toes of your boots to propel yourself forward."

Right, I thought. Oooch, eeeouch. Out of the blue, my training took over. The adrenaline kicked in, and I felt no pain. I had just one simple goal: To show those assholes how it was supposed to be done. The cadence came back, the chant, the images of strength: *Airborne—All the way—Every day—All the way.* And on I squirmed, oblivious to the pain.

The group of pleebs and Sergeant Lims followed my every move. I completed the obstacle course and jumped to the parade rest position in front of them. Lims closed his narrative with, "And that, gentlemen, is the way it is supposed to be done." Our eyes made contact. He flashed a smile and a wink. I just stood there and felt a growing warmth at the points of my elbows and knees. I looked at the pleebs' faces.

They were looking at my knees. The blood had saturated my fatigues. It was also running into my socks where the (bloused) fatigues were tucked into my boots. However, I took pride in seeing the fear in their eyes and faces. I relaxed out of the parade rest position and noticed blood all over my hands. The sight of that caused one pleeb to pass out. "Harry" Lims barked, "for Christ's sake, go clean yourself up, will ya?" I was covered in dust from head to toe, but I didn't care, I relished the fear of what was to come that I saw on the pleebs' faces.

A week or so later we were taking a break from running more pleebs through the obstacle course. One of the guys had a portable radio on. A few of the senior cadets at West Point were with us gathered under the shade of a large oak tree when President Lyndon B. Johnson addressed a press conference on Vietnam. He assured the American public, in the interest of justice and freedom, that he would commit more American soldiers to the Vietnam War. He promised a swift end to the reign of terror rendered upon the Republic of South Vietnam by North Vietnam's Communists. One of the cadets interrupted the speech to ask with childlike exuberance, "Do you guys think you'll be going?" Just then, Johnson stated he would send more troops from the 101st Airborne Division. One of the paratroopers nonchalantly responded to the cadet's question: "Well, we aren't teaching you battlefield tactics to play war. It may seem like a game right now, but let me assure you, it is, according to Jack London's writing, *The Most Dangerous Game* you'll ever play."

All of us troopers looked into the eyes of the cadets gathered before us and just stared. We stared until they broke their gazes. They, in the meantime, were looking for us to say more. For us, the paratroopers, there was nothing more to say. We knew we were next in line to go. They would not see us hollering and hooting with false bravado. We remained quiet, turning inward. This is it, I thought. Oh, shit. I'm going to Vietnam; it's just a matter of time.

~~~~~~~

I look up at the party crowd, amazed to see a dozen more guys and gals have gathered to hear my story of preparation to go to war. John Yard breaks the silence and extends his hand to shake mine, "Good luck, brother." A couple other guys shake my hand with similar senti-ments, when Beatrice says, "But Harry, it is an illegitimate war. We are mingling in a civil war. You should *not go*. You should just walk away and go to school."

As much as I feel for her and do not want to take a stand against her, I stare at her for a second and respond with the training that was so expertly instilled in me. "Ours is not to question why, Bea. Our government has determined our respective fates. I will go because that is the honorable thing to do; that is what our government has asked me to do. To do otherwise, I'd end up in jail."

The crowd's response is mixed. Some side with Beatrice while others support the United States of America and me. History will record who is right, but for the soldier, it doesn't matter. All we know is what we are told to do. If we don't follow orders, a dishonorable discharge will haunt us for the rest of our lives.

Suddenly I feel totally estranged from everyone in the room, so I gather myself and bid all of them farewell. It is painful to say goodbye to Bea, but it has to be done. No fanfare. I simply kiss her and state, "I'll see you next year. Goodbye." She begins to cry as I turn to leave, but I know she has the support of those gathered. Goodbye, my love, I thought. I love you more than you'll ever know. Duty, honor, and country—so it is, so it shall be. Ssshit!

Chapter 4

MOVEMENT TO VIETNAM

B ACK AT FORT Campbell, I am greeted by Steve Best as I come through the door of the barracks from my three-day pass. Steve is the second most senior member of the medical platoon; I'm number one. He hates the fact that, though I'm younger by some two years, I am his senior in the platoon. Steve is my best friend in the army. He is from New York City and stands just 5'6" and comes in a little too heavy at 160 pounds. I kid him a lot about that on both fronts, weight and age. I've known him now for eighteen months. Chuck Holt is also in the barracks. Chuck's from Chicago. He is younger than I by some fourteen months and has been in the service just twelve months. Both Steve and Chuck are close to me. Maybe it's because we are all from big cities—we all come from where the persona is to play tough—and maybe it's because we all are white. The majority of the platoon is black, but up until now I didn't give that much thought.

Because Chuck is younger than I, he looks up to me. He is one of the newest and youngest in the platoon. There are a few more white guys in the platoon, maybe a total of ten out of thirty-two; the remainder are either black or Hispanic. Blacks comprise the greatest percentage. Back in December of '64, the platoon was once damn near exclusively white. The old school of guys has been replaced with a higher number of blacks. Not that it is a big deal— it is simply a fact. In fact, our platoon sergeant, Flock, and all the squad leaders are black; all are Specialist 5 rank and up. A Spec-5 is just one rank above me. They may have more rank, but I have more time in the platoon than anyone else; Steve is a close second. And somehow I think that fact bothers most of them, because everyone, including Flock, is new to the platoon, and have come here within the past couple of months. Those they replaced left because they're getting out of the army within the next couple of months.

Sergeant Flock portrays himself as a bad ass from Missouri, a dark-skinned guy who is thickly built. He is basically an unhappy person—unhappy in love, unhappy in life. If you cross him, you'll pay the price. At thirty-two or thirty-three years of age, whichever he is, Flock isn't somebody you would want to jump on. He is street-wise and army-smart, and acheived the rank of Sergeant First Class, an E-7 paygrade. His only problem as I see it is that he was born. He's a certified asshole who lacks education and general intelligence, let alone common horse sense. How he got as far as he has is a mystery or an indictment of the army. He goes from hot to cold as if he were a psycho. We've had a problem from the get-go. He recognized me as the senior donkey, and that I have some kind of influence over those junior to me, and has attempted to discredit me ever since. Why? Go figure! I know my order in the food chain. Maybe it's because he knows I see right through him. I see him for what he is worth. That is to say, if I met him on the street I'd make certain it would only be a one-time meeting. You can pick your friends, but not your sergeant in this man's army. Simply put, if he were a civilian he'd make a great security guard at a cemetery, on the graveyard shift. Other than that he's a great guy!

SUNDAY, JUNE 5 1966

10 P.M. Dozens of guys are lined up at the numerous pay phones scattered throughout the barracks area. I want to call home, but the lines never seem to thin out. The call goes out to fall into battalion formation. Senior non-commissioned officers (NCO's) are pushing men away from the phones, ordering them to get in formation. Some of the guys are so desperate to say goodbye to their loved ones that they try to ignore the orders, but one by one they reluctantly turn away from

the phones and run off to Johnson Field, the area where we histori-
cally gather into a battalion formation.

As I walk to the gathering formation, I spot our platoon leader,
Lieutenant Edmore, saying goodbye to his wife and mother. All three
are crying like babies. The scene reminds me of my own family. Just
before I got on the plane the morning after the party with Bea, my
younger sister, Martha, gave me a "she-him" troll doll. Crying, she
came up to me and said, "Here, big brother, take my doll, it will bring
you luck." The little long-haired plastic troll doll stands three inches
high at most and is made of soft plastic. I put it in the elastic band that
runs around my "steel pot"—my helmet. Many of the guys wear such
paraphernalia to bring them luck. As I walk past the lieutenant, I ask
myself, when are you ever going to see a medical platoon leader on a
combat patrol? Shit, his chances of coming home alive are a hundred
times greater than mine. Although that thought angers me, I dismiss
it. After all, he has a family, and they are genuinely concerned for his
safety. The answer to my own question about this lieutenant going out
on a patrol is never.

10:45 P.M. As we approach the civilian jets that have landed at
our base's airstrip, I begin to feel what it must be like to be a cow.
NCO's keep contradicting each other's orders. The scene appears
chaotic. The jets' engines are running while the sergeants are yelling
at us to move along faster. I barely hear the statement, "Hey, you, you
with the green tuxedo, come here." I've been in the army too long to
fall for that one. I ignore him. But, as usual, some young kid responds,
"Yes, Sergeant, did you call me?" I look briefly at the sergeant long
enough to see a smile of triumph spread over his face. He then says,
"Yeah. Get down and give me twenty, asshole." I shake my head in
empathy for the kid. All of us have fallen for that age-old line at one
time or another. I continue to follow the man in front of me as we make
our way closer to the aircraft.

There are a number of civilians on both sides of the line that leads
up to the motor-powered staircase. I suspect the sergeant is putting on
a show for them, showing them how much power he has over us. The
sergeant is a World War II and Korean War veteran. He holds the
rank of sergeant major, the highest enlisted rank one can achieve.
With his background and experience, he feels that he is superior to

any of us. I can't argue that point, but I have developed a simple theory about background and experience—it is not what you have done that makes you who you are; it is what you can do. I look upon him with disdain.

He is at least forty-five years old and, a little thick around the waist and head. His name is Dow. You can't just call him sergeant. No, that will not do. You must call him sergeant major. What a prick! Whenever I have overheard him talking, it was usually about the "Big One," World War II, and how nothing could possibly compare to what he has been through. Yeah, right, I think as I pass him at the plane's entrance. We'll see, old man, just how tough you think you are. The senior NCOs and Dow will never be out on a ten-man patrol in the jungle. Their best shot at us is not in the jungle; it is here and now.

I developed a coping mechanism early on in life. Simply put, it is this: Whatever you throw at me, no matter how tough it may be, if anyone can take it, I can! In fact, I am so cocky that I made several mistakes. Earlier on in the army, when a sergeant said, "Give me twenty," I asked him which arm. Big mistake. I remember his response: "Both, but one arm at a time!" In an outfit like mine, everyone is here because they think the same way. Each feels he's tougher and stronger than everyone else. We are our nation's toughest all right, but not the smartest.

The war in Vietnam, when you break it down, is a way for the government to test us and for us to test ourselves. Very shortly our training will be called to contest. A crack fighting machine comprised of street toughs who were given the same choice as I—jail or the service—will be armed with state-of-the-art technology to destroy human beings, whoever they are and wherever they may live. We have, up until this point, been classroom students of war, but we are about to be let loose to apply theory to reality. Deep within me a little voice is saying, "This is wrong, Harry. This is insane." But I suppress it. I have to go. There is no turning back now. I understand all too well what is taking place. The bottom line is, as my father used to say, "If you're willing to play, be willing to pay." Yeah, sure. Right.

Part of me refuses to believe the reality of the situation; part of me accepts it. Inside, I'm screaming, time out, assholes, this is a joke, right? But the cadence comes swirling up from my subconscious, *Airborne—All the way*. I push the negative thoughts out of my mind. I have to go. I have to do it. Airborne!

3 A.M. The flight ends at Travis Air Force Base outside of Oakland, California. As we step off the airplane, I immediately take note of the surroundings from the vantage point of the powered staircase that leads to the pavement. Off in the distance, there's a line of buses three hundred yards long. The route to the buses is lined with military police. It is strange that so many MP's are present. What do they think, we'd run away? To where? There is also a small crowd of civilians by the fence that we will have to walk by to get to the buses. I suspect they are there to cheer us on. We congregate around the plane until our gear, our duffel bags, and rucksacks are unloaded.

When everyone has found their gear, we form a column of twos and begin the arduous walk to the buses. Each man is loaded down with an average of 150 pounds of gear. The walk is slow, agonizing, deliberate, and silent. No talking, no laughing. We are on our way to war. And we are not in the mood for joking around.

As I near the fence, I hear the teenagers—college-age kids—who have gathered begin to jeer us, poking fun at the strain we are under with comments like, "Oh, look at that one, he's cute," and "Man, look at that dude, he must be the machine-gunner." Good deduction, I think. How can they possibly tell? Maybe because we all have our weapons? Of course he is the machine-gunner; he's carrying a fucking machine gun. But I can't help but wonder, how in the world did they know we were coming?

We file by the civilians, an infantry outfit going to war. Not only are we wearing our steel pots, but our fatigues are different than state side issue. They are lightweight, thin cotton, and we do not tuck our shirts into our pants. On the uniform itself, we still have contrasting colors, which I'm sure isn't the smartest thing to have in the jungle. But I guess the brass wants the enemy to know what unit is attacking them and what our names and ranks are. White name tags, yellow PFC strips, and the red white and blue shoulder patch of the 173rd Airborne Brigade helps Charlie identify us before he blows our fucking heads off, I guess. Our boots, too, are different. Part black, part drab olive-green nylon—they are jungle boots, designed to let our feet breathe and dry out faster than they would in stateside issued leather boots.

It's almost 3:45 A.M. As we file by, an MP addresses the crowd, "Yeah, take a good look at these guys. These are the bad boys from Fort Campbell, Kentucky, the Screaming Eagles, the 101st Airborne Division. Take a good look; many of them will not return. They are going to protect your right to do what you are doing now."

In response, the crowd quiets down slightly, then I hear a guy say in a solemn tone, "You don't have to do this, man. It's wrong, you know?" I shoot him a look like, fuck you, asshole; you do not know what you're talking about, and shift the weight on my shoulder, not breaking stride. More shouts, more exchanges with the crowd follow us, to no avail. It is a done deal. We are going to war, but the crowd doesn't fit my preconceived notions of what it should have been like.

We press on toward the buses in silence. Occasionally the eerie silence is punctuated by a groan and grunt from a guy carrying his equipment or the teenagers poking fun at us. It is a strange feeling. No speeches, no fanfare, no "Johnny, go get 'em" rally. Not even a good luck speech. Just silence among us and the occasional jeering from the crowd of teenagers.

Dawn is breaking as the buses pull up to the ship that will take us to Vietnam. It is a monstrous-looking vessel—a cold, giant piece of gray metal. Waiting to board, we lay our gear on the tarmac as word spreads that a phone booth is nearby. The sergeants respond to the rumor: "No, you can't use the phone, goddamn it. Stop acting like a bunch of fucking babies."

At 12:30 P.M., Monday, we're finally allowed to board ship. We have been without sleep for about thirty-six hours, and it is beginning to show. We are shown our platoon sleeping area; there was a universal disbelief—thirty of us are to live and sleep in an area no larger than a fifteen-by-thirty-foot space. The bunks are stacked five high with about eighteen inches between each—just barely large enough to turn on your side while sleeping. The guys keep asking the sergeant to show us our real bunk area.

When it finally sinks in that it is not a joke, I claim a bottom bunk. Heat and smell rise. I am smirking to myself as I maneuver to claim my space when Sergeant Flock calls me over to him. "Spencer," he begins, "You are a pain in my ass, and you have been since I came to this platoon. Now, get down and give me twenty." Flock instinctively senses my dislike for him and goes out of his way to harass me at every opportunity. Because of this little encounter, I lose out on my choice of bunk, so I head topside to take in a view of the world we are leaving behind.

The sight of the Golden Gate Bridge and San Francisco is breathtaking. Despite the dismal rainy, foggy weather, it is an incredible view from the ship. We are on our way. Ain't no stopping us now. The color of the water, however, is disappointing. It is sort of a brown-green color. I look forward to seeing the true color of the ocean. I had heard there is no way to describe the beautiful hue of blue away from land. Up and down, back and forth, the boat pitches like a giant slow-moving roller coaster. I sit mesmerized for a couple of hours. I'll let those down in our bunk area fight among themselves for best bunk position. I resign myself to take whatever bunk is left unclaimed. After all, the trip only takes eighteen days.

Everywhere you go on this ship, you have to stand in a line a mile long, or so it seems. The officers and senior sergeants have separate sleeping and eating quarters. Although we cannot see those quarters for ourselves, we instinctively know they have to be better than what we have. I'm looking forward to returning home already. Body odor is beginning to pierce the air.

I make a casual comment to a fellow medic, Leon Dallas, a big brute of a man. I state that I am beginning to learn what it must be like, to not only be a black man, but how a black man must have felt aboard a slave ship bound for the New World. He responds, "Stay tuned, kid; you'll learn a whole lot more." Six foot tall and about 210 to 220 pounds, Leon is a compassionate man a couple years older than I. I purposely befriend him—not because he is black, but because he is a compassionate guy, a gentle giant no one would want to cross.

Minor fistfights are occurring with greater frequency. It must be due in part to the cramped space. No privacy—not even when shitting. The "head," as the merchant marines call it, has six commodes all within inches of each other. Demeaning and humiliating are the two best words to describe the environment. We, the grunts of grunts, are subject to incredibly dehumanizing conditions. It is pathetic to say the least.

Chuck Holt comes up to me, scared shitless. Someone has threatened to kick his ass. I grab him by the arm and lead him topside to get away from the madness down below. "Harry," he says, "I've got this terrible feeling I'm not coming back." His eyes are wide; fear is written all over his face

"Knock it off, Chuck," I say. "We all feel that way; come on, get a grip. It will be OK." Hell, I don't know if I will make it back, but I can't allow him to believe he is alone in his thoughts. His display of fear makes me feel stronger than I actually am. I play the strong role for the benefit of both of us. Most white guys instinctively stick together. Because I grew up in a racially mixed neighborhood, I drift between both races. My role from time to time is to act as an intermediary, explaining the different attitudes and calling for greater understanding and respect of our differences.

JUNE 8 1966

We hold a makeshift training class on battlefield wounds, from a sucking chest wound to arterial bleeding control. The training is conducted by a new guy to our platoon, Specialist Sixth Class Robert Crack. He's a tall, dark-skinned black from Louisiana—very competent, very articulate. Crack knows the ins and outs of first aid, and we all respect his knowledge and listen intently.

However, my mind drifts as I scan the guys, and I feel all alone. I have been in this very same platoon since December 1964. No one, save Steve Best, has been in the platoon nearly as long. I will be the first to be discharged, but that isn't for 386 days. Like prison inmates, we count how long we have to go before we're released.

Crack interrupts my daydreams, "Spencer is now going to demonstrate how to best administer a battlefield intravenous injection. Step forward, trooper." I set up the line, bag, and needle, and ask for a volunteer. Holt jumps up and within one minute the fluid known as dextrose is flowing into his vein. Others join in, sticking each other in the arms. A couple of riflemen walk by and see all the bags and tubes and the needles stuck into our arms and cringe. The paradox hits home. Here are a couple of guys, trained to be killers, cringing at the sight of needles stuck in our arms. Amazing, I think. Simply amazing.

The weather is getting a little warmer. While standing on the deck of the ship, I can actually feel the warm and then cold pockets of air. Down below, our sleeping quarters is becoming unbearable. The air below, by comparison to the outside's sweet-smelling breeze, is stagnant and tainted with a pungent odor of uncleansed humans.

The ocean is growing rougher as each hour passes. I still cannot eat properly. The food is terrible. I spend most of my time on deck thinking of what is to come. My thoughts both petrify and fascinate me. Everything I am experiencing is new to my senses. It makes me yearn for more. It is fascinating. My world is changing at a pace I have never experienced. I conjure images of little people welcoming us, cheering our arrival with signs of "Welcome G.I. Joe. Thank You For Coming To Help Us."

The ship's administration circulates a newspaper. Most, if not all of the information is on the Vietnam War. The most startling report is about our unit, the 1st/501st of the 101st Airborne. We are no longer that unit! Our new unit designation is the 4th Battalion of the 503rd Regimental Combat Unit in the 173rd Airborne Brigade. 4th/503rd of the 173rd. Holy shit, what a bombshell. I always wanted to be in the 173rd, and now I am. Patches with the insignia of the 173rd are passed out within an hour of the release of the newspaper. Background colors that house the wings we wear on our hats are also distributed. Gone is the Screaming Eagle patch of the 101st Airborne. Sewing the patches on our uniforms consumes our time for most of the day.

At day's end, I lay on my bunk, highest in a vertical stack of five. My thoughts drift toward home. I think about that party I went to where I told John Yard and the others how I came to enlist in the service. I think of my little sister, Connie, hugging my leg as I said goodbye to my folks at Detroit Metro Airport.

My mind flashes to my family getting the news of my death. How would they react? Would my baby sister remember me? Try as I might, I can't shake the feeling that I will not make it through Vietnam. Invariably the questions arise: Why? How? Where will I get hit? I keep saying it is for God and country, but I can't buy it. We are not defending America's shores. No one is invading our country. Hell, it isn't even a declared war, and yet we all know it is a war. We are kept abreast of other infantry units' encounters with Mr. Charlie, the Viet Cong, or, worse yet, the North Vietnamese Army (NVA). The NVA is trained just as we are; the only difference is that Vietnam is their turf, their backyard.

JUNE 9 1966

I am awakened as usual by the barking of the squad leaders. "OK, you dogs, *on your feet!* Let's go, first call, assholes. Move, *move!*" If we wait for the second call, we end up on KP. Invariably, we learn to time our movements by the sergeants' footsteps. We stick together— black, Hispanic, and white guys. If your buddy is moving too slow, you push him to get him moving. This cohesion generates a form of *esprit de corps*. We need to feel good about something; it might as well be about each other. Instinctively, we know it is us against them (them being both our own sergeants as well as the enemy). We, therefore, demonstrate compassion from time to time amongst ourselves in this otherwise sea of despair.

Sergeant Flock continues to inquire as to whether I still have my diary. I insist that I do not know what he is talking about. He knows better; someone must be telling him that I have it. He threatens to confiscate it if he ever catches me writing in it. I plead my case, saying that someone, somewhere should know what it is like to be an infantry medic. He walks away, saying, "If you have it, you better get it right— you better mention my name, too." Sometimes he winks as he makes that statement and sometimes he just breaks out in a small grin. I appeal to his ego, and it works every time. I know he wants me to document what is going to happen because he occasionally makes a statement like, "If you don't write that book, I'll personally look you up and kick your ass." He always sends me mixed signals—very much like the relationship I have with my father. Still, I'd rather not cross him if I don't have to.

He has the power to make my life miserable, and he has the power to send me out on every patrol he desires. Therefore, he has the power of life and death over me. Fortunately, for me, I can out-maneuver him mentally. I am no rocket scientist, but he is far from being an Einstein.

9 P.M., Thursday. I go up onto the deck. The air is warm, and the sky is full of stars like I have never seen before. In fact, they are so bright I can write in my diary without the aid of the pen flashlight I always carry. Stars from horizon to horizon. What an absolutely beautiful sight. I know I will never see more of the universe than I see tonight. It is an incredible sight.

I let my mind separate me from reality. After all, this can't be reality. I know I'm going to wake up and be at home, in my parent's house. Home, where it is relatively safe. Home, where I feel relatively secure in my surroundings. Home, where I can be myself. Here and now, I am not myself. I am a product of someone else's doing. In fact, any attempt to be myself is looked upon with consternation by the watchdogs of behavior, the senior sergeants. If your attitude isn't what they want it to be, you're considered a potential threat. You learn quickly the type of behavior the army wants out of you. Even if you are unaware of the psychology being deployed, you learn. I wish I did not have the intelligence to be aware of what's happening and why. I almost feel it's a curse to be aware. Most of the others haven't got a clue.

I think about home again and calculate that it's about 1 or 2 A.M. there. Everyone's asleep, cozy in their respective worlds. I trust all is well. My little brother, Bobby, comes to mind. He is six. Just before I left, I bought him a small fatigue shirt with all the markings and insignia of my uniform. He was happy to get it. I called him my little paratrooper. As I look up to gaze at the stars, I'm reminded of the song, "Up on the Roof," and the stanzas: *"At night the stars put on a show for free, and, darling, you can share it all with me."* The song reminds me of Beatrice. She was at the party before I left Detroit. Afterwards, I purposely broke up with her because I felt I wasn't coming back. I called it off only because in the event of my death, she would be free without remorse. A lot of guys did the same thing with their girlfriends. I am simply following along with the norm set by the army. No, the army did not tell us to break up with our girlfriends— it was something we did because we all felt it was the right thing to do.

Silent tears well up inside. I allow myself to feel human for just a moment and then the cadence and the words gush forth: *Airborne— All the way—Every day.* Screw it, I think. If someone's gotta die,

OK, let it be me. But, if it's going to happen, please make it in the first thirty days, not the last thirty. Please, I plead, as if I am speaking to some entity who controls life and death.

It is impossible to differentiate between days of the week. No longer are there normal hours or weekdays or weekends. Instructional classes are held at any and/or all hours of the day and night. A first aid class is held at 10:30 P.M. Afterward, we go up on the deck to exercise by the light of the stars. Nothing, absolutely nothing, is normal. The world I knew is becoming more and more distant to me. The only routine is the absence of a routine. The only thing certain is the uncertainty. I suspect it's all part of the scheme to prepare us for what is to come.

JUNE 11 1966

After five days at sea, I sense we're all changing. It's difficult to describe, but tensions are mounting. We look at ourselves differently. Perhaps it's sinking in; we're actually going to war. This is not just another drill. The officers and sergeants sense the change in group dynamics. More discipline of mind and body is demanded. More classes, more physical exercises are conducted. I find it demeaning to be part of it all, but I'm powerless to do a damn thing to stop it. Our living conditions are nearly intolerable. Some of the guys are not taking showers, and the odor below is overwhelming. "Get used to it," bellows one sergeant. "Where you're going makes this shit look very comforting." I suspect they're poking fun at us, the animals, while we're in our cage, so when they release us we'll strike out in anger at Mr. Charlie or his cousin, the NVA.

The combat-hardened World War II and Korean veterans are all senior sergeants now and are not letting up on us. They assault us both verbally and physically by having us do bullshit work details like scrubbing the deck with brushes and soap—on our knees! Tonight, the guys in the bunk area adjacent to ours are talking about what they would do to these sergeants if they ever went out on patrol with them. Bullshit, they're just venting. Killing our own does not register in my mind; I put that thought out as quickly as I hear them say it.

More classes are conducted, only this time it's not about saving lives. The classes are on the nomenclature of the .45 caliber pistol as well as the M-79 grenade launcher. As I sit listening, I think of the paradox: medics learning to use weapons to kill.

JUNE 12 1966

At church today we pray for a safe return. I'm sure all of us pray for the same thing. Even Charlie probably prays for peace and victory. We sing a few songs and try to distract ourselves from this reality. Later I went to see a movie with Chuck Holt, but I couldn't sit through it. I'm too restless and edgy. The ocean is choppy, full of whitecaps, but the ship is taking it in without any difficulty. Three hundred and eighty-three days to go, and I'm out. That is, provided I make it.

As the days go by, I'm learning more and more about this ship. Today, I ran into an empty compartment with bunks and air conditioning. Meanwhile, we're crammed together in our area without air conditioning. It makes no sense whatsoever! But then, this is the army, and if I've learned anything in the past two years, it's that nothing makes much sense.

JUNE 19 1966

Saw land today for the first time since our departure of June 6th. Here in the middle of the ocean stands a monstrous volcanic rock that juts out of the ocean. It's a strange sensation to see land, but then again, it is only a rock sticking out of the ocean. No vegetation, no life, just a rock. The weather is getting warmer and warmer as each day passes. The sea is very calm, almost mirror-like. They piped air conditioning into our sleeping area today. Boy, what a relief. The trade-off is that the motors that are running the air conditioning are close to deafening. Still, I'll take it over the constant yelling and cursing. Besides, the sound of the motors running will block out the snoring of the guys. In all those World War II movies, I never heard any mention of the deplorable conditions of troop ships going to war.

A fight just broke out between a white guy and a black guy. Leon Dallas is running to break it up. All I can think is, hey, fellas, pretty soon we'll all be armed to the teeth; let's try to get along before we kill ourselves. Besides, whites are outnumbered four to one. My white brothers should wake up and smell the coffee. Racial tensions run high. Insane. We're supposed to be on the same side, and yet we can't get along among ourselves.

We are advised today that our little "rendezvous with destiny" is a mere four days away. Four more days on this stinking ship in these incredible conditions. I can't wait to get off, even if it means coming face to face with Mr. Charlie himself. Word is filtering down that we may be in for a welcoming party by a couple of North Vietnamese Army divisions. That information takes our minds off of our differences and allows us, for the moment, to focus on who is the real enemy.

JUNE 21 1966

I spot a ship along our starboard side; I also spot some buoys. We must be nearing land. The ocean is changing color from brilliant blue to a dark, almost black appearance. I remember the color changes when we set out from San Francisco. Exercise is now taking place three times each day. Men are quick-tempered, and fights are a daily occurrence. Unfortunately, these fights involve members of different races: White against black, black against Hispanic, and occasionally white against Hispanic. The situation is nearly out of control. With all our animosity toward one another, what in the world is going to happen when we get there and we're all armed? In the meantime, I'm glad that I'm a medic. In comparison, we are definitely a cut above the others, meaning the riflemen. They're animals without restraint.

A lot of them are looking forward to their first kill. They speak as if they are going hunting for deer and not "the most deadly game." Deer don't fire back. What a bunch of idiots. A fight breaks out to my immediate left between a black and a Hispanic. I scream at the two, "Save it for Charlie! We're supposed to be on the same team; now knock it off!' They stop but give each other looks that say, "I'm going to kill you."

That nice little quiet area I found early on our journey proves to be the brig. I sneak off and catch a nap there from time to time. It is a welcomed reprieve from the crowded conditions everywhere else aboard ship. I show the brig to Steve and Chuck, but they're afraid to go in for fear of being disciplined.

I feel like I am coming down with a cold or some other virus. I am tired when I should not be and decide to lie down to catch some zzzzzzzs. When I wake some eight hours later, my gums are bleeding. Sick Call diagnoses it as "cutting a wisdom tooth." I take some pain meds and drift off to sleep again in our bunk area.

When I wake, I am told I missed a mandatory class and that I will be put on KP as punishment. "KP," I think. "You've got to be kidding? Spec-4s don't pull KP." I get more pissed when I learn another person, a black guy, missed the class as well, and nothing is going to happen to him. It appears that the squad leaders in our platoon covered for him even though he is one rank lower than I. Well, that's bullshit. Screw them, I'm not going on KP. I'll just tell my story, and all will be forgiven. This racial division is bullshit. Prior to this event, I was passed over three times for Spec-5 by black guys who are my junior. A white man, normally, does not think discrimination is aimed at him; I just figure they don't like me, forget that color of skin nonsense.

My mind is made up to take a stand. After all, the acting company commander is a white guy; he'll have to understand. So the stage is set; the cast of characters in place, and I'm ready. I even did some investigating and lined up witnesses on my behalf who will testify that not one, but two black guys missed the class and that Spec-5 Willie Runner covered for the pair. The next morning the play commences. Sergeant Flock comes up to me and states, "Spencer, report to the mess hall, you're on KP for the next twenty-four hours."

Man, was I ready, so I just ignore him. He repeats himself, only this time his tone was more combative and definitely louder, "Spencer, did you hear me? Report to KP, now."

I turn to look him in the eye, and if looks could kill, he'd already have a headstone. Then I state, "No!"

He responds as if he just got hit in the stomach. His eyes widen as he attempts to gather himself, thinking of his next move. He expands his chest a little, steps back rocking on his heels, takes a step forward and says, "What did you just say?"

I reiterate my point with more clarification than just saying no. "Sergeant Flock, I'm a senior Spec-4, and Spec-4s don't pull KP. Besides, you and I both know two other guys missed the class, and someone covered for them. You know that, and you know that I know that. So get off my case, will you!"

It isn't a question. It is a statement to back off.

Flock is flabbergasted by my audacity and summons another sergeant. Once the other sergeant arrives, Flock begins again. "Specialist Fourth Class Spencer, I hereby am giving you a direct order. Report for KP duty *now*."

His face is in my face, even though he is four inches shorter than I. He must be standing on his toes, but no matter. I stare right back at him and say, "Kiss my ass, Sarge. Take me to the company commander. I respectfully request to speak to him on this issue."

Flock turns to the other sergeant and asks if he heard me disobeying his direct order. When he acknowledges that he did, he turns back to me with a sneer and says, "Boy, your silly white ass is all mine. You will curse the day you were born before I'm through with you." He leans closer and whispers, "I'm going to see to it that you are killed motherfucker. It's going to be legal, and I will get away with it; do you understand me?"

I have to admit I am taken aback and somewhat frightened. But, being young and foolish, I respond with equal venom. I whisper back to him, "Sarge, if I catch your fat black ass out on line, you're all mine." Somehow I manage a smile once the words are out of my mouth. He jerks back, eyes wide in amazement at my raw nerve. I don't really mean it, but I believe he meant what he said. I am simply fighting fire with fire. I look at the sergeant who witnessed the incident and ask him if he heard Flock threaten to kill me. He cynically smiles and says, "I only heard you refusing to follow an order to report to KP."

Well, I'll be a son of a bitch. I've just been had. Still, I think, once I get to the acting company commander, Lieutenant Wronges, I'll simply tell him the whole story. It will be simple . . . right?

Flock is livid. He screams at me that I am under "house arrest" and that I am to lie on my bunk until he returns. He actually puts one of the platoon squad leaders in charge to watch over me. I scream back that it's absurd to be put under house arrest and have someone guard me. "Come on, where would I go? Overboard! You stupid son of a bitch!" Squad leader, Dan Reynolds, a light-skinned black with whom I have a decent rapport, tries to calm me down and says, "Hey, man, be cool. Be quiet, you'll only get yourself in more trouble." He is pleading, but I don't care at that point, and scream, "Kiss my ass, Sergeant Flock! You racist bastard!"

At this point all my fellow medics try to calm me down. Steve Best bursts through the crowd and yells, "Harry, you're playing right in to his hands. Now shut your fucking mouth!" I trust Steve enough to know he is only trying to help, so I stop raving like a lunatic. I shake my head in the affirmative at Steve and start punching someone's bunk. I flail wildly at the pillow, which, in my mind, is Flock himself. Minutes later, Flock reappears wearing a .45 pistol strapped to his hip, flanked by two other sergeants. I assume they are there to kick the shit out of me if I resist.

Amused by the whole scenario, I resign myself to my fate with a sneer for good measure aimed at Flock. OK, pull yourself together, Spencer. Be cool, just tell your side of the story to the acting company commander. The three sergeants escort me to the company commander's office. They tell me to wait outside in the hallway and not to enter until they summon me.

One of the sergeants waits in the hallway with me. Under his breath he whispers, "You're screwed, you know that, trooper?" I pay him no attention, but suddenly I feel I have been in this position before. Deja vu. Shit. This is just like the time I was arrested back home in Detroit. I feel the weight of the world falling on me. God, I'm mad at myself. I screwed up again. Way to go, you stupid asshole, I tell myself, way to fucking go. Still, there's a ray of hope. If I can only convince the lieutenant, if I only could tell him my story and he hears it from my witnesses, I might be able to . . . .

The command to enter is given, "Report." I open the door and walk right to the front of the lieutenant's desk. I come to attention and salute with all the military precision I can muster. "Specialist Fourth Class Spencer, reporting as ordered, Sir."

Lieutenant Wronges barks, "Get the hell out of my office and come back in here in a proper military manner, trooper. Don't you know how to report to a superior?"

I spin an about-face and walk back out. What the hell did I do wrong? Then it hits me. I was supposed to knock first. Yeah, OK, that's it. OK. I got it.

Seconds after closing the door the command, "Report," is again shouted. I bang on the door to the point of hurting my fist. "Come." And again, I walk to the front of the lieutenant's desk, snap a crisp salute, and state, "Specialist Fourth Class Spencer, reporting as ordered, Sir."

The lieutenant doesn't even bother to look up and says, as if he were annoyed, "I'll give you one last chance to try it again. Get out of here. And come back in with the proper military manner of a professional soldier."

There were four senior sergeants lined up behind him; all of them are standing at the parade rest position. Two are stone-faced while the other two, Flock and the World War II-lifer, Sergeant Major Dow, are smirking at me. In fact, Flock is rocking on his heels and toes and staring at me with a look of death in his eye. As I make eye contact with him, he smirks triumphantly.

I pivot to about-face and march out of the office, I know I have just one last shot at it. With my heart racing and adrenaline flowing, I beat on the door again, not waiting for the command. Bam. Bam. Bam. Bam. I hit the door with such force I break the skin off my knuckles. I hear the command, "Come." Once again, very deliberately and at a much slower pace I walk up to his desk, begin to salute him, when that little voice inside of me takes over. "Fuck it, Spencer, you can't win. So do something that'll blow their fucking minds."

So I drop my salute before my hand comes up to my forehead and put my hands on my hips. I gaze at all the sergeants whose smirks have disappeared and give them my best "screw you" look. This time I'm the one smirking at them. The company commander's head bolts up from some bullshit piece of paper he's pretending to read and shouts, "What in the hell do you think you're doing? Atten-Hut." But I don't move. I just stare down at him. His eyes widen at the realization that I am not going to play his game. "Goddamn it, trooper! Atten-Hut!" he shouts. I just snicker at him and relax my stance. Putting my hands on top of his desk, I lean forward and say, "Kiss my motherfucking ass . . . Sir."

His eyes look as if they are coming out of his head; his mouth drops open, and he is speechless for a few seconds. He begins to stammer, searching for the right words to counter such stalwart insubordination. Shaking his head in disbelief, he states in a low somber tone, "I don't believe I heard you say what I think I just heard you say," and he looks me in the eye. "Would you mind repeating what I think I heard you say?"

I smirk again in triumph. It is worth it. At this moment I have absolutely no control over my life, so to suddenly speak as a man, not fearing repercussion, and to see him, as well as the senior sergeants in a state of shock—it's worth it.

"No," I said. "I don't mind repeating what you think you heard. What I said was, *'Kiss my motherfucking ass, Sir.'* Can you hear me now?"

With that, he jumps to his feet, pulling out his revolver and runs around his desk to get me. But I don't flinch. In fact, I smile at all of those sergeants who are still stunned at what I have just said, when the lieutenant grabs me by my fatigue shirt, jerking me toward him and puts his .45 caliper pistol to my temple. "I ought to kill you right now, trooper. Do you understand me?'

He is searching for some form of capitulation from me when I respond, "Go ahead, Sir. It's your move."

He pushes me away, ordering the sergeants to throw me in the brig for the remainder of the trip to Vietnam. "No, on second thought, put him on KP and post a guard to watch over him," he shouted as the sergeants lead me away. "You'll have a court martial waiting for you once we're in-country." He continues to shout as I walk down the ship's corridor toward the brig.

At that point I don't care what he has to say. However, that nanosecond high I felt in telling him what he can do with himself is fading fast. Now I am spinning toward earth at mach ten as I figure I have just screwed myself again. I feel empty, void of feelings, numb to the world. The only feeling I have for sure is that I don't care—about anything! Nothing matters. All my hopes and dreams are gone. Try as I may to conjure up visions of how that is going to effect the rest of my life, it simply does not compute.

Instead of going directly on to KP duty, they march me to the ship's brig, where I am left alone to deal with silence and total darkness. No lights, no sounds, just me and my inability to grasp what I have done. I begin talking to myself. I know I was out of line. I know I have screwed myself. I also know I have a story to tell and that one day, in some way, I will somehow get the chance to tell someone. There has to be someone in the world of this army who would listen and understand, not only why I did what I did, but also, that there was a conspiracy that caused me to act as I did. Someone, somewhere, but who, and when? I don't have an answer. So I sit in silence and dark for the next twenty-four hours.

The next day they come for me and march me off to the mess hall for KP duty. As I enter the cafeteria area, the early birds are already eating breakfast. When they see me, they start cheering, clapping their hands and whistling. Most, if not all who are cheering are either Hispanic or white. I have mixed feelings about my reception because I know they will not be with me when I have to face the music. I have been in the army long enough to surmise what is in store for me—a demotion, hard labor, and a monetary fine. Maybe one, maybe all three.

Chapter 5

ARRIVING IN VIETNAM

THE SIGHT OF land and knowing it is Vietnam is both breathtaking and terrifying. Word has it that we'll stay aboard ship for another twenty-four hours, disembarking tomorrow for our duty station in Bien Hoa. The heat is unbearable. We've truly had a false sense of how hot it is because the ship has been moving between fifteen and eighteen knots for the past eighteen days.

Stopped in the harbor of Cam Ranh Bay, the steel gray ship is soaking up the heat and reflecting it back at us. Just standing on deck and not moving, we sweat profusely. Within an hour of stopping, we, the medics, are ordered to pass out salt tablets to the infantry platoons we're temporarily assigned to. Guys are getting sick and vomiting from the intense heat. The distribution of salt tablets is my first involvement in looking after my brother grunts. We're ordered to move about as little as possible, "Do not exert yourself any more than is absolutely necessary." That order is the first one that makes any sense on this voyage of the Grim Reaper.

The Vietnamese people are, if I may, very foreign looking, which is ironic because I'm really the foreigner. This is their land. As I stand on deck, the "boat people" paddle out to get a closer look at the newest troops to arrive in their country. Then I hear automatic weapons fire. It is coming from the opposite side of the ship. Holy shit, we haven't been issued any ammunition yet, and we may be coming under attack! I instinctively respond—someone may be hit!

I've got to go check it out. I push my way through the crowd of guys who are also trying to see what was happening, making my way to the guy who is doing the shooting. As it turns out, he's a military police officer, an MP.

A platoon of MP's came out on a small watercraft with an official welcoming party from the army. His fatigues are not green. Faded by the sun and the number of times they've been washed, his fatigues look dingy when compared to our newly issued fatigues.

Information has it, the "boat people" were getting too close to the ship, and the MP's are under orders to keep them at a safe distance. They do so by firing into the water very near the small boats' hulls. The MP's have no reservation about firing their weapons to keep the boats at bay. It is somewhat perplexing. They're just small Vietnamese people coming to greet us . . . smiling, waving their hands, clapping and shouting in broken English, "Hello, G.I., Welcome. You number one Joe," pointing to no one in particular. I also hear one of them plead, "Food, please, food, G.I."

It breaks my heart to see these people, so pleasant, so friendly, beckoning us to help them. Hell, they don't appear to be a threat to me. So I approach an MP and ask, "What gives here? Why all the fire power?" He shoots me an indifferent glance and returns his gaze upon the "boat people." "Stick around, trooper," he says. "If you're lucky you'll learn not to trust anyone. Young, old, male or female, even your fellow paratroopers—every one here is a potential threat. And given the right conditions, they will not hesitate to blow your fucking head off."

He then spots a boat straying too close and lets off a short burst from his M-16 rifle. Within a second after he pulls the trigger, at least five rounds spew into the water very near one of the boats. He shouts at them, "Dee Dee Mao! Motherfuckers. Dee Dee Mao," as he waves his arm for them to back off.

Man, I think. That's one cold dude. These people are just glad to see us, but this asshole MP is firing at them. I feel sorry for those people. They are simply begging us for substance and welcoming us. Sure, some are bolder than others. Some ask us for money, some ask us if we want a "short time," which is vernacular for sex.

As I stand there and take in the surreal setting, I see little kids rubbing their stomachs and hear them say, "Please, Joe, candy?" I scan them all and realize that they are indeed a small race of people. Their skin tone is different than anything I could have imagined. They do, in fact, have a yellowish skin tone and a frail thin look about them. Growing up, I was told, in so many ways, that the enemy possesses yellow skin, slanted eyes, and big smiles. Even the "Hi, G.I." fits the programming. It is an eerie feeling.

Today, I'll write in my diary about my arrival to Vietnam, the unbearable heat, and my punishment for insubordination. The punishment will not be a court martial, but something less, an Article 15. An Article 15 is just this side of a court marshal in terms of increments of punishment per the Uniform Code of Military Justice. Now there is an oxymoron if I ever heard one—military justice! Yeah, right! Sergeant Flock informs me that they want to give me a Section 8 discharge, which is basically an honorable discharge with the stigma "unable to adjust" clause. He told me that he went to bat for me only because he wants me to die in battle rather than be discharged that way. I remember what he said when we had our little disagreement: "I'm going to see that you're killed." Only now, I'm starting to believe him. But then I think, OK, cool. If I catch him out on the line, he's all mine. Two can play this game.

The next day proves to be very interesting. Our final destination is our base camp just south of the air base at Bien Hoa, which is on the periphery of what is called War Zone C. The trip itself takes just about everything I have in me. We are loaded into the familiar five ton "cattle trucks" for the first part of our trip to Bien Hoa. The mood is solemn, no laughter, no excessive moving around. The heat is a great equalizer to being tough. The "cattle trucks" drop us off at an airstrip for a short jaunt to Bien Hoa. C-130 aircraft are the ticket to war. I have jumped from C-130's before; they are a familiar sight in an otherwise unfamiliar setting.

As we unload from the "cattle trucks," the planes are already fired up, their props turning. The temperature is totally foreign. It is like breathing in a steam room. The heat stings our lungs with every breath. Meanwhile, the sergeants keep prodding us to hurry, hustle, move. Christ, we're burdened down with an average of 150 pounds of equipment per man. Combine the heat, the weight, and the barking of the sergeants—it is cumbersome to say the least.

What really bothers me though is, what's the hurry? But the sergeants never let up. They are mentally beating us while the weight of our equipment is physically killing us. Still, we try to adhere to their commands. We hustle for the sake of pride; after all, there are non-airborne personnel all around, watching our every move. No one wants to wimp out.

So we push ourselves, some of us to the breaking point. As we near the planes, the noise intensifies. So does the heat. A few steps in front of me a guy falls face first on the concrete. My first thoughts are: Why did he fall? Was he hit? What's going on? And then, as if someone just flipped a light switch, my training kicks in, and I make my way toward him.

As I get closer to him, the prop blast from the plane's propellers hit me as well. Jesus Christ. It's difficult to breathe. The air is so fucking hot it burns my nostrils when I inhale. I fall to my knees alongside of him and gasp for air. Oh, God! I can't breathe! I again gasp for air, trying to remain calm. It's not working. Oh, shit, I'm in trouble. Suddenly, I'm hoisted to my feet by two air force guys with handkerchiefs covering their faces. Before I know what's happening, I'm onboard the aircraft.

They lay the unconscious guy at my feet. His face is bluish gray; he is not getting any oxygen. I peel off my rucksack to be more mobile and check his airway. There, that's all it takes. I straighten out his windpipe, and he begins to cough and gasp for air. When he opens his eyes, he sees me first. He is, however, in shock. I pour water from my canteen onto some gauze and wipe his face gently, reassuring him by yelling in his ear that he'll be all right, that he simply passed out from the heat. I have to yell because the throttled-up engines are deafening, and everyone else is screaming to be heard. He acknowledges my presence with a slight nod of his head. I know then he will be all right. All I have to do at this point is to keep him from being trampled by those still coming on board the plane.

The sweat from my forehead stings and burns my eyes, blurring my vision. "Will somebody please turn the steam bath down?" I yell. A couple of guys close enough to hear me give me a nod and a wink as they pass by. I think, God, how hot is it? It is hotter than anything I have been subjected to in my entire life. A guy I've known for about a year passes me. Doug Coughner, a cool guy, taps a friendly smack on top of my helmet. I hadn't recognized him in all that gear he's wearing. It's not easy to recognize guys you know when they are dressed up in combat garb. Next stop—Bien Hoa. "All aboard!"

Again, the "cattle trucks" are waiting for us as we disembark from the aircraft. I'll give the military credit for one thing: they knew logistics and the movement of men and equipment. I like the precision and certainty of it. It makes me feel that somewhere, someone knows what they're doing. I take comfort, in an odd sort of way, knowing that.

Once on the road, which is a one-lane road to our base camp, we soon spot others wearing the shoulder patch of the 173rd. Whoever they are and whatever they are doing, they stop to watch us go by. Most of them give us a big smile, a wave or a thumbs-up sign. Some, on the other hand, simply shake their heads. We all know what that means—you sorry bastards; you don't know what you're in for. They're all very tan compared to us. Our long-sleeve fatigue shirts are rolled up, and the sun's rays burn our exposed skin, neck, face, and arms. Another item of interest: most, if not all of our fellow paratroopers look thin, no spare reserves of fat on them. No, Sir.

We arrive at our prepared battalion area. There, standing empty, are rows and rows of large tents. Once the trucks stop, the sergeants continue where they left off, "You," one of them yells. "Yes, you," some asshole among us responds. "Get down and give me twenty." I think to myself, they've got to be kidding. In this heat? They're nuts, absolutely nuts. The command to "fall in" is given. Because I am aboard one of the first arriving trucks, I hold my arm up in the air and shout, "Medical platoon, here."

Soon men all around me are shouting out the titles of their respective platoons. "First platoon, A Company here, Signal Platoon. Form up here," and so on until the entire battalion has come to order in proper formation. The battalion sergeant major, "Top," as he is sometimes called, welcomes us and reads off our respective tent numbers. The medical platoon is assigned tent number thirteen. Not that I'm superstitious, but of all fucking numbers . . . thirteen. Great. Once all tent numbers are assigned, we are dismissed to seek and find our respective tents. This will be our home until we are either killed or wounded in action, or on a brighter note, "rotate" back to the states, having served our twelve months in-country.

The tents are large enough to house upwards of thirty guys. The sides of the tents have screens built into two-by-four-foot studs. The floor is a slab of concrete. Our tent has been entirely closed up, causing the stagnant air inside to be at least 150 degrees. I mutter, "What stupid bastard left the sides down, Jesus Christ? How fucking stupid."

Unbeknownst to me, Sergeant Flock is within earshot and hears my comment. "You think its hot, Spencer, do you?" he asks. "Well, let's just see how hot it can get. Get down and give me fifty."

Fifty? He's out of his fucking mind. But I am not about to exacerbate an already-strained relationship, so I drop down and begin the count. During the repetitions, the sweat is pouring off my face onto the concrete, at nearly a constant drip. Finished, I jump to my feet in a show of "no sweat," when the world begins to whirl around me. I fall backwards before I know what has happened. The others simply laugh at me, but I don't think it's funny. Hell, I'm in shock. As they laugh, I think, this shit is crazy. We're in a war zone, and he's got me doing pushups; this is insane. God, get me out of here. The temperature on our very first day in Vietnam reaches a record high of 122 degrees.

Later, Flock informs me with his usual smirk that Captain Martin, our regular company commander, wants to see me. Shit. Martin is a hard-nosed son of a bitch. He, along with other upper echelon officers, including our medical platoon doctor, Jim Pierce, has been in country for two weeks before our arrival. Captain Martin is a Korean vet. He earned his Combat Infantryman's badge as an enlisted man, working his way up to direct commission as an officer the hard way. Make no mistake about it, it's impossible to run a game on this man. He is unmerciful and a bastard at heart. Martin considers most other officers to be lily-livered punks without backbones. He never liked me, but I feel the same way about him. Only now, I fear him more than ever and what he'll do to me after the incident on board ship with Lieutenant Wronges.

As I enter his makeshift tent/headquarters, his tirade is immediate. "Just who the fuck do you think you are? And where the fuck do you think you are, trooper?" I don't think he wants me to respond so I simply stand at attention like a tin soldier. "You really fucked up, didn't you? You little punk!" Again, I know better than to give him some kind of plausible answer. He continues, "Do you have any idea what the good Doctor Pierce did for you while you were en route to Vietnam?" I stare straight ahead, not flinching, and certainly not responding. "Well, let me tell you," he growls as he walks up to me and puts his face in mine, "He convinced me that you were worthy of being promoted to *buck sergeant.*" Shit, I think. Oh, shit!

The rating of buck sergeant as opposed to that of specialist fifth class denotes not just achievement, but true leadership among the ranks. Spec 5's are subordinate to buck sergeants. I have already been busted from Spec 4 to PFC (Private first Class). "Did you know that, Private?"

I respond with dismay, "No, Sir, I was unaware of that."

"Well," Martin continues. "While you were on your way to this little picnic, he went to bat for you and convinced me you deserve to be promoted, and against my better judgment, I went along with him and had orders cut promoting you to E-5, a three striper, a buck sergeant. You stupid son of a bitch!"

Martin is nearly screaming while he waves what I presume to be the official orders of my promotion. As he berates me, I know he is on the edge of losing it. His eyes burn right through me. He is certainly a tough-looking guy with a long scar running the length of his face, from just underneath his left eye socket down to his outer jaw line. Rumor has it he got sliced in hand-to-hand combat in Korea. Martin stands about 5'7" and weighs about 175 pounds. He not only acts tough, but he has the build to back it up. He scares me. But I just stand before him absolutely still, hoping I will leave his office with my face intact. His raspy gravel voice and ice blue eyes pierce my soul. It is nearly impossible to look him in the eye. If the devil is alive, he is alive in this man.

He continues nonstop, his nose just inches from mine, even though he has to look up at me. "Spencer, you have embarrassed a lot of people, good people who, for whatever reason, believed in you. You not only let them down, you let yourself down. But let me tell you one thing, I've had your number right from the start; you are a weasely ass punk. How you ever made it through jump school is a mystery to me. So, let me make this perfectly clear: I am going to make your life as miserable as possible. You are going to wish you had never been born by the time I'm through with you. Do you understand me, trooper?"

Ooohhh, yeah, I think. I understand all too well. Martin has the power and brains Sergeant Flock can only dream about. Right on the spot, I resign myself to my fate. I figure I'll never make it home alive.

"Spencer," he then says, "You're dismissed, get your sorry-ass self out of my sight." I snap him a salute, pivot an about-face to leave his tent, when he gives me a parting shot. "Oh, by the way, if you ever pull the shit on me that you pulled on Lieutenant Wronges, I promise you I *will* blow your fucking head off. Now, get the hell out of here." As he speaks, I turn to look him dead in the eye. I wish I hadn't; I believe him.

Sergeant Flock and Dr. Pierce are waiting for me outside the tent. They heard the entire one-way conversation. I feel totally humiliated, defeated, and genuinely remorseful. I snap a salute to Dr. Pierce and state, "Captain, I'm terribly sorry I let you down. I humbly apologize, and I ask that in time you forgive me." He is a compassionate man whom I admire. His eyes tell me he understands and that he is sad for me.

He acknowledges my statement without speaking, nodding his head, casting his eyes downward, when Flock jumps in, "OK, trooper, let's go, follow me. We need an ammunition storage dump dug. Your hard labor punishment starts now." He leads me to an area two hundred feet away from our compound of tents adjacent to the road that winds through, not only our battalion area, but other battalion areas as well. At the site where Flock wants me to dig, an armed guard holds a shotgun cradled across his arms. White chalk outlines the size of the proposed ammo dump; it's twenty-five-by-twenty feet and six feet deep. Lying next to the chalk line is a stack of shovels and pickaxes. The time is 4:30 P.M.; the temperature a blistering 112 degrees, cooler than the 122 degrees at noon. I know this because temperature gauges hang off every tent, and, because the ammo dump is near the latrine tents, I can look up any time and check the temperature.

However, the hard labor detail will have to wait until morning. Our first priority is to dig what we lovingly call a mass grave alongside our platoon tent. It is nothing more than a trench three feet wide, four feet deep, and forty-five feet long. The grave is where we'll take cover should we come under attack. Thirty of us medics labor in the

100-plus-degree heat until 9:30 P.M. The rationale for digging well into the night is that Mr. Charlie occasionally pays a visit, striking most often under the cover of darkness. A rumor circulated among us while we were still aboard ship: Mr. Charlie or his cousins, the NVA, will provide us with a welcome party, an obvious metaphor for an attempt to kill us. With that thought, we dig fast and hard. No one wants to be caught out in the open should the "party" begin.

JUNE 26 1966

Off in the distance, somewhere on our base camp, artillery fire missions are taking place as I write. With no electricity in our tents, I write by light of candle. I remember the posters that hung all around our battalion area at Fort Campbell with "Seven Days A Week" laid over a map of Vietnam.

It doesn't feel like Sunday. People are working and fighting everywhere here. The air force's runway is a mere half of a mile from our base camp. It seems as if jet aircraft are taking off or landing every ten to fifteen minutes. Though we have been subjected to the noise of the C-123s, C-124s, C-130s, and the Huey helicopters, the noise from the jets is louder than any one of us could have imagined.

The temperature right now is ninety-five degrees, even though it's 10 at night. We're eating c-rations until the mess hall is up and running. Four more days and I will have been in the army two years. Some of the guys who were in the platoon, but who transferred to the 173rd three weeks ago and flew here by commercial airliner, stop by to say hello. Johnnie White is among them. It is good to see them, even though I wasn't close to any of them. That is, it is good until I ask about Fred Torrent. "Fred's dead, got hit last week," replies Johnnie White.

Holy shit, what a jolt! Fred Torrent went to Fort Campbell with me, Rocky Southern and Johnnie White from jump school; then we all went on to medical school together at Fort Sam in San Antonio, Texas. Fred . . . dead! I wonder what my fate will be. Freddie, dead . . . man, what a shock.

Rain, rain and more rain. I suspect it's Mother Nature's way of cooling off this god-forsaken inferno. But, when the rain stops, the humidity becomes unbearable. It's like living in a steam bath! The smell of this place is foreign to me, too. It smells like shit with no breeze and no wind to move the air. If there was a breeze, it might be tolerable. Then again, maybe it has something to do with the start of my punishment. I began digging the ammo pit today, and low and behold, it's next to the damn latrines. The latrines themselves are wooden structures covered on top with canvas about fifteen feet by twenty feet. Inside there are holes cut into plywood so you can sit and take a dump into a fifty-five-gallon drum just below each hole. Wwwoowwee. it stinks!

Digging is incredibly hard given the heat, humidity, and the stench from the latrines. I can only dig for about ten minutes before I have to take a break. While I rest, I decide the other thing about this place that is foreign is that everybody accepts rain as part of the reality of living. Nobody attempts to get out of the rain. We walk, run, and work while it rains. Being wet from sweat or rain is simply part of our existence. Now that is strange.

As I dig in the rain, my hands slide on the wood. Looking at my hands reminds me of when I was a kid and spent too much time in the bathtub; they would shrivel up with squiggly lines that were non-existent when dry. While looking down at my hands, I also notice that in the last couple of days I've lost some weight; my waistline also looks foreign to me.

After four hours of digging, I am ordered to join the others for a "forced" march in full field gear. The idea is to have us become acclimated to the temperature and humidity with the weight that we will normally carry while out on patrol. They even issue us ammunition prior to the march, which makes sense—just minutes before there was an armed guard watching over me. Now I'm armed to the teeth with 700 rounds of M-16 ammunition, and, yes, I even have my M-16! Only in the army!

Our march takes us throughout the entire brigade area. Men are spread apart fifteen feet on both sides of a roadway, which is maybe twenty feet wide. Some are talking, some lighting cigarettes, all laboring under the weight of rucksacks, heat, and humidity. Knowing that we are all armed makes me feel as if we are a force to be reckoned with. We know our strengths as well as our weaknesses. I count on our strengths to make up for the weaknesses. Our weak spot is the fact that ninety-nine percent of us have never come under enemy fire. Our strength is the collective power of our weapons. We know our weapons like we know our serial numbers. And, because of live-fire training exercises, we know what our weapons can do. After all, we are our nation's fiercest fighting force—we are United States Paratroopers, members of the elite 173rd Airborne Brigade. The Rock Troopers. The Sky Soldiers! I smile with pride at that thought as I march on.

A lot of the guys are candid about encountering Charlie. They want that first kill and the medals that go with it. I, on the other hand, could care less if we never make contact. Hell, I don't have anything against these people. They haven't done anything to me. And if anyone should be upset, they should be. We are, after all, on their soil. Beatrice's words while at the party come to mind, "It is a civil war between the North and the South, just like our own Civil War." It made sense, but I didn't have much of a choice. I sure as hell was not going to stay with my folks after graduation. And the judge didn't give me much of a choice either. Besides, if I question the war, my ass will be put in a healthy sling. Each time I've opened my mouth it has caused me nothing but grief. No, I'll go along with it all. Just another 360-some days, and I'm outta this place.

After the arduous four-mile march, which took about two-and-one-half hours, we are spent. The heat has taken its toll. I had to treat five guys for heat exhaustion because they insisted on carrying an incredible sum of 2000 rounds of ammo instead of the mandated 700 rounds per rifleman. I tell one guy he is nuts for carrying the extra load on top of the required seventy pounds of equipment we are required to carry. His response is, "I'm not going to run out of ammo. I'll be just fine, just give me a minute." M-16 rifles have the capability of spewing out 750 rounds per minute. Theoretically, if we just carried 700 rounds as required, we would be out of ammo in one minute! Although that could never happen for a number of reasons, most of us carry a little more ammo than required.

On top of the rifleman's supplies I carry, I'm also weighted down with my own large medical bag, loaded with everything from bandages to pneumatic splints. The aid kit also includes three pints of intravenous fluids, a gallon of water contained in three separate bladders, drugs, cravats, pressure dressings, plus 700 rounds of ammo for my M-16, and forty-nine rounds of ammo for my .45 caliber pistol. Additionally, a small first-aid kit is strapped to my waist belt so that when we come under fire, I can slip out of my heavy rucksack and gain the maneuverability to treat my patient. With the rucksack on it's nearly impossible to move quickly and get to the injured. In all the war movies I have ever seen in my life, no one appeared as burdened as we are. I guess it doesn't make for good footage to see a man stumbling around and falling under the weight he carries!

Back in my tent and rid of my rucksack and other hanging-on items (grenades, etc.), I notice how everyone's fatigues are as soaked with perspiration as mine. I am tired, and, like everyone else, I want to crash on my cot, but Sergeant Flock has another idea. From outside our tent he yells, "Spencer! Front and center, come out here, now!"

What the hell does he want now? I get up from my cot and walk out to him. "Yeah, Sarge, what's up?"

With perspiration pouring off his face and into his eyes, he snarls at me, "Report back to the ammo pit. You've got four more hours to dig before day's end. Now move it, trooper."

He has the same look in his eye that he had when he said he would see to it that I am killed. I try to dismiss that look and simply walk slowly toward the ammo pit. Screw it, there's not a damn thing I can do.

As I walk toward the ammo pit it starts to rain, again. Shit. Although I know the rain will cool me down while digging, I don't welcome it. Two more guys—a white guy and a black guy—are at the pit when I arrive and are already digging. I ask what they did to deserve the honors. The white guy answers first, "Shit, man, I didn't do a damn thing. Just told my squad leader to kiss my ass. He wanted a full field inspection upon returning from that chicken-shit march, that's all, man."

The black guy interrupts him with a raised tone of voice, "Now, come on, asshole, you know you told him more than that." He looks at me and says, "Doc, that stupid cracker told the squad leader he would cap him when they go out on patrol together."

Wow. Another threat to kill one of our own, I think, and respond, "Look, guys, if you're really serious about offing someone, at least have the brains not to advertise it! Stupid move, Jake."

Jake responds with a childlike deflection, "Well, why don't you ask him what the hell he did to get here?"

I don't respond other than to pick up a shovel and join them in the ever-deepening pit. The rain continues as the guard stands over us with a shotgun and a shit-eating grin. As I dig, I think of the insanity of the whole situation; there's a guard standing over us, and we have weapons and ammo back in our tents.

The next four days are a repeat of the first day. After four days of digging in the rain and mud, my hands begin to break apart. Blood under calluses is not a good sign. Each shovel full of heavy earth takes its toll. We live in mud and filth, and we have nothing to eat but c-rations. I'm trying to adapt to it all, and it seems to be working. Nothing in my past made much sense either, and I coped. I'll be all right. I just got to keep it in perspective. In one year this will all be history. But then again, a million dollar wound doesn't sound too bad either. Maybe a bullet through the forearm or a small shrapnel wound. Yeah, a million-dollar wound, a Purple Heart and a ride home. That's the ticket!

Back in my platoon tent at 2130 hours, we're still without electricity. Candles or flashlights still are the only form of illumination. The communications boys are working around the clock, laying wire to provide us with electrical power. I miss the luxury of a light switch. The other luxury I miss is a toilet seat. Most of us are suffering from digestive problems—probably due to the heat and eating nothing but c-rations for the past few days. Imagine the smell of being close to the latrines with 500 guys suffering from the shits! They didn't talk about that shit in those war movies either.

God must have a master plan. When I woke up this morning, my lips were so swollen I could barely talk. Something must have bit me during the night. God must have created this climate as a breeding ground for *bugs*. Christ, the mosquitoes here are as big as an American horsefly. Back in the pit, I mumble my dilemma to my digging buddies. The black guy, Tyrone, had a field day with me and the swollen lips on a white guy! He tells Jake and me a funny anecdote, "I think I'm gonna train some of those mosquitoes to pick up my big black ass and fly me home. Shit, man, you think you got bit by something bad, check this. I swear, last night, as I laid on my bunk, they is flying around me in formation." His eyes grow wide with theatrics. "And let me tell ya, they can talk too. I swear they's debating which tent I should be sleeping in." At that he can't continue, he laughs at his own performance. Even the guard laughs with us.

It feels good to laugh. I can't remember the last time I laughed so hard. I treasure that moment. I do not want to forget what it is to genuinely laugh.

My hands are really starting to concern me. As I dig yet another day, alternating between marching under a full combat load of equipment, I wrap them in gauze. Just as they begin to form a scab while sleeping, they're ripped open once I start digging. The bandages offer little protection from the persistent rain and mud. I'm not sure how long I can continue.

We take some sniper fire in the night. It is our first taste of coming under fire from Charlie. Nothing overpowering, just an occasional "pop" from a small caliber rifle and a second later we hear the bullet buzzing past us. We estimate him to be nearly a half-mile from us. We stand in our trench that we dug next to our tent and listen. We feel somewhat comfortable with our collective firepower; we don't feel threatened, just fascinated.

But what is really strange is that I can actually tell where the bullets come from and where they head. Our perimeter guards at first withhold a response. They sit in an elevated, fortified tower—four of them—and are in constant communication with the officer on duty. No doubt that officer repeats the standing orders to them, "Do not, under any circumstances, return fire without confirming the origin of such fire at least twice in the exact spot you saw it the first time!"

This little cat and mouse game goes on in the dark for about fifteen minutes. And with every shot Charlie squeezes off, we state, while crouched down, "Sight him, guys, confirm sighting, get him, goddamn it."

Suddenly we hear the sound of a helicopter approaching and, simultaneously, Charlie makes one small mistake. He fires a bullet that was a tracer round. That's all it takes, and our guys on guard duty open fire. M-60 machine guns, one on each tower, open the gates of hell on Charlie. The sound from all four machine guns is deafening compared to that little "pop" we heard from Charlie. Seconds after the machine guns start firing, a Huey gunship shoots past us at about one hundred knots. Just as he flies over us, he opens fire with rockets. Wow! What a sound!

Between the noise of his turbine engine, his rotary blades chopping through the air, and the ssswoooossshh of the rockets leaving the pods, we are beside ourselves with exhilaration. It is an incredible show of force. But, I must say, I have to respect Charlie's raw nerve. If he lived through that barrage of bullets and rockets, next time, he'll triple check and make sure he doesn't fire any tracer rounds.

Back in the ammo pit I let my mind drift. Anything to take my mind off these conditions. June is all but over. Time is flying by, but when I look at how long I have to go before all this is just a mere memory, it feels like forever. I can't help but think that this is not war. Nobody gives a rat's ass if I'm killed or not, outside of my immediate family, of course. With each shovel full of earth I throw, I ask myself, what the hell is this all about? There seems to be as many American civilians here as soldiers. Everywhere you look some form of construction is taking place. Of course, the main people in the work force are the Vietnamese, but the brains, the engineering, are all American.

In the short time I've been here, I get the strange feeling that we're all here to turn this country in to a little America. Based upon my observations, I get the distinct impression someone, somewhere, is making a financial killing. And I know if I speak up about those observations, I'll get myself into hot water, more than I am right now. Mine is not to reason why, mine is but to do or . . .

Tomorrow is payday. I have elected to receive just $50 a month. The remainder, about $200, will be sent home to a savings account. There is not much to spend your money on here. Cigarettes are only ninety cents a carton at the Post Exchange. And toilet articles are dirt cheap. Might as well try to save some so when I get out of the army, I'll have something to fall back on for a while.

We are still in weather acclimation training. We march longer each day throughout the brigade compound. As we go by those who have been in country longer, we're harassed with brash expressions like, "Hang in there, guys; it gets far tougher." Or, "If you guys had any brains, you'd shoot yourself now to get the hell out of here."

None of it makes any sense to me. We keep silent as we slowly march by them and listen to their comments. It's difficult to comprehend how and why things are as they are. Guys are drinking far too much, too often. As a result, a general breakdown in behavior is occurring. Beer is readily accessible at any hour of the day. In fact, the first building erected was the Officers and Enlisted Men's Club. Although they regulate the hours we can purchase beer or whiskey, they do not stop us from overbuying and stocking up a personal inventory. But who wants to drink warm beer? Ice is a missing condiment to cool drinks. Still, some guys drink warm beer. Can you imagine that?

Also, as incredible as it sounds, there is a lot of stealing going on. Items stolen are fenced to the local black market vendor. I have yet to see this for myself, but I hear that if you have the cash you can buy damn near anything. Some of these guys would sell their mothers' eyes for the right price. This frightens me as much as encountering Charlie or the NVA. Here we are, fighting for the right of the Vietnamese people to exist as a free sovereign nation, and with us comes some of the ills of a free society—theft, lies, deceit, and cheating.

At 2000 hours I stop digging and make my way back to my platoon, exhausted. Upon entering the tent, a guy from another battalion approaches to say hello to someone in our platoon. As he follows me into the tent, a group of guys are talking about the black market. The guy and Tyrone, a fellow medic, exchange some words, and, because this guy has been in country longer than any of us, I ask him how the black market vendors get such items as M-16 rifles and ammunition. He smiles coolly and asks, "What do you carry into the jungle for fire power?"

I respond, "Generally, an M-16; why?"

He then looks me dead in the eye, and says, "Let's put it this way, dude, if your platoon or squad comes under fire, and you're outnumbered and overpowered, people getting hit all around you, and you drop your M-16, would you stick around to pick it up or run for your life?"

I'm mesmerized by his tone. I don't answer. I just continue to listen. "Look, kid," he says, "the only real hero is on the movie screen or six feet under. There is no right and wrong in the heat of battle. It is simply a matter of survival. Many of the items we leave behind are picked up by Charlie." As he continues to ramble on, I think, why is it that everybody who has been here longer than I appears so angry?

I tune back into what the guy is saying. "Look, in the ten months that I've been here, I don't think we are what we have been led to believe we are. And, by the way, the ammunition and weapons we leave behind are picked up and used by the enemy. What he can't use, he sells. And he does not want to be caught with what he sells. But you can best believe, some of the bullets coming your way in a firefight are made in the good old US of A."

He continues, "Oh, yeah, one last bit of information, in a firefight, you are not fighting for God and country—you're fighting to stay alive. You're fighting to go home the way you came here, if that's possible. But know this," his voice rises while pointing to all of us, "we are not the good guys in this country; we are the invaders of this country's civil war." My thoughts immediately transcend the miles and time to where I heard those words before. My soul feels vexed. Something is not right.

He is a black guy, about twenty-one years of age, medium build, and comes across much older and wiser than his age might otherwise dictate. I don't like hearing what he is saying, so I ask, "OK, brother, tell me: where do you stand? If it's not about motherhood and apple pie, what's it all about for you?"

With a toothpick in his mouth rolling from side to side, he flashes me a smile and states, "Look, white boy, all things being equal, which they ain't, we black folks left nothing much behind when we came here and ain't got much coming to us when we return. Like on the streets, it ain't about nothing but surviving, that's all brother."

He then holds his hand out to one of the black guys for him to slap him five. He turns and strolls out of the tent with a couple of black medics trailing him.

As I open my footlocker this evening to write today's activities, I notice that someone has gone through it and stole the $20 I had put aside for an emergency. I'm incensed and can't believe that someone would have the audacity to not just steal, but to go through my diary as well. Absolutely incredible.

Based on this revelation, I cannot help but think what it will be like when we come under fire. Shit, if we're breaking down now, in base camp, what's it going to be like under fire? The military police officer's words come to the fore of my thoughts, "If you learn anything here in Vietnam, you'll learn not to trust anyone." Christ. I thought he was talking about the enemy, not the enemy from within our own ranks! It is a terrifying feeling to be at war's edge and not be able to trust the person sleeping next to you.

I have been programmed to think that going to war is a time-honored tradition. To serve the interests of the United States of America and all its people. All people include my people, my loved ones—my little brother, Bobby. He is a cute little kid. I love him. I conjure up visions of mothers and daughters embracing me upon my return, grateful for the service and dedication to them. I also have visions of what might take place if I am killed; they will be proud that I made the supreme sacrifice, that I died defending the principles of human justice and freedom. These thoughts, however, don't erase the vexation and doubt that are brewing just beneath the skin.

JUNE 29 1966

It's raining like hell. Bugs are having a field day. We still do not have electricity. I was issued a mattress today, but I don't see much need for one. The canvas of the cot has been just fine. In my mind, the mattress will serve to collect the perspiration as we sleep and then stink to high heaven. I tell Sergeant Flock about the mattress, and he responds in his usual negative manner, "You don't have a choice in the matter." I don't need another run-in with him; I'm still digging that ammo pit. So I back off and go about my business.

My hands are getting worse each day. I'm not sure if I can continue to dig, but I'm not sure how to get out of hard labor. Morale is low. Everybody is talking about what they want to do to the guy who is stealing if they catch him.

Another amazing development occurs today. After digging with the barrel of a shotgun pointed at me, today I played "armed guard" for the company commander, Captain Martin. Today is payday and men file by me one by one to receive their monthly pay in the form of military script. Only in the army can things be as screwy as this.

After the detail, which takes about two hours, I head down to the Post Exchange. There, in neat rows, are the goods that you'd find in any small grocery store. It is somewhat comforting to see all the stuff they have for sale. It serves as a tie to the "real world" we left behind.

Later in the day I drive Captain Pierce through the village of Bien Hoa; I am fascinated by the Vietnamese people—they are a small and frail-looking race. And women are now beginning to look more attractive.

Bicycles and small Honda motorbikes are the main form of transportation. In fact, if a Vietnamese has a motorbike, he is a cut above on the food chain. The traffic congestion is unlike anything I have ever experienced. It's damn near a lawless state when driving. The prevailing rules of the road are simple: "Go for yourself." If you do not assert yourself when driving, you won't make much headway. Pollution from the motorbikes, Lambretta motor scooters, and a wide assortment of other motorized vehicles, is choking. New York or Los Angeles people only think they have problems with pollution. Man, they have no idea what pollution is. The lack of a breeze coupled with the heat and humidity makes it difficult to breathe. The sight and smell is distressing.

Merchants are, surprisingly, foreigners themselves. Indians from India hawk their wares from both sides of the dirt road. Their goods range from silverware and rugs to jewelry and clothes. Boy, it is different from anything I could have imagined. No one ever said it would be like this. It doesn't fit the images I have been programmed to expect.

The street is packed with not only vehicular traffic but hundreds and hundreds of people too. Children outnumber adults by about five to one. I think, yeah, that's about right, born and bred to die. Most of the Vietnamese kids are completely naked up until about the age of five or six. After that, their genitals are covered.

Whorehouses seem to outnumber all other forms of merchant buildings. As I continue to drive down the main street of Bien Hoa, we are constantly hailed with offers for sex from either the girls or the pimps themselves. I am overwhelmed with their lack of modesty. Some pimps are as young as ten, and say, "Hey, Joe, you want young cherry girl?" Yeah, right. Let me park right here, leave the doctor in the jeep and jump on this cherry. Sure. But curiosity gets the better of me. "How much?" I ask one of the pimps. Sensing he has a bite, he points and says, "For you, Joe, three hundred 'P'" (which is the equivalent of $2).

The crowd presses alongside the jeep as we barely move with the flow of traffic. I make the mistake of asking the pimps a question. They read that as a sign I am interested and begin all sort of inquires, offering all sort of wares. Dr. Pierce casually admonishes me for addressing the guy. As they surround us, I tense, thinking that any one of them could shoot us dead in a second. I check my M-16 that's laying across my lap and feel for the safety switch. Pierce, sensing we are in a bad situation, yells at the crowd and, waving his arm, says, "Dee Dee Mao," meaning back off, get out of here.

After a couple of hours of sightseeing, we make our way back toward base camp. Driving in silence with Pierce next to me, we are locked in our own thoughts. I spot a teenager urinating right alongside the road, in full view of everyone. People are walking by him, not paying any attention to such behavior. Amazing! What a different world this is.

Just prior to turning into our base camp, Dr. Pierce spots a laundry, and we pull over to inquire about prices and time frames to clean our uniforms. The Quartermaster laundry has not yet been set up to clean our uniforms. Currently the only way to clean your uniform is to wear it while taking a shower. Having a laundry service clean and press your clothes is a necessary luxury, especially for an officer.

Once I park, we walk in the direction of the laundry, and I notice a small cart with hundreds of small trinkets for sale. Scanning the cart, I notice bullets for sale. They were M-16 bullets! I shake my head in disbelief and think about the guy from the sister battalion who talked about the black market.

Dr. Pierce and I begin negotiations to have our uniforms cleaned. I have never bartered before, but I know the basics. I have heard they might even extend credit if they are comfortable with your presentation and sincerity. Xin Van Dam is the owner of the laundry and a family man. He is a warm and friendly man who appears to be about forty. At twice my age, I feel he is an old fellow. He makes no effort to hide the fact he has an arm missing, waving it as he speaks. I try not to stare at its blunt, jagged-edged stump.

His wife is a typical mamason. Her most pronounced feature is her red-stained teeth. She chews what we call beetle nut, a local bean that provides a slight high when consumed in large doses. She, too, is warm and inviting. I bid her good day with a slight bow of the head and the words, "Chao, mamason." But, when she smiles, I lose the appetite that was growing within. Gross would be a nice way of saying how she looks. Dr. Pierce speaks with mamason while I speak to papason.

"Aha, you toupar," papason smiles at me, making a gesture with his hand to show the shape of a parachute, then points to the wings sewn on to my fatigue shirt.

"Yes," I respond, "Paratrooper."

We nod at each other while he pats me on the shoulder and says, "You number one toupar. You OK."

I return the gesture saying "You number one, too, papason."

This warm encounter bridges the gap between two separate worlds of experience and culture. His shop is simple and neat, no furniture except for a small desk to set your clothes on. Mats for sitting are strewn onto the floor. The hut is primarily made of sheets of corrugated steel, which is commonly used by the military to construct fences or barriers, and in some cases, quonset huts.

This sheet metal is augmented with flattened beer cans that make up the walls and ceiling. This man must have flattened 20,000 beer cans that became the walls of his laundry and his home. And he didn't do it for some kind of commercial or artwork. Our discarded beer cans became his home and his place of business. I stand humbled before this man who, with one arm, built his family a home and a place of business from items we Americans call trash! I am truly amazed and fascinated by our different yet strangely alike lifestyles.

Papason's daughter, Lum, is strikingly beautiful. She is about seventeen years old, about 5'1" and, in comparison with most Vietnamese women, well built. When her father introduces Dr. Pierce and me, her face lights up. She smiles with a set of pearls that would be the envy of any actress. As papason speaks through a lot of hand gesturing, sprinkled with a dash of broken English and Vietnamese, I learn Lum runs the business. I will have to barter with her. As she speaks, I look her over from head to toe while, of course, trying to hide the fact that I think she is beautiful.

She returns my penetrating gaze with her own form of seduction inherent to Asian women seeking a mate. God, she is beautiful. She asks my name again, and I reply, "Harry." She immediately giggles, connecting "Harry" with "cherry." Vietnamese know the word cherry is sexual slang for virgin. Papason barks something to her in a harsh tone, and Lum returns to her business demeanor.

Aside from her physical attributes, she speaks remarkably good English. Up until this point, the only English I have heard from the Vietnamese is, "Hi, Joe, you number one," or, if they don't like you, "You number ten thousand." And, of course, the ever-present pimps hawk their women with their limited English: "You want short time, G.I.? My sister number one for you."

Lum's grasp of English mesmerizes me. Within a few minutes, we hash out the terms of her doing our laundry. Lum will wash, iron, and starch our fatigues along with other miscellaneous items for $10 a month. Then she throws me a curve, "Cash up front. Cash in advance before any commencement of work." Hell, I don't know these people. For all I now, they'll stiff me and skate with my money and my clothes.

Lum senses my displeasure and mistrust and, without missing a beat, says rather apologetically, "Harry, sometime you not come from jungle. Sometime you die. Sometime you not come for clothes. I need money for papa and mamason and babies." She points to her two little brothers who appear to be two and four years old.

Wow. Now that's blunt. That is cold. She is obviously speaking from experience, but the way she says it belies her femininity. That rattles me, and Pierce knows it. He interrupts, saying, "That'll be fine, Lum," and hands her a twenty dollar bill (military script) to set up the account. Lum holds out her hand in a gesture for me to pay as well, but I state that I have to think about it for a while and that I'd get back to her. She nods in agreement, and we part company.

As I drive Captain Pierce back to base camp, I can't get Lum's statement out of my head, that I must pay my bill before I go out on patrol because, "sometime you not come from jungle." Bullshit.

Once back at base camp I have to go back to the ammo pit. After digging a few minutes, my hands begin to bleed through the gauze dressing. Calluses and blisters both break loose from the skin. The raw skin is exposed; an infection has set in. Gggrrreat!

Chapter 6

BAPTISM OF FIRE

TONIGHT PIERCE, CRACK, and I visit a small Vietnamese maternity hospital. A white stucco wall approximately seven feet high, capped with orange clay tiles, encircles the hospital. Inside the walls there are four buildings with the same stucco design and color scheme. It was some wealthy Frenchman's mansion at one time, but has since been turned over to the local government to use as it deems appropriate. The main building houses the hospital itself while the other three flank it on three sides: one on the left and one on the right, while the third lies directly in back of it. It is impressive to this day, even though it was not maintained. I can only imagine how majestic it must have once been.

Today the adjoining buildings are occupied by young women with children in tow, waiting to go into labor. The average age of the women appears to be between seventeen and twenty. Women stand at various window ledges and shout across the courtyard, exchanging small talk. A dozen four-to-eight-year-old children scamper about in the dirt-covered courtyard and play tag with each other. In all, there appears to be between seventy-five and one hundred people in the compound. Men are noticeably absent. I reason the women are recently widowed, divorced, or their men are in the South Vietnamese Army.

The atmosphere is light-hearted and neighborly even though it is almost 9 P.M. I have come here tonight with Dr. Pierce and Specialist

Crack to stand guard as they help the locals deliver newborns. Crack is very proficient in applying his trade. Among the medics, he is the most skilled and well trained. To get to the specialist sixth class rating, he has to be knowledgeable in the fields of obstetrics, orthopedics, intensive care, and, of course, emergency treatment of the injured.

The only difference between an army paramedic and a registered nurse is that, in the army, we do not have the luxury of someone on staff looking over our shoulder to guide us through the process of treating and stabilizing the patient. There is no one to consult, no one to rely upon for a second opinion. We are out there in the jungle all on our own, for better or for worse. Early on in the army, I learned that my life, as well as the life of my patient, is my sole charge. Whether shooting my M-16 or applying a pressure bandage for a sucking chest wound, it is up to me to make the right move. The responsibility for life and death is a monumental weight for a nineteen-year-old. My biggest fear is not living up to that responsibility. I know Crack can be counted on, but I am not sure if I can. How can I know? I have never been tested under fire.

After parking the jeep in the courtyard, we all go to the delivery area. The room is nothing more than a large room with wooden benches lined up in two rows of three. Almost all the tables are occupied. Most of the women are young. An older nurse, or midwife, takes exception to our presence. But after speaking with Dr. Pierce and Crack, she realizes who we are and why we are here. Dr. Pierce asks me to step outside and guard the area. It is not uncommon to have hospitals attacked by VC Sappers—suicide squads, men hell bent on killing others at the expense of their own life.

One of the classes on board the ship when en route to Vietnam dealt with sapper squads. I listened because I thought it was macabre and because it went against everything I have been taught to believe in. After all, you've got to be one crazy son of a bitch to do some shit like that.

Crack gives me one last piece of advice as I leave the room, "Never turn your back on the entryway to the courtyard. If they're going to come in, that is the only way in. Stay alert. Stay alive." I wink at him as I turn and tell him not to worry.

Once outside, I scan the compound—the walls, the gates. The buildings are two stories high. Young mothers chat incessantly to one another across the courtyard. Children scoot about with an energy only the young have. The kids appear too small, by American standards, to walk, let alone run. Here in Vietnam, a five-year-old looks to be about the size of a two-year-old American child. The kids are either half-clothed or nude, but totally oblivious to it. The mood is festive, teeming with life and with energy. As the minutes tick by, I become enchanted with them as they dart about looking like midget kids. I think they are equally enthralled by my physical characteristics. Standing six foot, I'm huge to them. And by their standards, I have a pointed nose.

Within an hour, we begin to communicate in a strange sort of way. The younger ones come up to me slowly and hug my leg. I pretend that I am shocked to find them there and let out a slight groan of bemusement, and off they go, running away so the giant has to run and catch them. I fake a gesture of "I'm going to catch you," which makes them more excited. Then they huddle as if they're coming up with some sort of game plan, and the game repeats itself. It's the White Giant against the little yellow boys and girls. I am on a natural high.

Suddenly one of the mothers hanging out of a dorm window sill shouts something that causes the kids to scurry as if a bolt of lightning just struck. I catch the looks on a couple of the kids' faces. They are scared to death as they run in different directions. At the time of the shout, my back was to the compound's gates, and I was in a crouched position. So, now I naturally stand and turn around to find out what in the world has scared the kids so much. I glance at my watch; it's about 10 P.M. All is quiet. The air is still. No breeze. Not a sound.

And then I see them—three men, slender with short bodies, walking slowly toward me. They are not in a hurry. The one on the left has a white long-sleeve shirt that is far too big for him, with tan polished cotton suit pants and sandals. The one in the middle also has on a long-sleeve white shirt, black pants that are too short, and worn-out white gym shoes, no socks. The third has on an oversized pair of black shorts, a tank top T-shirt and no footwear.

As they slowly walk toward me, they are smiling, while nodding their heads in an affirmative gesture, but they are speaking to each other. Seventy-five feet separate us. The one on the left appears to be in charge. He is better dressed than the other two who are about my age, maybe younger. As they close the distance between us, they talk to me in hushed tones. The one on the right puts his finger to his lips, gesturing for me to be quiet. It is deadly silent. However, I can now hear Dr. Pierce and Specialist Crack making small talk with the women in the birthing ward. I couldn't hear them seconds before while I played with the kids.

The laughter of the women emanates from their location. In the birthing room there is an air of gaiety, laughter, and security. Out here, things don't look so good. I feel as if I'm going into shock, not knowing what is happening, though a little voice within me is screaming for my attention. I don't see any weapons! The guys are even smiling and laughing at me when a sudden wave of fear comes crashing through my consciousness. Danger. Danger. Danger.

Because an adrenaline charge shoots through me like 220 volts of electricity, my breathing becomes labored as if I have just run a marathon. Oh, my God! They want to kill me! It's fight or flight time. My mind races to comprehend what is developing right in front of me. Instinctively, my training takes over. I no longer have to think; my moves become automatic.

My rifle is cradled with the butt on my right hip, nozzle pointed to the sky. Because of safety concerns, I had the bolt pulled back and locked in position. The weapon's safety is also on as a secondary safety precaution. The chamber is empty even though I have a full load in the magazine.

The men are now just fifty feet from me and begin to spread out. They are still smiling at me. They sense my fear of them and try to console me with their words, "You OK, Joe," and, "You number one G.I," almost at a whisper.

Then they speak again amongst themselves in a tone I sense as serious. This belies their smiles and friendly words. Their eyes give them away, darting back and forth around the compound nonstop, as if looking for something or someone. All the while, they're gesturing for me to believe all is well. A foreign taste in my mouth grows as each second passes. I nod at them, trying to swallow and speak simultaneously. "Chao, good evening, guys. How are you?" They like that and respond in kind.

They're now just twenty-five feet from me. Because my weapon is still on my right hip, I reach over with my left hand and let the bolt slam forward with the flip of a button located on the weapons side, near the trigger. The sound shatters the silence—metal hitting metal with an authoritative clank. Immediately afterwards I flip the weapon to full automatic. I scare myself with the boldness of my moves. I don't even think about doing it; I'm on auto-pilot. The swiftness with which I arm my weapon startles them more than me. They freeze momentarily in place, trying in their own language to calm me down.

Because I grew up in the inner city of Detroit, I know a sucker punch in the making. I have used the psychology myself. Tell the joker you're about to hit, anything he wants to hear to disarm him, to lull him into a sense of false security. Get close enough and then knock the living shit out of him. The only thing we could lose on the streets was our pride or, at worst, a couple of teeth. Here, the stakes are much higher. But, where in the hell are their goddamn weapons? Show me a weapon, and I'll do you in, I think.

The standing orders creep into mind, *"Do not fire unless fired upon."* Shit, they're now just fifteen feet in front of me. The one on the left is at my nine o'clock, the one in the middle at twelve, and the one on my right at three o'clock. This is a set up if I've ever seen one. I scream, *"Dee Dee Mao,"* in their language, and, *"Get back, go away,"* in English.

Again I think, where are their damned weapons? I don't want to kill you guys. I try consciously not to pull the trigger. But my training takes over and I remember, *"Pan left, shoot right against the recoil of the weapon that naturally pushes to the left when fired."* Also, *"The M-16 trigger takes only 3.5 pounds of force to discharge the projectile; that's a bullet, to you street boys."*

The men are attempting to calm me down. I find myself apologizing to them mentally, "Sorry, guys, nothing personal." As I start to pull the trigger, Specialist Crack's voice bellows from the building behind me, "Spencer, are you all right?" He and the Doc are to my left rear when suddenly, from my right rear, two voices in Vietnamese scream out. It is a horrific scream of anger and terror. Despite this confusion, I do not to take my eyes off the targets. The three men attempt to spring into action, but not before several shots ring out in rapid succession. They never had a chance.

They fall where they stood just seconds earlier. I stand there not moving, thinking that I will be next. After a couple of seconds, I force myself to turn slowly to face whoever just killed these three guys. As it turns out, they are South Vietnamese Paratroopers who were visiting someone and were just leaving. But I just stand there as if glue is on the bottom of my boots—in a state of shock. Two of the guys are lying on the ground twitching from post mortem muscle spasms.

The Vietnamese Paratroopers scream at the fallen men and run up to them and shoot them again, only this time in the head. Dr. Pierce and Crack slowly come out of the hospital with their weapons drawn and ask what happened. Their tones are tainted with fear, disbelief, and puzzlement. "What happened here, Harry?" Pierce asks with deadpan expression, even though I know him well enough to know he is scared senseless. After I explain, he moves toward the fallen bodies to check them for signs of life. One of the two Vietnamese guys stops him with strong defiance. After pushing Doc back, one of the Vietnamese Paratroopers slowly rolls one guy over and pulls at the man's shirt very carefully, exposing a belt full of grenades—American grenades, at that!

The grenades are strapped to an ammo belt under the oversized white shirt of the guy that I thought was in charge. One of the paratroopers orders us out of the compound. "You," he screams pointing at Crack, Doc, and me. "You! Dee Dee Mao, you go."

We are in shock, but look at one another, shrug our shoulders, and decide rather casually that it is a good time to go. But first Doc Pierce, being a conscientious officer, turns to me and asks, "Harry, did you fire your weapon?" When I respond, "No," he says, "OK, we're out of here." We quickly gather our belongings and split, trying hard not to show how scared we are.

I think it odd that as we drive back to our battalion area, which is about fifteen minutes from the maternity hospital, not one of us says a word. But then again, the encounter was queer to our senses and training. It did not fit our expectation of war. However, we knew that night that war is very real. It came close tonight, too close for comfort. Eyeball to eyeball. One thing I learned for sure is that killing someone is very personal shit. I also know now, more than ever, how very much I want to live. And I am no longer in a state of fascination about being in Vietnam. The novelty has been erased this evening. I now know the look of death; it is stark, ugly, shocking, nauseating, and it comes when you least expect it.

The next day I find myself driving Dr. Pierce to a field hospital. As we pull up to the 93rd Field Evacuation Hospital, a "Dust-Off" (a medical helicopter) is landing. One of the wounded looks dead as they rush him by us. He has that chalky pale look of a cadaver. Pierce follows them in, and I trail behind him. I cannot believe what the nurses and medics say about his vital signs. "Doctor, I've got a BP of fifty over thirty, we're losing him, Sir." One of the staff doctors responds harshly. "Not on my watch, let's move people, stick to your jobs, let's go!" As frightening as that scenario is, I like what I hear. It is good to know that if I get hit, an attitude like this is waiting for me.

We stay at the hospital all day and most of the night. What I see frightens me. More of us are dying than I ever thought possible. I pray that God will help me. Please, dear God, help me get through all this madness.

JULY 2 1966

They put me back on hard labor today. Another day of digging. I try in vain to dig myself out of this place. With each shovelful of dirt, I reason that if I dig deep enough, I will come out somewhere near my home in Detroit. It is a comforting thought that keeps my mind occupied and off the returning pain in both hands. I dig from 10 A.M. until 2 P.M. in 110-degree heat with nearly ninety-five percent humidity, stopping only to eat another box of c-rations.

While I'm digging, Captain Martin stops to check up on me. When he arrives, the pit is about six feet deep and seven feet wide. Five more guys have joined the crew. The sight of Martin no longer makes me jump. For whatever reason, I no longer fear him. If anything, I feel disdain for the man and how he intimidates people. He plays macho with savagery. As he walks up to the pit's edge and stands with his hands on his hips, I simply ignore him. The guard tips me off, saying with a smile, "Hey, Doc, your favorite officer is coming this way. Better look sharp."

As Martin approaches, the guard snaps him a salute while simultaneously shouting, "Detail, Officer on the grounds." Because I know military protocol well enough, I know I do not have to salute him. Instead, I simply acknowledge him by temporarily taking a break from digging.

"Spencer," he growls in that raspy voice of his, "Where in the hell did they teach you to dig a ditch?"

I know better than to respond. I resume digging like a good soldier on hard labor. He repeats himself. Oh, I think, he is asking for a response. I stop digging and turn to look up at him. With a smile and all the satire I can muster, I state, "Top of the day to you, Captain, How are you?" I know he wants to be called Sir, not Captain.

He growls back at me, "It's Sir to you, Private. You got that?"

I reply, "Captain is your rank, Mr. Martin, is it not? Please tell me if it is illegal or in violation of the Uniformed Code of Military Justice to call you by your rank or your name, Captain." If looks could kill, he's history.

He knows it too, but simply responds, "Ever the smart ass, aren't you, Private?"

I ignore him and continue digging. He smashes his swagger stick against his thigh. He always carries it as if he were General Patton and responds, "We'll see just how long you last, Spencer. I'm going to break you my way." He turns and marches away. As he does, he lets out one final salvo, "Guard, if that man tries to escape, I'm giving you a direct order to blow his motherfucking head off. You got that, trooper?"

"Yes, Sir," snaps the guard.

The guys that are digging with me and the guard immediately smile at me when one of them states, "Boy, that man want a piece of your ass real bad. You betta watch out, he be the man." Another comment was, "You're some bad ass or stupid ass dude to be messing with the Man. Better chill, dude, he be the devil man."

At this point, I am enraged. Where the hell does he think I can run? Jesus. He's crazy, simply crazy drunk with power. As I continue digging, I think about all the Martins in this Army. They think they are tough bastards in base camp; I'd like to see just how tough they are out in the "bush" under fire!

Earlier I had asked the guard to summon help for me. My hands have had it. A few minutes after Martin leaves I look up and see Sergeant Flock standing over the pit with two fellow medics, Karl Lesnau and Mark Badwin. Flock simply smirks at me saying, "Do we have a problem here, boy?" He mocks me by saying in a motherly tone, "Oh, what's a matta? Do we have a little boo-boo?" He orders Karl and Mark to jump down and take a closer look at my hands. When they reach me, they are shocked at how bad the wounds actually are. Mark, a specialist fifth class, says, "Jesus, Harry, how long have you had this problem? This didn't just happen." Karl, meanwhile, has opened his first aid kit for some saline solution to pour over my hands so he can get a better look at the extent of the wounds.

As soon as they see the depth of my wounds, Badwin looks up at Sergeant Flock and says, "Sergeant, this man cannot continue on this detail; he is not fit to continue." His tone is authoritative, yet pleading.

Flock does not like what he hears. "Well, then get his sorry ass out of the pit and take him to the aid station." Turning to walk away, he shouts over his shoulder, "I'm not through with you, Spencer." But I am in too much pain to give a rat's ass what he said. But I remember his threat to murder me and get away with it. That, I can never forget.

As we walk to the aid station, the artillery battery comes alive with another fire mission. The cannon fire is in support of our guys out in the jungle. They must have made contact with the enemy. The artillery barrage is very intense. From my training, I know that they are "firing for effect," laying a wall of molten explosives—hopefully around our guys as opposed to on top of them. We, the ground-pounders, don't have greatest confidence in artillery support. Back at Fort Campbell, they sometimes missed their mark and came dangerously close to annihilating us. As we walk toward the aid station, my thoughts drift to the medics in the field. God be with you, guys. Be safe.

Eventually, the doctor prescribes rest so my hands can heal properly. Flock is not happy one bit at that call. He snaps at me as I walk out of the aid station and head toward my tent, "I'm not through with you, Spencer. You got that?" He steps in front of me in order to stop me and drive his point home.

"Yeah, Sarge, I got that." My head and posture indicate submission. My hands throb with the pulsing of my heart as I walk to my tent, when I think, how in the world am I going to wipe my ass with these heavily bandaged hands? I feel hollow, weak, and exhausted. I hit my cot and fall fast asleep, despite the heat in our tent that is least ten degrees hotter than the ambient temperature outside of 110 degrees.

I awake as A Company is going out on a night patrol. Night patrol scares the hell out of us. To begin with, there are about 120 men in a company, and 120 men walking through the jungle make a lot of noise. Then, you can't see a damn thing in front of you. No one likes going out on night patrol. Five medics leave with the company. I watch them leave the perimeter of our base camp and move out across "No Man's Land," a swathe of land barren of vegetation approximately two football fields deep and extending the length of the 173rd Brigade base camp, which is approximately a half mile in length. Gray trees lie on their sides by the thousands; it's not fit for man nor beast.

A group of us who are not going out go to the base camp's edge to watch them walk by and give words of encouragement. Gino Washington, a small wiry guy and fellow medic, is in line and hunched forward to offset the weight of his rucksack. His face glistens with perspiration. "Take care, Gino!" I say, giving him the thumbs-up. He returns my gesture without zeal. "Yeah, man. It'll be cool. I'm cool," he says while shaking his head from side to side. He isn't too convincing.

"Airborne!" someone yells to the group of men leaving base camp. One of the guys going out on patrol responds, "All the way, man. All the fucking way." The other guys are strangely quiet as they file past us. I can't help but think it's strange: A group of men are going out to do battle, yet there is no hype, no bantering and very little talk among them. In fact, as they file past us, not one speaks. It feels like they are in a funeral procession. Minutes later, it starts to rain. Again.

That night a group of us sit together listening to the Armed Forces Radio Network. We need to talk. Others stay near battalion operations to keep abreast of A Company's movements. A Company is out on a "search and destroy" mission. Moving around at night is not a good idea, however, one trooper says, in order to make us feel a little better, "If you have to move at night, it's in your best interest to do so while it rains. Rain, for the most part, drowns out the noise that one or 120 people make as they forge through the jungle. The rain is on their side tonight."

Then Willie Sykes, a tough-talking guy from Georgia, makes a comment that sticks in my craw, "Hey, brotha, all things being equal," his eyes widen for emphasis, "better them than us."

Leon Dallas, the thickly-built giant of a black man, lets out a sigh as he looks skyward and says, "Forgive me, brothas, but better anyone of yous than me," and permits himself a small chuckle.

To me, both of those statements are cold—extremely cold-hearted. But it is also the raw truth that we all feel. Living on the edge brings out feelings that, under normal conditions, we'd never give any thought to, let alone say.

My education in survival is just beginning, but I already want out. However, I am too afraid, so to speak, to raise my hand and ask to be sent home. Yeah, right. Like they'd send me home just because I want to. Fat chance. Besides, that would bring total dishonor to my very being. From my earliest years, I always knew that someday I would be called to war, just as my father, and his father, and his father were. Therefore, regardless of how tough it gets, I will not "punk out," as the expression goes. I'll choose death over "punking out." As another saying goes, "death before dishonor." Soon, however, I instinctively feel some among us might think otherwise. Some of us just might choose punking out over death. Reality often cannot and will not be recorded accurately.

As the evening draws to a close, each of us go our separate ways to turn in. Tom Brown, the guy they gave my buck sergeant stripes to, makes a comment to no one in particular, maybe he is just thinking out loud, "What the hell do they mean 'search and destroy?' Ourselves?" As he walks away, he is shaking his head. He extends his arms out from his sides and continues, "They've taught us to fire and maneuver; now they tell us to not fire unless fired upon. They've taught us to kill 'gooks,' but where are they? What the hell do they look like? Why don't they stand and fight? The elusive bastards!" Shaking his head harder, he persists, "Jesus God, we can't hit what we can't see. Show me my enemy. It's too difficult to hate someone or something you can't see."

As he reaches the doorway of the tent, I stop him saying, "Hey, Tom, did you ever stop to think you can see the enemy?"

"What the hell do you mean, man?" he replies with irritation, turning to look at me.

I reply, "The enemy is within each one of us. We are him; he is us—the enemy within."

"Where the hell you coming from, Spencer?"

"Tom, man has dominated man to his own injury. Look it up, it's scripture."

"Good night, Spencer."

"Good night, Tom."

As I blow out the candle that lights my bunk area, I make one final comment, "Lights out, brothers."

Someone speaks up, "I'll give you lights out, Spencer. Where in the hell did you get that stuff from? That shit's heavy."

I want to tell him more of the wisdom from the Bible, but the time is not really appropriate. I don't bother to respond except to say, "Good night, asshole."

That elicits a few light laughs from the others in the tent. In the dark, all falls silent.

While waiting for sleep to overcome me, I think about my fellow medics out in the jungle. Fighting to walk in the dark without falling, swatting the swarms of mosquitoes, sweating while moving, and freezing while resting. Fear and fatigue are ever-present companions. I'd like to meet them, Fear and Fatigue, in the flesh. I'd kick the living shit out of them.

The following morning I am rudely awakened by rainwater dripping through the tent's canvas roof. Rain has pooled in the canvas right above my face and it begins to drip rainwater rapidly. I immediately bolt to an upright position and shake my head as if to rid myself of a bad dream. Then I jump out of my cot in a state of shock and look for the asshole who poured water on me.

A couple of guys who have already been to the mess hall, (which finally opened this morning) and are sitting on their footlockers drinking coffee, start to laugh. "Good morning, Spencer," says medic Art Gamesmore, smiling as if I just made his morning. Jim Chiefoot, who is sitting opposite of him, laughs so hard that he spills his coffee. When he regains his composure he states, "Looks like you owe me a buck, Gamesboy." "Yeah, just by five minutes. Don't get a big head over it Indian man," Gamesmore retorts.

Apparently the two had a bet on how long it would take before the tent started to leak. Jim won. Art, and I, lost. Pulling myself back together, I ask them if any contact has been made by A Company.

"Just sniper fire," Jim states, "No casualties. Our guys are doing fine. They are 17,000 meters out."

"Jesus Christ," I respond in amazement. "17,000 meters! That's a long way out humping at night!"

"Well, maybe it is 7,000," Chiefoot replies, "I'm not sure."

Art interjects, "Chiefoot, you're so full of shit your breath stinks. Think about that. 17,000 meters would be about ten miles. There is no way in hell those guys could have made ten miles while humping the boonies, in the rain, at night. No way, man."

"Whatever." Chiefoot casts his head down to sip at his coffee, and says rather sarcastically, "Chill, man. Taint no big thing."

"Fresh coffee?" Art asks as I begin to put on my boots.

"Great, thanks," I respond. "Mess hall's finally up and running, huh?"

Chiefoot responds, "Yeah."

"Great," I state as I hurridly strap on my boots. "Fresh coffee sounds good."

Later around noon, I'm back to driving Dr. Pierce, this time through the countryside. I don't particularly like the idea of driving around back roads and through remote villages without an armed escort. An American doctor and a medic get a high bounty by the Viet Cong, but Dr. Pierce dismisses my objections with, "Harry, nothing's going to happen. We'll be just a couple of miles out from base camp."

I respond, "Doc, Charlie is probably a lot closer than you think. I'll go, but I don't like it."

I take twenty magazines of ammo as opposed to the usual three to five on jaunts like this. (There are twenty rounds of ammo per magazine.) Prior to leaving, I look over the vehicle, throw some c-rations and first aid supplies in the back of the jeep, check the radio, and my weapon.

We drive out of our compound, through No Man's Land. This is my first real close look at that dead, gray vegetation that looks like the aftermath of some volcanic fallout. Tree trunks six inches in diameter stand tall, but without branches. The color of the wood looks as if it had died thousands of years ago, petrified by the passage of time. The underbrush is thick, but it, too is gray. No leaves of any kind. Even the dirt road looks different than the normal orange sandy clay of other dirt roads I have driven on. It looks sterile, gray in color, and void of life. I wonder how it got this way.

Three miles out of our base camp, we run into a little village. The people are poorer than those I saw in Bien Hoa. These are the folks who work by the land and live by the land. Straw huts line the road. I feel as if I have gone back in time some five hundred years. The village is primitive by any measure. All we see upon first glance are old men, old women, and young kids.

I slow the jeep down to nearly a crawl, taking in the sight that is foreign to our eyes. Because we are as foreign looking to them, the youngsters flock toward us and beg for anything we might give them. Their best form of English is, "Hey, G.I., You number one," while smiling and reaching out with one hand and rubbing their stomachs with the other hand. It makes me realize how sheltered I have been from the realities of the world, how rich the United States is, and how good I had it growing up.

Dr. Pierce orders me to stop. "This is as good a place to stop as any. Stay here, I'm going to seek out the village elders." I know Pierce is attempting to learn the state of the health of the villagers. He is the type of person who will help anyone, anywhere, applying his trade of caring for the sick and injured.

I turn off the engine and am immediately surrounded by more than two dozen kids—boys and girls ranging in age from two to twelve years old. God, are they cute. I have an urge to just sweep them into my arms and magically transport them to the United States. All the kids are filthy. Some are completely naked; some touch me just for the sake of touching. Others, mostly the older ones, pull at me to get my attention.

To communicate, they make gestures of eating food and rubbing their stomachs. All of them are vying for my undivided attention. One spots the case of c-rations I brought along and their excitement grows in anticipation of receiving food. Concerned that I won't be able to control them, I reach for my M-16 and immediately their faces lose the smiles they all wore a second earlier. They have a fear of weapons—it comes across loud and clear. Some run away screaming; most, however, stay, but all back up in submission with fear written all over their faces.

Some of the kids have expressions that plead, "Please, help me." I hold out my free hand to try to calm them down and reassure them that everything will be OK. I mean no harm to them. I open some c-rations. I don't have enough to give each one a full meal box so I open some cans with my P-38 army-issued can opener. The kids immediately return and begin jumping for joy, literally. Some of them are curious as to why my hands were bandaged, exhibiting signs of concern. But all their faces glow with anticipation. Of course the older ones are dominant and push their way to the front. I managed to open about a couple dozen cans, placing each in a row on the back seat of the jeep despite being pushed and pulled by the growing sea of kids surrounding me. I feel like Santa Claus. And I can't wait to see their reactions to the different food I am about to give them. I leave the lids intact by the narrowest thread of tin so if they don't eat the whole can, they can fold the lid down to keep the insects out.

Content that I have opened enough cans, I grab two open cans in each hand and turn to them to pass the food out. I am immediately mobbed as a fight breaks out among some of them who vie for the best position to receive the goods. Meanwhile, I am pulled, tugged, and shoved by the kids. "Whoa!" I shout. "Stop it! Get back!" I hold the cans high over my head and out of reach of even the oldest among them. I have to do something to gain control, and it seems to work, but not before an older kid becomes upset with a little one's ability to scoot in front of him.

By God, that older kid, who is twice as big as the small boy, punches him dead in the nose. Not a slap, his fist slams right into the little kid's face. The little one is so shocked that he falls backwards onto his butt, crying with such abandon that he turns blue from lack of oxygen. His nose is bleeding profusely. Like the shutter of a time camera, my mind flashes back to having my own two front baby teeth knocked out in a fight with a kid twice my age. Oh, God, what have I done? All I wanted to do was help, and I've created a negative situation here. I feel terrible and sad. Somehow I manage to get through to the kids even though I know they don't understand a word I am saying. The situation eventually comes under control, but barely.

Within minutes all the c-rations are almost gone. The kids who are tall enough to see into the jeep become anxious, fearing they won't receive any food. A pretty little girl, whom I had tried to get a can to on two separate attempts, catches my eye again. She is shy in comparison to the rest of the kids, and very small, standing just knee high to me. We have made eye contact several times. Her eyes say that she is shy, scared, and timid. Her hair is coal black, parted in the middle, and flows to about chin length. As the others push and shove, she simply flows with the crowd. Not pushing back, not yelling, just staring at me with those big beautiful eyes that say, "Please, please help me." I decide to make it a point to give her the last can even though I have already tried twice to get to her through the crowd of kids. Both times, as I extend my hand to her, someone grabbed the can from me before she could reach up for it herself. All the while her eyes were glued to mine.

Finally, I am down to the last opened can. I'll make this last offering special. I stop the usual way I have been passing out the cans, hold it high over my head and say, even though I know they can't understand me, "This one is for a special little girl." I scan the crowd, teasing them a little with my body movements. They are all jumping for joy except that little girl. She is standing quiet with one finger at the corner of her mouth. Our eyes make contact again. At this point she realizes that the last can is for her and only her.

For the first time since I honed in on her, she allows herself the pleasure of a smile. It is a warm genuine smile that says she can't believe this one is for her. As I reach out with my arm fully extended, her face is aglow with an angelic expression, as if I am about to give her the best gift of her young life. Just as she reaches up to meet my outstretched hand, someone pulls the can from me with such force that the lid slides across the base of my thumb-slicing it open like a razor blade. I recoil in pain.

Most of the kids knew that she was going to get that last can of food and resigned themselves to their fate of not receiving any food. They didn't know however, that I was planning to give all of them something anyway.

The blood spills forth from my thumb with such a force that I am dripping blood on them before I can pull it back. I immediately pull out my handkerchief and apply pressure to it. After a few seconds, I take a look. Holy shit. I need stitches for sure! Here's another fine mess I've gotten myself into, I think.

At this point, some of the older kids begin to leave. However, the younger kids display genuine concern that I am hurt. Some are so worried they want to look at my wound. It is touching to witness such concern for me, a perfect stranger in their midst. My hands are already bandaged and wrapped in gauze because of the friction wounds I received from digging the ammo pit. That in and of itself elicited curiosity earlier. But I paid no attention to their attempts to have me explain what's wrong. Now, however, their curiosity is genuine. A couple of them actually hug my leg and lay their heads on my thigh to comfort me.

At this point, we have been in the village for about thirty or forty minutes. Holding my bleeding hand, I look around and try to spot Dr. Pierce. And then I see three teenagers crossing over the road about fifty yards away from me. They are wearing black pants and black shirts and carrying rifles. Oh, my God! "VC!" I yell to the doctor with a voice of alarm. Normally, I address the doctor with the appropriate title of his rank. This time however, I yell, "Pierce! Get your ass out here, Sir! We've got trouble! We've got to go!" The children scatter in different directions. Some of them disappear into the tree line; some run and then stop and stare back at me. They sense something is wrong.

I jump into my jeep, no longer paying attention to the kids. Damn it! The jeep won't start! Shit! I start to panic. The kids are taken aback by my sudden change in demeanor. They look where I was looking when I spotted the VC and talk among themselves. They put it together very quickly though and run in different directions. Seeing them run confirms my suspicions. I scream again, "Doctor, goddamn it, let's go!" The jeep still will not turn over. I reach for the radio microphone, and, son of a bitch, it is gone!

Pierce arrives at the jeep without any visual signs of distress, despite my calling out to him the way I did. "What's the matter, Harry?"

Trying to conceal my growing panic, I respond, "The jeep won't start; our radio mike is missing, and I just spotted three VC with rifles fifty yards up the road."

His eyes widen as he looks toward the area of the road where I saw the VC. "OK," he says, "Keep calm, relax, don't panic, stay cool."

"Stay cool? Come on, Doc—we're in deep shit here."

He bolts back in the direction he came from as I continue in vain to start the jeep. He returns in seconds with about six adults and demonstrates that he wants them to push our jeep. They finally catch on after what I think is too long. Pierce and the others begin to push. I depress the clutch, put the jeep in second gear, and wait a bit before I pop the clutch.

"Oh, God. Please, please start you goddamned piece of shit jeep!" As I yell the jeep responds. Cough, cough, cough, cough, pop. Varrooom! Yes! It starts, and Pierce jumps in while the jeep is still rolling. My legs are shaking so bad that I don't think I will be able to keep the accelerator pedal pressed to the floor. My hand is glued to the steering wheel, and the cut at the base of the thumb is bleeding really bad, the blood running down my forearm. Pierce notices and asks if I have been hit. As I flip my hand over to show him and tell him what happened, we hear shots ring out. A bullet suddenly smashes through the windshield between us. Holy shit! I begin to zigzag down the road toward base camp at breakneck speed.

I have escaped death once again. Though part of me feels like "Lady Luck" is riding on my shoulder, the other part of me feels that two encounters in the last couple of days is not a good sign. The cut requires six stitches to close. The motor pool mechanics repair the jeep, only this time, before I take delivery, I demand they put twenty-five miles on it rather than take their word that it is fixed. My fellow medics harass me jokingly, stating that I don't have to go out on patrol to make contact with Charlie; I'm a magnet for the enemy. Great, I think, just great.

JULY 5 1966

Saigon is crowded beyond belief. Traffic is a menagerie of bicycles, small motorbikes, and scooter taxis as well as Vietnamese police and American Military Police jeeps. Like in Bien Hoa, traffic obeys no law. Again, the exhaust fumes are unbelievable. Hot, stagnant air coupled with high humidity makes it difficult to breathe.

Whole families appear to be living on the crowded streets of the city. Small fires are built to serve as a place for cooking food. Young mothers sit on the pavement, openly breast feeding their babies. Everywhere I look, there are youngsters running about playing games known only to them. Kids outnumber adults by at least five to one. Born to die young. The temperature hits 105 degrees.

Once back at base camp, I learn A Company made contact while out on patrol, though there are no reports of any injuries or casualties. I know that very soon it'll be my turn to go out; it's just a matter of time.

Even though I'm no longer in the ammo pit, they've got us planting trees and laying out foundations for sidewalks. My hands are so swollen that it hurts to write in my diary.

I find a strange correlation between the uncertainties of my existence here in Vietnam and that of growing up at home. I never knew when some form of punishment would be rendered upon me in my parents' home, and here there's no telling where or when Charlie will show himself. That thought makes me think back to a moment in time when I was in elementary school.

I started playing the trumpet when I was in second grade. As time went by, I noticed that those getting promoted in the band invariably owned their own trumpet. After one of those super sales pitches by my music teacher, Mr. Lacey, I went home all fired up and begged my mother to buy me a trumpet. I was so hyped at the thought that owning my own trumpet would result in a promotion to first trumpet position, I wouldn't take no for an answer. My mother gasped at the price and said, "Harold, you know we don't have that kind of money; seventy-five dollars is a lot of money. The answer is no." Being only about ten years old at the time, I cried, pleaded, and begged my way right in to the bedroom. I was grounded for being insubordinate to her.

There were two bunk beds in my bedroom, one bunk for each boy with four boys in a room approximately nine-by-ten feet. We couldn't even close the door because one of the bunk beds blocked the doorway. As I lay on my bunk, I thought maybe God could help me.

Brought up Catholic, we were taught that God could perform miracles, so I started praying, "God, it's me, Harry. You may not know me. I live at 5851 Limley in Detroit, Michigan. My phone number is LU2-1418. God, I need a trumpet. But my Mom says we can't afford one. So, if you would, please put a trumpet right here next to me. OK? I mean, well, I've been a pretty good kid. Not too good, but not too bad, either. Yeah, I know I've done some dumb things, but I'll be better if you'll just let me have my trumpet."

As I lay on my back and stare at the ceiling, tears rolled down into my ears. I whispered, "Now, God, I'm going to close my eyes now and count to ten, and you put my trumpet right here next to me. One, two, three, four . . ." I opened my eyes, and there was no trumpet. But I was not through yet. I tried again, "OK, God, maybe you didn't understand me. Maybe you don't speak English. Hello, God, can you hear me? It's me, Harry Spencer, I'm ten years old and I live in the United States." At that point I began to cry uncontrollably, burying my face in the pillow to keep my mother from hearing me, and drifted off to sleep.

Some time in the middle of the night, I awoke to the harsh tone of my father's voice as he made his way to my bedroom. "I'll give him a sons a bitching trumpet. Where is he?" As the door to my bedroom flung fully open, I tensed, knowing full well what was coming. I caught the shape of his body as a silhouette in the doorway. He was a monster of a man, and not just because he was my father. He stood around 5'11" and weighed close to 230 pounds. By anyone's measurement, he was a stout, thickly-built man quite capable of causing great bodily harm.

To a skinny ten-year-old, he evoked fear simply by raising his voice or glaring at me with his icy stare. His belt hit the mark over and over. I knew based on other beatings that the more I squirmed, the harder and longer he'd whack on me. So I had to stop moving and allow him to hit me with his belt until he felt I had had enough. Afterward, one of my brothers asked in a whisper, "Harry, you all right?" Of course I wasn't all right; I just got the crap kicked out of me, but it was the way we looked out for each other. If we could speak after a beating it meant we were OK.

Once my emotions were under control and the pain diminished to a tolerable level, I apologized to God. "All right, God, I won't ask you for anything again. You must be on my father's side. Sorry I took up your time. Honest, I'm sorry and I won't bother you again."

In a very bizarre way, I have been programmed to tolerate the fear and uncertainty of Vietnam. My upbringing provided me with the ability to cope with and dismiss situations that others around me struggle to tolerate. It gives me some kind of edge. Flock, as I see it, is my surrogate father; the army is my school, and the jungle is my playground.

The condition of my hands has kept me out of the jungle so far; however, I know that I am slipping closer to going out on patrol. What was meant as punishment has turned out to be a blessing in disguise. Every time Flock schedules me to go out on patrol, the doctor overrides his orders because of the condition of my hands. That enrages him, and he doesn't try to hide his anger. After arguing with the doctor in one of their morning meetings, Flock comes up to me and states, "The doctor is saving your ass, but sooner or later he won't be able to keep you out of the jungle. I'm going to get you, Spencer, make no mistake about it. You're dead but you don't know it . . . yet." I stay as far away from that man as I can. I know he is serious, but I am powerless to do anything about it. Who would I tell? Captain/Sir/Mister Martin? I don't think so.

The sound of machine guns and artillery fire on the perimeter going off from time to time no longer causes as much concern as it did when we first got here. It is accepted as the norm. Tonight, just before we drift off to sleep, someone says that No Man's Land out on our perimeter is being sprayed for mosquitoes by helicopters or C-123 aircraft. Sounds good to me. Perhaps they should spray some of that shit over our tents to help reduce the mosquitoes that are hell bent on making my life miserable.

Chapter 7

INTRODUCTION TO THE BOONIES

JULY 21 1966

I'M ACTUALLY OUT in the jungle now. Flock finally won. My hands are better. I'm not "on the line," but at what is called "BSOP." (Battalion Supply Operational Point). It's a base camp in the jungle where platoon patrols leave at dawn and return at dusk or leave at dusk and return the next morning. The sounds are strange, nothing like I ever heard back at base camp.

BSOP is nothing more than a clearing in the middle of the jungle about the size of two football fields alongside one another. My job is to help set up a field evacuation hospital to accommodate the inevitable casualties of war. I sleep in a large tent with the few remaining medics who are considered "ready relief" should one of my brothers take a hit. Being out here makes me realize how nice it was back at base camp.

Because of monsoon season, the ground is saturated, with standing water on the surface. Just walking around, we sink into the earth right up to the top of our boots. It's impossible to stay dry or clean. I'll never complain about base camp again after going through this. The bugs are so thick that I've got to be careful or I'll inhale them. My days at Fort Campbell were rough from time to time when we were out in the boonies, but we always knew the comfort of our barracks awaited us when the training exercise was completed.

Here, it's the real thing. There is no relief and no comfort. But the guys out on patrol have it far worse than I. BSOP is base camp to them. BSOP is a luxury to them. Christ, I can't comprehend how difficult it must be. It frightens me to think how tough it actually is out there. I'm anxious to get out there and get it over with. The anxiety is playing on my nerves. When I ask the guys how it is on patrol, the response is universal, "Just wait and see. Words cannot describe the hardship, the fear factor and the fatigue that accompanies it." I feel that a lot of the medics have a mental edge on me—ninety percent have tasted actual patrol; fifty percent have had some form of contact with Charlie, though no one brags or boasts about encounters with the enemy.

Off in the direction of C Company's position a sniper is firing. It's a small caliber weapon. He shoots off about a dozen rounds before our guys respond with an M-60 machine-gun. Christ, the noise difference is amazing. M-60's have far greater power and sound much louder. The machine-guns settle into a familiar five-round burst pattern, alternating between two of them. They are followed by the dull thud of an M-79 grenade-launcher when fired and finally the thunder of the grenade exploding. I can actually see the foliage disintegrating. It's as if I am a spectator to war; this is amazing.

C Company's position is about a football field away from us. We feel no immediate threat. So we watch, listen, and wait as the guys do their thing. It is an incredible experience. How in the world can I possibly describe this to my friends and family? I'm at a loss for words, but some day, some way, I've got to try. I reaffirm my resolve to take notes in my diary to capture each and every experience. It seems so unreal, but it is happening.

Fear suddenly engulfs me. Christ, they could be setting up a diversion and hit us from a different direction. Lieutenant Edmore, our platoon leader, runs out of his tent and demands to know what is going on. One of the guys responds, "Better get your ass down, Sir, or you might never find out." Edmore drops to the ground at the realization that the firing is not an exercise. Even from this distance I can hear men yelling to one another between bursts of fire. "They're over there," someone yells. "Where? Goddamn it, I don't see them," someone else screams back, and another five rounds from the powerful machine-gun burst forth. At this point I am hugging the ground, listening to the bullets whiz past me as Charlie tests and probes us, looking for any signs of weakness.

As I lie there, powerless to do anything, it dawns on me. I don't have my aid kit with me. I have my M-16 and ammo belt with three magazines of ammo in each ammo pouch, but, as a medic, I feel compelled to get my first aid kit. I crawl toward our tent. Anyone, anywhere around here could get hit at any time, I think. I'm not prepared to help them. No, this is not good. I've got to get to it. As I crawl I become soaked with mud and water, but I've got to be ready, just in case.

While crawling I notice no one else is moving. They're all firmly ensconced in Mother Earth. When within ten feet of the tent, the shock waves from several explosions vibrate through me. Holy shit! This is not good! This is not a drill!

Then, just as suddenly as it started, it stops. A dreadful dead silence follows. My ears are ringing; my senses are numb. What the hell happened? Has C Company suddenly been eradicated?

Lieutenant Edmore is the first to speak. "Roll call," he hollers. We know that we'd better speak up. We are trained that after a fire-fight, the senior man among us is to account for all men under his charge.

I start, "Spencer, I'm OK."

"Gerrilleo, I'm cool"

"Smitty's here, Sir."

"Sergeant Flock here, Sir."

Shit. Why couldn't that son of a bitch been hit!

"Beatty's here"

"Perez."

"Georgie Porgie is with you, Lieutenant."

"OK, men," Edmore says. "Am I missing anyone? Sergeant Flock, can you think of anyone I missed?"

"No, Sir," Flock responds, "they're all with us. But I can think of a couple of assholes I wish weren't."

"That'll be enough of that talk, Sergeant. Let's just give it another few moments before we get up. All you men, stay put in position."

"Like, where in the hell do you think we'd go, Lieutenant?" asks George Shepherd, whom we fondly call Georgie Porgie.

Edmore responds, "Knock it off, Shepherd, I don't need a smart-ass right about now. Just lay low for a minute."

Off in the distance, we begin to hear the thunder of helicopters, Huey gunships. It is an unmistakable sound we all have grown accustomed to. Helicopters are to the Vietnam War what the jeep was to the Korean and World War II—our ticket to do battle or our ticket to safety. They're a welcome sound. "Sounds like three, Lieutenant," Flock yells. "Stay down, men. Hellfire is a comin'."

We know what that means. To call for air support means that the officer on line has direct contact with Charlie. Oh, shit! Here they come. Just before we can see them, we hear what sounds like a freight train, swoosh . . . hiss! As I look up, the rockets are coming our way. Jesus Christ, they look as if they're coming directly at us. *And the rockets red glare.* The projectiles are seeking and finding their targets.

Suddenly, we see the helicopter come over the tree line of the clearing at full throttle. It's over us and gone with near lightning speed. Holy shit! Another one comes in from a different angle. The pilot configures his aircraft into a straight line, sixty-degree bank, giving the door gunner a clear view of the enemy while the M-60 he has mounted on a sling from the choppers ceiling spews forth fire into the tree line. The door gunner is not firing in any familiar burst pattern, which our guys do. Jesus, look at him. He's standing up, leaning out to get a better view, and he's not letting up on the trigger. It's the longest burst of fire I have ever heard. His tracers lead him to his target, like a magic wand of fire—hell fire. And, just as suddenly as it appeared, it vanishes over the tree line. Man, what a sight.

And the bombs bursting in air. Now, here comes the third chopper. Wow! He's raking the area with his nose-mounted mini-gun. It sounds like a jet's turbine engine as it spits out bullets at three times the rate of an M-60 machine gun. God, am I glad they're on our side. As it shoots by us, empty shell casings fall from the sky like rain. It is raining brass metal from the sky. Ouch. Damn, they hurt. A couple hit my thigh and lower back. I grab one as a souvenir. Ooh, it's still hot! I fight to control my emotions—fear, jubilation, exhilaration, excitement, joy, and sorrow.

Gerrilleo is the first among us to speak as the roar of the encounter subsides. "Man, can you believe that shit? That, is in-fucking-credible." We have had numerous contacts with helicopters back at Fort Campbell, but never did we see them display such speed and angle of attack. Smoke begins to engulf the tree line where the choppers directed their fire. A few minutes later, word is passed along that we have some injuries. Someone on line got hit.

Lieutenant Edmore and Sergeant Flock are working the radio and try to speak to the medics assigned to C Company. Edmore grabs the microphone and speaks in pre-assigned call signs, "Twisty Swamp Connecticut Lima," meaning C Company Commanding Officer. "Mike Papa here, what is your sit-rep? Over."

The response comes back in an excited tone, "Stand by, Twisty Swamp Mike Papa; as soon as it is available, we'll reply same, over."

Edmore immediately depresses the microphone button, "Roger, Connecticut Lima, Mike Papa out."

The airborne army takes great pride in maintaining radio discipline by using words that are very difficult for Charlie to enunciate. Charlie has captured our radios before after they won a particular encounter with us. Although extremely rare, such an encounter occurs on small squad-size patrols. Squad patrols are inherently dangerous because we only have somewhere between ten and twelve guys out on patrol. It's easier for Charlie to overtake a small unit as opposed to a platoon or a company-size patrol. There is strength in numbers. We know that, and Charlie knows that. We've dubbed squad patrols "Death Patrols."

All of us medics are gathered around the radio, which is located in our tent. All of us want to know three things: First, how many enemy are out there; second, which platoon is involved so we know which medic is tending to the wounded; and, third, who is injured or killed.

Flock has his assignment roster out with all the guy's names and their assigned platoons. The radio is busy with the voice traffic of C Company's commander speaking to his platoon leaders who are out on perimeter holding defensive positions.

By monitoring their exchanges, we learn the second platoon has taken the brunt of the hits by the enemy. "That's Mark Badwin's platoon, Lieutenant," Flock says to Edmore. "Advise them to have second platoon switch to their alternate frequency; I want to speak to Badwin."

Edmore depresses the mike button and with an air of authority, interrupts those speaking, "Break for Mike Papa, Break for Mike Papa. Request Dust-Off sit-rep. Over."

Mike Papa means medical platoon leader; Dust-Off sit-rep means he is looking to talk to the medic involved in order to gain information and to support him as necessary. "Advise your Papa Lima involved to come up on Alt-Freq (Alternate Frequency), acknowledge receipt of this transmission prior to shift, over."

C Company's commanding officer responds, "Serria Papa Lima (second platoon leader), switch to Alt-Freq in three, two, one. He's all yours Mike Papa."

"Roger," Edmore states and the radio operator switches frequencies. "Serria Papa Lima, this is Mike Papa Lima, do you copy? Over."

In an excited yet controlled tone, the second platoon leader responds to Edmore. "Yeah, gotcha MPL. Sit-rep is as follows: Three friendly's down, two stable, one critical. Dust-Off Chopper en route with an ETA of thirty minutes, over."

Flock grabs the mike from Edmore, "Serria Pap Lima, let me speak to my guy, over."

"Stand By Mike Papa."

A minute or two later, Mark is on the radio. His voice is shaky and unsteady; he is laboring to catch his breath. He struggles to remember the code of call signs. "Mike Papa, this is Serria Papa Medic. Cannot get an I.V. started on critical. Faint pulse. Pupils unreactive; the guy has lost a lot of blood. It doesn't look good, Sarge. Wounds to head, neck and chest are extreme. Two others have shrapnel wounds to their stomach, arms . . . arm. Oh, I don't—I can't . . . they'll be all right though." I feel for him. He is obviously scared shitless.

Mark holds the rank of specialist fifth class, an E-5 paygrade. Although junior to me in the army, he outranks me by two paygrades. He is also older than I am—a straightforward, mature guy. I am a little surprised to hear how upset he is, and that scares me.

Flock responds, "Relax, son. You're doing fine. Dress the wounds, control bleeding, and keep an eye out on the airway. Dust-off en route. Do you copy?"

Mark's response is markedly different when he responds to Flock in a softer tone of voice, "Ah, Sarge, bleeding not a factor—airway, not a factor either."

We know what that means, not only by the words, but by his tone of voice. The guy is dead, and Mark is taking it hard. I turn away just like most of the others and walk out of the tent. I don't need to hear anymore. I glance in the direction of the smoldering jungle where I know Mark is, trying to dismiss what I have just heard, and in a fit of anger I kick at the ground. Then cadence begins. Yeah, I think. All the fucking way. For what?

Word spreads quickly. The guy who took the hit was Dutch Coughner. And here's the kicker—he and two others were hit from "friendly fire." The rockets fired from the chopper took them out. "Friendly fire"—what an oxymoron. Friendly. Who in the hell ever thought of that one? A few minutes later, the Medevac chopper, the Dust-Off, is landing a short distance from us. Accompanying it are two gunships.

One of the gunships lands along with the medical chopper while the other one circles at treetop level. I run toward them to see if I can help in any way. By the time I get to the chopper, Mark Badwin and a few others are carrying the dead and wounded. I assist as best I can without interfering. As I turn to leave, I hear a faint sound of someone calling my name. The noise from the two choppers, their blades whipping and snapping against the wind, makes it nearly impossible to hear.

Out of the corner of my eye I catch a glimpse of a door gunner in the gunship waving at me. He flips up the shaded lens attached to his helmet and with a smile he screams, "Harry!" Then he points back at himself, again shouting, "Louie Blade!" While protecting my eyes from the churned up grasses, I squint in attempt to recognize him, when it hits me. Louie! Louie Blade! Jesus, I haven't seen him or thought much about him since jump school. We wave frantically at each other until the chopper's turbine engines gain take-off RPM, gearing up to get airborne. I take note of the chopper's numbers. I'll make it a point to look him up when I get back to base camp. My ole fellow musketeer, my buddy. God, it was good to see him. His smile is still the same, confident and cocksure.

I flip him the thumbs-up sign as his chopper goes airborne and fades from sight; Louie acknowledges with the same. Man, was it good to see him. I wonder how in the world he went from being an airborne grunt to that glory job of being a door gunner, and in no less than a gunship. Wow. I am impressed. Once I get back to base camp, I've got to go see him.

Nightfall finds me on the line as a medic for B Company's second platoon. Flock relishes his words as he orders me to relieve a fellow medic, Mike Sand. "Spencer, it's your turn. Report your skinny white ass to B Company's first sergeant." He points in the general direction where I need to go. "It'll take you about twenty minutes to get there. And once you get there they'll be about fifty yards into the tree line. That will be your new home until I decide otherwise."

"No problem, Sarge," I respond. This is it. It's my turn, and, of course, it starts to rain as I begin to walk toward B Company's position.

Well, this is what I've trained for. My mind begins to conjure up various conditions that I might be confronted with. *Sucking chest wound—seal it off from any air. Excessive bleeding— apply a tourniquet.* The checklist: Flashlight, check, got it. Mosquito repellent, check, got it. Morphine, of course, I had to sign for it. Patient tags, yeah, I've got six of those. Ammo—twenty magazines full, that's 400 rounds, 300 more are still in boxes in my rucksack. Small aid kit, yeah, strapped through my ammo belt. .45 (side-arm pistol) attached to the ammo belt, check. Two magazines for it, yeah, one in each thigh pocket. I'm cool, I think as I continue walking.

After I find B company's position and check in with the first sergeant, he states, "Yeah, we've been expecting you." Pointing to my left, he says, "About forty yards that way, you'll come across Staff Sergeant Garcia's platoon. He'll put you in position to find and take the place of their medic. Listen to his directions very carefully. You'll be our first line of defense out there; keep alert and good luck, trooper."

I nod and begin to walk away from him and say, "Thanks, Sarge. Good luck to all of us."

He grunts back and resumes reading the map on his lap. The rain beads roll off the waterproof sheaf that covers it.

By the time I find Sergeant Garcia's platoon, dusk is fast approaching. When I introduce myself, a big smile spreads across his face as if he is glad to finally know me. It seems strange to get such a nice, warm reception. I take comfort in his ingratiating demeanor. Then, in a blink of an eye, his mood becomes serious with the dos and don'ts while out on the line. "If you must talk, do so by whispering only. You'll be put into the exact position I want you in. The only time you are to move is either because I tell you to, or because someone has been hit. If you've got to piss, you do so while in the prone position. *Do not stand at anytime.* There will be a man to your left and one to your right about fifteen feet away. Make sure you see them; make sure to acknowledge them once in position. Do not smoke, and do not take a shit. If for some reason you must shit, you will give your position away to Charlie just as if you lit a candle for him to draw a bead on you. But if you must shit, do it in the prone position. And bury it immediately. Got it?"

"Yeah, sure," I respond.

His voice is steady, serious, and direct. He speaks with authority but almost at a whisper. The seriousness of what I am about to do causes me to shudder. I am getting cold already. A light misty rain is still falling. Everything around me is soaking wet just like I am fast becoming. Then he takes the lead as we head out towards the line . . . the real line.

Talk about perspectives.

There was a time when I thought the boonies at Fort Campbell were tough, then the conditions of the ship coming here, base camp, and BSOP, just a mere two hundred yards from where I am now. Damn, I'm chilled, and my skin is starting to look as if I stayed in the bathtub too long again. Ouch, these fucking mosquitoes are everywhere. Christ, I can't even think about writing in my diary here. I stumble and nearly fall trying to keep up with Sergeant Garcia. Hell, he doesn't have anything to carry compared to me. He's only carrying his M-16 with an ammo belt and a couple of pouches full of magazines. I'm lugging everything but the damn kitchen sink. The jungle is so thick. Smack! A vine snags my helmet, nearly knocking it off my head. Man, it's getting dark fast. Really dark.

We finally make it to my destination. As I scan the area, I look up at the clouds that seem to be just a hundred feet above our heads. The jungle appears to have a life of its own. Then I spot Mike Sand, the fellow medic I am replacing. Boy, he looks rough. He's filthy too; mud covers most of him. He has dug a small indentation in the ground to conceal himself from the line of fire. When he sees me he shakes his head as though to say, "Thank God, you're here. I'm outta here."

We do not talk but simply pat each other on the shoulder as we pass. Just before we break contact, he tugs on my rucksack to get my attention. I turn slightly to look at him, and he winks at me while nodding his head, giving me a thumbs-up. I return the same but not with the same conviction.

Garcia gets my attention with hand gestures. He wants to make sure I can see the guys on either side of me. I look in the direction he is pointing, but I don't see anyone. I look again, straining to find the guy and shrug my shoulders. I can't see him. Garcia shows signs of being upset with me. He flashes ten fingers followed by three and points.

Again, I look, and the guy decides to help me. I spot foliage moving. The guy has foliage stuck into his uniform to camouflage himself. That's pretty good, I think. If he hadn't moved, I would have never spotted him. I see him smiling at me. He is obviously pleased with himself and his efforts to blend in with the jungle.

Garcia then directs me to look in the opposite direction, and again, I can't see a damn thing; try as I might, I cannot find him. Garcia motions for the guy to stand up. The ground seems to come alive just five feet from me. Boy, is he close! Realizing he is that close, I jump back, a bit startled. I find it hard to believe that someone could be that close and yet I couldn't see him. The guy's face is painted with crayon camouflage too; numerous large palm leaves cover him.

When we make eye contact, he doesn't smile. His only acknowledgment is to make his eyes larger than life. Oookaay. Now that we're done with introductions, I slip out of my rucksack and make myself as comfortable as possible in what the riflemen refer to as a "grave." Comfortable. Ha.

As I settle down, I hone in on the different sights, smells, and sounds of the jungle. The first thing I notice as I look at the area directly in front of me is that it's as noisy as a wetland in the spring when all God's creation comes out of hibernation. Funny, I hadn't noticed it until now. And then it dawns on me—the jungle and those billions of insects, birds, monkeys or whatever they are—they are my friends. They go quiet when they hear any movement that varies from their normal world. After an hour or two of just sitting, staring, and listening, I notice that my new friends are also quiet when it rains hard. The jungle is alive as if it were one entity. Its tentacles are made up of billions and billions of insects and organisms. My senses are overwhelmed. I am awestruck with fascination. Fascinated by a multitude of thoughts buzzing, vying for my attention as if they are sperm squirming in competition to be the first to the egg.

It proves to be too much for me to assimilate. In my imagination, I speak to my brothers and sisters. "You guys should see this. It's incredible." But then I realize where I am. No, it's better that it's me here than any of them.

God almighty, I am on the primordial edge of mankind's existence. No, we're not throwing stones at one another; the stones have changed shape. Today we call stones bullets. How far have we really come from the stone age? Then, without prompt, the beat and the words spill forth from the deepest recesses of my mind: *Here we go— All the way—Airborne—Every day—Wine—Women—No good —Mud—Death—So good—Airborne!*

I refocus and come back to reality shaking my head as if I just woke from sleep. Rain, dripping down my helmet finds its way onto my neck and flows directly down my spinal column. I flinch and grit my teeth in an effort not to move too much. Hell, if Charlie can survive out here, I sure as hell can. But then a twinge of doubt creeps in. This is his land, his home, and his backyard. He is as comfortable here as I would be running through the alleys in my neighborhood.

Another solemn thought comes to mind. Charlie is just as committed to win here as I would be if I were in his shoes back home, where he would be the invader dictating some bullshit doctrine I should live by. They must hate us. Water is beginning to pool in my shallow grave. When I move the water feels very cold, but if I stay perfectly still it feels warm.

Charlie, I say to myself, I'm sorry for me that I'm here, and I'm sorry for you I'm here. I've got nothing against you. I just want to put in my time and go home—home where it is safe, home where it is comfortable, home where the only thing I have to worry about is the light bulb burning out (besides, of course, my father kicking the shit out of me). But, if you are going to try and kill me, I've got to protect myself and my fellow paratroopers. Nothing personal, man."

Swallowing hard, I slowly reach for one of the magazines of ammo I laid out in front of me. I slip one bullet out of it and put it in my breast pocket. I do not think I can surrender if we are overrun; that bullet is not meant for Charlie. My heart races as I make the choice— surrender or die. God help me. Please stay with me. Then I begin to argue with myself. Should I or shouldn't I? But I keep the bullet in my breast pocket. Somehow, despite the rain, the cold, and the insects buzzing all around me, I drift off to sleep.

I know my turn to be on guard is a couple of hours away, 2300 hours to 0100 hours. In what seems like seconds, someone pokes my shoulder, which has about the same effect as if I had just been poked with a cattle prod. I jerk in response. I didn't even realize I had fallen asleep. The guy's lips are very near my ear. "Shoosh, quiet. We've got movement, forty to fifty feet at your ten o'clock. I've been watching and listening to it for the past forty minutes. I cannot make out anything for sure, but there is definitely something out there." I can barely control the shaking inside; it's like lightning bolts pulsating through my body.

He hands me the hand-held generator, which is attached to a Claymore mine set somewhere out in front of us, and whispers, "You've got the watch, Doc." I suddenly feel the gravity of the situation. Christ, if we make real contact, it is my responsibility to squeeze the lever on the generator to send an electrical current to the Claymore, thereby detonating it upon the incoming enemy. He then slowly, very methodically crawls back to his position on his hands and knees. My heart is racing. The responsibility of watch is now resting solely with me. It is his turn to sleep for two hours, after which I will crawl over to give him back the generator.

It has stopped raining. The sky is partly clouded with big low nimbus cumulus clouds that appear to be a mere fifty feet overhead. Between the clouds, moonlight shines down, illuminating the night like giant laser beams penetrating the jungle, allowing me to see much better than when I first came out here some four hours ago. Strange sounds capture my attention—typical but scary sounds indigenous to the jungle. I stare out into the darkness and try to see whatever or whoever is out there. We control the day; Charlie owns the night.

We were told the most likely time Charlie will strike is at night. Within an hour into my watch, despite the adrenaline rush when the guy woke me up, I begin to nod off. I don't even know I've nodded off until my face falls into the mud as my muscles relax. Awake, realizing I nodded off, another adrenaline surge shoots through me with such force that I become short of breath. It would be easier to stay awake if I could move about, but that is not possible. If I move, without the cover of rain drowning out the sound, I'll be setting myself up for a sniper's hit. I keep that in mind in an effort to scare myself into staying awake.

At about midnight I hear someone, or something, breaking branches. I blow at the mosquitoes buzzing around my face. In order to hear better I take off my helmet. The helmet allows sound to echo off it and reverberate into it, creating distortions. The jungle is backlit by the low-moving clouds. Just as I zero in on the direction of the intruder, it starts to rain once again, blocking out any further sounds of movement I could have detected. Shit, rain is always in his favor. I freeze in position and try to keep my breathing down for fear that whoever is out there will hear it.

If I stare too long at something, that something appears to move. My mind is beginning to play tricks on me, so I change the direction of my gaze every second. Oh, shit, there it is again! I wrap the electrical cord that runs to the Claymore mine around my finger. If Charlie is going to attempt to move it, reverse its direction (which is his favorite trick), I want to feel him move it, and then blow his ass to Kingdom Come. We learned in our training that Charlie likes to sneak up on us from time to time, especially on new units to Vietnam, and turn the Claymore mine 180 degrees so that it faces us. Then he pulls the line or makes a sound and we, in turn, panic and detonate the Claymore mine. The mine then explodes directly at us. A simple but effective way to have us do to ourselves what we intended to do to him.

But I feel nothing. No movement detected. The line is not moving. Rain begins again and runs down my face and into my eyes while the mosquitoes have a field day about my face and neck. I blink excessively in an attempt to see more clearly. My view is foggy. I slowly reach to change my weapon from single-shot mode to full automatic. My mind shifts to the last time I felt this scared—back to those three guys who entered the hospital compound. The big difference now is that we are in a "free fire zone." That is, if Charlie's out there, he's fair game. I do not have to allow him the privilege of shooting first.

Millions of thoughts run through my mind like a fast spinning roulette wheel, first to Beatrice, back home. When I get back, I've got to hook up with her again. She is a beautiful American/Japanese girl. Then my thoughts shift to my little brother, Bobby, and sister, Connie, playing baseball on the school playground across the street from where I grew up, boxing at the Boys Club; what it would be like to die . . . and then, I hear it again. Only now, I'm convinced that it's not my imagination. Someone is out there. I strain to see him.

My heart's beating so strong it's hitting my chest. There it is again! They're walking from my left to my right; I hear distinct movement. Goddamn it, rain or sweat is dripping into my eyes. I can't shoot blind; that would be suicide, giving them my exact position. Cool it, I tell myself. Get a hold of yourself and don't panic. Yeah, don't panic. It's as if I'm speaking to two distinctly different people within me. Be cool. The rain begins to stop while the bright moonlight penetrates the jungles canopy again. Oh, God! There he is! He's up in the tree sitting on a branch alongside the trunk. A fucking sniper. Jesus Christ, the Claymore is useless.

Charlie's only about fifty feet out and just as I spot him, the clouds block the moonlight and obscure my line of sight. Everything is pitch black again. Shit. It's as if someone just put a blindfold on me. I can't see five feet in front of me. I shift slightly and get into a more comfortable position to fire, taking aim in his general direction and wait for the clouds to open up again. Ah, shit! The guy who gave me the Claymore generator is snoring. I want to scream at him to shut up. But instead, I chance movement and throw a clump of mud in his direction, hoping it'll hit him to get him to stop snoring.

I reposition myself, ready to fire if I see Charlie again, but there's nothing. All is quiet. Even the insects have stopped their incessant noise, confirming something is out there. Five minutes go by. Ten minutes. I begin to think it must have been my imagination. Is he really out there? Did I really see him? Doubt grows by the second.

Oh, oh, the clouds are breaking up again. I haven't moved. I am still aiming my M-16 in the area where I last spotted him. Moonlight moves like some mystical force through the jungle. Here it comes. Get ready, Spencer, I say to myself. If he's there, just do it.

The sound of the bullets exploding deafens me while the muzzle flash blinds me. I hold the trigger down longer than the norm. At least ten to fifteen bullets have been expended. Immediately those on line with me open fire. The noise is beyond comprehension. Thirty men are firing their weapons as if they are shooting at a thousand charging enemy soldiers. The jungle is disintegrating under the barrage of bullets. I, however, stop shooting. I just stare where I had shot to see if he is still there.

Tracer rounds from the weapons being fired pierce the jungle and look as if they are laser beams. After a minute or two, I shout in between bursts of fire, "I got him! I got him!" The guys hear me and slowly each of them stops firing. "Cool it guys! I got him!" I say, primarily to get them to stop shooting. Christ, talk about overkill. We probably killed a couple million mosquitoes with all that firepower.

Sergeant Garcia's voice suddenly fills the air. "Cease fire, cease fire. Second platoon, B company, cease fire." A couple more shots are fired and then all falls silent. "Cease fire, Goddamn it. Who opened fire here?" He walks out to us on line, stumbling in the dark as he crashes through the foliage. A couple of guys respond, "Not me, Sarge," "Not me," says another, "It came from over there."

I spoke up, "I did, Sergeant Garcia. Over here."

"Who the hell is that?"

I can tell he doesn't recognize my voice so I say, "Me, Spencer."

Stumbling closer, Garcia asks, "Who? Oh you, the medic! Why in the hell did you open fire?"

I respond, trying to control myself, "There was a sniper in the tree about fifty feet out at my one o'clock, Sarge. I think I got him."

Reaching my position he crouches down and speaks with a lowered voice. "Are you sure, son? What do you mean he was in a tree?" I repeat myself with a growing confidence. "OK," he says, "Men, settle down, stay alert; Doc here thinks he took one out in a tree. Check your weapons. Nobody move. We'll do a sweep of the area at first light." He then bends down again and asks, "Where is the Claymore generator?"

I respond, "I've got it right here."

He takes it from me and rips off the wires. "The damn thing is useless now; he might have already turned it around on us. We'll check it out in the morning." He stands up and stumbles into the darkness. "Keep alert men, and for Christ's sake, don't panic." As he walks away, silence permeates the landscape. Not even the buzzing of the omnipresent mosquitoes is heard. I don't think any of us drift off to sleep the rest of the night . . . I know I don't.

Within a few hours, dawn begins to make its presence known. My mind races with a million emotions—one of which I can't shake. I have killed a human being, and I don't feel heroic. I feel nauseous. I try to rationalize that it was either him or me, but that doesn't ease my mind. I keep thinking maybe he's still alive, and maybe I'll feel better; it'll ease my conscience if I can find him still alive. The remainder of the night I kept talking as if to him, saying, "Don't die, man. I'll get to you as soon as I can. Just don't die, please."

When there's sufficient light, I whisper to the guy to my left, the one who alerted me to movement, that I am going out to look for the sniper. He shakes his head but doesn't speak. His eyes tell me not to be crazy, stay put. I feel so bad that I don't care. I feel compelled to get to him, to help him. He is, after all, a human being. I have to get to him. I move forward, taking only my .45 and my small aid kit. I leave my steel pot behind too; I can hear better without it.

I crawl very similar to how I crawled while demonstrating the maneuver at West Point. Only this time, I do it with as much stealth as possible; this isn't practice. Speed kills. My heart races. I have to stop to catch my breath. The adrenaline is flowing so fast that I can't even swallow. I try to spit because I can't swallow, but there isn't any saliva. I have a terrible copper taste in my mouth. Christ, my heart is beating so fast that for a moment I think I am having a heart attack. I have a feeling I am going to crawl up on the muzzle of a rifle pushed right into my face. But I regain my composure and inch forward again. Then I see it.

It is some kind of monkey—small, frail, and gray. Of all things, a monkey. Holy shit! I feel such a huge relief that I smile, put my arm in front of my head and bury my face in it. I want to scream with joy; I don't have the death of another human on my conscience. I do, however, apologize to the little monkey and say, "Sorry, little guy, I didn't know. I couldn't tell." I stand up, holding him over my head, and shout to the guys, "It's just a monkey!" I then gently place him down on the ground and walk back, feeling partly relieved, partly guilty, and largely stupid.

The guys just smile upon my return to the perimeter and state, "Good job, Doc. It could have been the real thing. Where did you learn to shoot like that? That was a damn good shot, man, for a medic." I dismiss that comment. If there hadn't been anything out there, my ass would be in a healthy sling for discharging my weapon without an identified, verifiable target. Well, at least now the sergeants will know I'm on my toes. I hope that counts for something.

At around 0700 hours, Sergeant Garcia, along with B company's first sergeant, pay me a visit. I had to stay out on line until they came. Those who were out all night with me have been relieved. I was told by one of Garcia's squad leaders to stay put. As they approach my position, I sense they are going to ream my ass for starting the phantom encounter with Charlie. And sure as shit the first sergeant speaks up as he gets within earshot. "It's my understanding, Private, that are you the person responsible for initiating fire last night. Is that a correct assumption?"

I am bone tired, and a confrontation is the last thing I need. Christ, I have been sweating and freezing my ass off for the last twelve hours out here. My nerves are shot. As he speaks, I think, why the hell is he so damn condescending? I mean, I'm out here on line, protecting them, in the first line of defense, and his attitude is so damn negative.

Gracia interjects before I can respond, "Who gave you permission to fire, Spencer?"

I look at him dumbfounded and respond, "I didn't think I needed permission, Sarge. It's a free fire zone."

With a demeaning tone, the first sergeant hollers, "I ought to give you an Article 15 for disobeying Sergeant's Garcia's orders. He told me he specifically informed you not to fire unless fired upon."

My eyes shift to Garcia in disbelief. "First Sergeant," I state, "Sergeant Garcia never said that, And if he did, Top, I'm sorry. I did not hear it."

"Sorry doesn't cut it, Private; get your sorry ass out of my sight. Report back to the medical platoon. Flock's waiting for you there."

Feeling totally defeated in mind and body, I bend down to gather my equipment while they turn and walk away. As I put my ammo magazines back into their pouches, Karl Lessnau, another medic, walks toward me to relieve me. Good. I'm so tired, and I feel a little nauseous.

"Hey, Spence" Karl states. "Hi, how you doing, guy?" I respond. "I'm OK," and he continues.

"Man, you're in deep shit with Flock. He told me to tell you to report directly to him after I relieved you. We heard it was you who started firing last night." He smiles broadly shaking his head, "Man, you scared the hell out of everybody last night. What made you do it?" After I explain, he shakes his head. "Shit, they ought to give you a fucking medal for being alert instead of screwing with you. Hey, man, for what it's worth, I think you did all right."

A rifle platoon squad leader and another trooper walk up to us. "Hey, Doc, did you turn the Claymore mine toward us?"

My eyes grew wide, "No, why?"

"Well," he says, "someone did. We just checked it and it was turned facing us. You sure you didn't do it?"

"Of course not Sergeant, come on." I continue putting my stuff together and reluctantly walk back to the medical platoon tent.

As I walk, stumbling on the uneven terrain, I wonder who the hell . . . ? Then it dawns on me. Maybe Charlie was out there. Maybe once he turned it around to face us he slipped away and released that monkey, thinking one of us would blow the Claymore. Nah, can't be. Maybe one of the guys did it to add some bullshit excitement to the scenario.

When I reach our tent, Flock throws open the entrance flap with a vengeance. "You stupid fucking asshole; so you panicked out there, did you?" He points at me. "Well, guess what, we need a communal latrine trench dug. Report to Squad Leader Reynolds; he'll give you the location and the dimensions." His eyes burn right through me.

"Sarge," I plead, "can I get some shut-eye first? I'm exhausted."

"No, you can't, you fucking pussy! Get moving, *now!*"

Anger builds within me. It feels like a volcano deep inside, but somehow I manage to suppress it. This isn't a fucking war, I think.

This shit is insanity. It's a massive exercise designed to eradicate compassion and humanity. We have prepared ourselves for this shit for two fucking years, and it comes down to *this*—digging ammo pits and latrines, shooting at what I believe to be the enemy and getting my ass reamed out. This is insanity at its finest. Hell, nobody has even asked me what I shot at.

A couple of medics try to lighten the air. They sense I am distraught and near the boiling point. "Hey, Spence," Ted Dziengelewski calls out, "Cool it, man. How many more to go?"

I look his way and nod in recognition with a slight smile, aware of what he's doing. "Thanks, Ted, about 340 days and a duffel bag drag." Ted's words help me put things in perspective.

"OK, Specialist Daniel Reynolds, where do you want me?" I ask, reporting for duty. Reynolds is cool with me. I like him. He is about twenty-four, has been in the army nearly four years and has two more to go until his current enlistment is up. He is a black guy, as are all our squad leaders, but, unlike most of them, he is compassionate and caring.

As we near the spot where the latrine trench is to be dug, he asks if my hands are OK to dig. "Not really," I respond, "but they'll be OK." And then he steps closer to me so no one can hear and says, "We heard that Charlie turned the Claymore around on you. Why didn't you blow it?"

"I don't know, Dan. I didn't think I needed it. I spotted what I thought was him in the tree. Verified his position three times, and on the third spotting I let him have it."

He leans closer, eyes darting back and forth, and says, "I would have done the same thing, man. But I probably would have blown the Claymore first and then opened up on him. In my case, I'd be dead. Don't let anybody tell you otherwise; you did good, Harry." He winks at me, "You did real good, kid."

Chapter 8

TAKING THE PLACE
OF A DEAD MAN

JULY 28 1966

I LOOK FORWARD TO flying in a helicopter; the view of those gentle, rolling hills is always breathtaking. This operation is our second. Each search and destroy mission is given a name; this one is Aurora II. Our helicopter is so heavy with men and equipment it's difficult to get airborne. The other choppers are already airborne. Our chopper is the last one on the ground. The pilot spools up the engine to the point of red line and then pulls on his collective to try to get us in the air. But the chopper lurches, slides sideways a little, and settles back down on the tarmac.

The pilot studies his instruments, attempting to determine the problem. He twists the turbine's accelerator, trying to gain the necessary power to lurch forward and ascend as normal. Christ, of all the times I have been on a chopper, I have never heard the sound this engine is making. The door gunner is speaking to someone on his mike. Because I'm facing the rear of the chopper with my back to the copilot's seat, I twist my head to see who's speaking in the cockpit and try to identify the problem.

Again, the chopper begins to lift off. It noses slightly forward while the blades beat the air and try to respond to the pilot's commands. The metal vibrates throughout the aircraft. The door gunner has his blackened sun visor down so I cannot see the expression on his face. He leans out, attempting to see the tarmac, checking if we're off the ground. This is not a good sign. Let's just call it off.

I notice my platoon mates staring at each other with weak smiles. We're trying very hard not to show fear, but it's there. Someone yells, "Let's go, motherfucker! Airborne!" But no one picks up on the prompt. It's so damn noisy we can barely hear the guy who's still shouting something else at the top of his lungs. So we all pretend we don't hear his "Airborne" cry. Because I was the last one to climb aboard, I'm on the outside edge of the chopper and will be the first one out when we land.

Finally, the chopper is airborne, but I wish it wasn't. I have a terrible gnawing in my gut that indicates something is wrong, terribly wrong. The pilot pushes the aircraft to the point of redline in an attempt to catch up with the other dozen or so of choppers flying ahead of us in close formation. I crane my neck to look at the indicated airspeed, and I'm shocked to see the needle pegged at 130 knots. Man, the fastest I ever remember a chopper flying was about 100 to 110 knots. The chopper begins to vibrate as I have never felt before. Fear dances in my head despite the numerous times I have flown. I don't like this. Something is out of sync, so I say a little prayer and check my weapon, making sure it's cleared.

We have standing orders: *"No weapons are to have rounds chambered while in flight."* We have our magazines in the weapons, but the bolts are locked in the open position with safety switches on. We are, therefore, forced to rely on the door gunners to lay down a field of fire as we land.

We are flying at treetop level blasting through the air. Wow, what a rush! A few minutes later we slow and climb to flight level. I stick my head out of the open door to see if we caught up with the others. Yep, we're closing in on them. Man, what a sight.

As our chopper slows, we pull up so close to another chopper that it looks like we're going to hit each other's blades. What are these guys trying to do, scare us? Air pockets cause the choppers to suddenly lose or gain altitude. It's as if we are on a giant roller coaster, rising and falling. I secretly wish it were just a roller coaster.

I recognize the guys in the chopper next to us; they're from the second platoon of C company. Hey, there's Karl Lessnau. He's sitting on the edge of the chopper's opening with his feet hanging out. We wave to each other, exuberant at recognizing one another in such a bizarre setting. I nod my head and he does the same. His chopper hits another air pocket and drops suddenly about ten feet. Just as suddenly, our chopper drops even with them. Wow! This is an unusually rough ride. Then his chopper ascends with such force it's like someone has a long string attached to it, violently jerking it up.

Lessnau's chopper suddenly banks away from us. Our pilot pulls a bank just as suddenly to follow him. The angle of bank is so sharp I can look straight down at the earth. I get a clear view of the guys in the other chopper who are looking up at us. But, my God, they're not pulling out of the bank. I strain to focus on Karl. What in the world happened? Have they been hit? Have we been hit? Shit! Shit! Oh, shit! They're going to crash! The blades of their chopper are not turning fast enough. They can't maintain altitude. I close my eyes as the chopper makes contact, splattering itself and those on board into the ground.

Our chopper continues to hold a sixty-degree bank, circling. I can't look anymore. I'm not dreaming. I take a deep breath. Vertigo disorients my senses as the chopper banks and then hovers over the crash site. I push my back up hard against the copilot's seat to try to ward off the dizzying effects of vertigo and take in a few breaths of air. I'm still alive. I put my hand over my face so I can smell life, my life.

We circle a few times over the crash zone. It is clear though—no one survived. Our chopper pulls away and resumes its course to war. Goodbye, my friend. God be with you.

As a result of Lessnau's death, I am assigned to his former platoon—that is, to those of his platoon who were on a different chopper. Four crewmen and ten of our guys were wiped out in the blink of an eye. Instead of helping set up a first aid station at BSOP, I am ordered by Flock, "Take the place of the dead man and pray it isn't contagious." He is an emotionless bastard. I hate him. I suspect he is toying with me when he says, rather mockingly, "You knew Lessnau, didn't you, Spencer?"

I look at him with resignation and respond, "Of course I did, Flock. You know I knew him. What's your point?"

His eyes widen with disbelief and anger. I forgot, in my present state of mind, to address him as sergeant. He drops what he had been holding and walks toward me. "Looky here, boy," he says, pointing his finger within an inch of my nose, "Lessnau was one hell of a man, and I don't think you're good enough to fill his boots, but I want you to try. Do you get my drift? Private Spencer?"

If I say yes, he will construe it as a sign of cockiness; if I say no, I am admitting that I am not good enough. "Where do I report, Sergeant Flock?"

Our faces are inches apart. Without flinching, he growls right into my face, "You're assigned to C Company. Lieutenant Redy is your platoon officer. It's off that way," he points. I don't look in the direction he is pointing. Our eyes lock in some bullshit battle of wills.

"Fine," I say as I turn away from him and with one last shot I snap, "I'd rather deal with the enemy out there than the enemy here."

He fires back, not missing a beat, "You've got that one right! I am your worst enemy and don't you ever forget that."

With my M-16 in hand, I briefly entertain shooting the bastard.

As I approach the area where I think C Company should be, I ask a radio operator where I might find Lieutenant Redy and the second platoon. He grunts and points in a direction without saying a word. I guess he knew some of the guys who had perished in the chopper crash. We are all affected. We all know that it could have been any one of us.

I spot another radio operator. I know the man in charge is always near his radio operator. "That's him," he says, pointing to a small guy a few paces away. "Lieutenant, Sir," I salute, saying, "I'm your replacement medic, Harry Spencer."

He immediately snaps, "Put your stupid motherfucking hand down, Private. Don't you ever salute me again in the jungle." He points his index finger at the tip of my nose. Startled, I apologize. Then he puts his hand on my shoulder, forcing me to the ground with him. "Look, Private, thanks for the salutation, but out here, never salute an officer. If Charlie is watching, you just targeted me. Do I make myself clear?"

"Yeah, sure, Lieutenant, sorry."

"Sorry doesn't cut it; you got that?" he retorts.

I nod my head in the affirmative. My mind races back to every time I was chewed out by an officer for not respecting his rank or not saluting him fast enough, and now this SOB chews me out because I do salute. Out here he's trying to melt in with the animals; out here he wants to play like he is just one of the guys. But the enemy knows that under fire the only person who ever moves is the medic. There is no fucking way for me to melt in, and here is this officer, a would-be hero, running this crap on me. Bullshit.

However, within a few minutes, he takes the time to get to know me. We talk for about thirty minutes. He turns out to be a likeable guy. He is twenty-three years old and received his commission through a ROTC curriculum. He just graduated from college a year earlier. He is trained as a mechanical engineer and has no aspirations to stay in the service longer than his obligation. He doesn't have the stereo-typical condescending "lifer" attitude that is so prevalent in most other officers. I decide he is cool.

Later, he walks me out to the perimeter's defensive positions where the remainder of his men are stationed. It is about twelve noon, and, for the first time in a long time, it is not raining. Lieutenant Redy takes me around to meet every man, who are entrenched on the banks of the creek and spread out about fifteen feet from each other. The waterline permits them to dig a slight indentation into the bank and still be five feet from water's edge. Not bad. I can live with it; at least it isn't raining.

One by one I am politely introduced to the men. To each man I meet, I ask for help. "If we come under attack, and God forbid you're injured, please call for Ben Casey. Charlie knows the word medic, so please, if you need me, yell for Ben Casey, will ya?" Each guy is exceptionally polite and responds with kind comments, "Glad to have you aboard, Doc," "Welcome aboard." It rapidly changes my mood. Out here I'm welcomed; out here I'm respected. Back at BSOP and base camp I'm shit on.

Despite the constant fear, I like being out on line. Each man is calm and collected and professional. At each of their positions, all pertinent equipment is laid out before them. One of the guys even taped his ammo magazines together so that when one is emptied he simply ejects and flips it 180 degrees and has another twenty rounds to shoot. Another guy has at least forty magazines of ammo laid out in front of him, half of which are taped. All of them have numerous hand grenades placed within reach so they can pick them up and throw them as needed. Not one of them is smoking. Their mood is sober but confident. In a strange way, I like this. It isn't too bad. Then I snicker to myself; in all the war movies I remember seeing, all of the men smoke. Here and now, reality dictates otherwise.

Today I received a letter from my folks and, of all people, Beatrice Davis. I have always been attracted to her and plan to get to know her better as time goes by. It appears our break-up has not dampened her interest in me. I relish in the thought of her beauty and how I feel when I'm with her. I believe she feels the same for me. I've known her for what seems like a lifetime. When I first saw her, a bell went off in my head. I've never been able to stop it from ringing every time I see her or when we're together. She lights up my life. I think I'll write her back and ask if she's interested in flying to Hawaii when I decide to go on R&R. I'll pay her airfare with the money I'm saving. Boy, that would be great.

The thought of her possibly becoming my wife makes me want to be a better man. I like that thought. It makes me smile to think about her and invokes a warmth that contrasts with the cold emotions I must wear here. I'm not myself here in the jungle of Vietnam. I've become something someone else designed.

This search and destroy mission proves to be uneventful. No contact with Charlie or the North Vietnamese Regular Army. Just sweat, mosquitoes, and the uncertainty of contact on every patrol. One thing is for sure: if we do make contact, Charlie will have the advantage. We are always so tired from humping the boonies that we sometimes let our guard down. Fatigue is wearing us down. Given the conditions here, sleep does not come easily or last more than an hour at a time before something wakes us up—bugs, mosquitos, or the screeching of animals in the jungle.

We get up at dawn to begin the trek of getting the hell out of this godforsaken jungle. Rather than airlift us from this operation, they decided to have us hump to a predetermined point where we'll board "deuce and half trucks" (two-and-one-half ton cargo trucks). I'm still with C company's second platoon. Each platoon takes a different path as we wade into the jungle. Because the second platoon lost ten guys in the chopper crash, it is the smallest unit on patrol with just twenty guys. Charlie picks his targets carefully, and we're the smallest group in this patrol. As I penetrate the foliage, I pray Charlie doesn't spot us. We are the weak ones in the fold.

Pushing onward, we struggle with the weight of our equipment for about two hours. Certain areas we walk through are swampy; waist-high water is infested with bugs, water snakes, mosquitoes, and leeches. The man in front of me signals, using his hands to indicate that we are infested with leeches. "Break time."

I look down at my legs and boots; I'm covered with them. I pull and swat at them. If they're not burrowed into your skin, they'll fall off with just a flick of the finger. Pulling out my pants that are tucked into my boots, I check if there are any on my legs. Sure enough, there are about a dozen or so blackish-purple leeches two or three inches long and about as thick as a small worm. I try pulling, but wait, shit. A few of them have burrowed into me.

I reach for the mosquito repellent I carry on the side of my helmet, which is held in place by an elastic band running the circumference, and pour it over them, and, like some magic potion, they fall off. Sometimes I can feel them if they are on me for a while. It feels like a slow drawing, sucking sensation, like getting a mini hickie; however, that hickie has no relationship with ecstasy.

We've all heard the stories about what would happen if leeches stay on you too long or if they somehow manage to get to your private parts. I wince at the thought and try to dismiss it. Ouch! I pull up my fatigue shirt to where there is a gnawing pain on the side of my stomach, just below the belt line. Ah shit, one of those suckers has burrowed his way into my appendectomy scar and died. His body is loose and hanging off of me, but his head is stuck inside the scar. I can't get him out of me, but I pull on him anyway. Shit, the body separates from the head. The head is stuck in me! Gross! Oh well, I'll have to wait till we get back to base camp to get that one out.

The deuce and a half trucks are a welcome sight. We wave to the MPs and the drivers. We are in a jubilant mood; we've made it out of the jungle unscathed, without contact, and we're going back to base camp. Seeing the uniforms of the MP's and the truck drivers makes me realize just how dirty we are. Their uniforms are much greener than ours and, in comparison, our uniforms are dingy and dull. En-route to base camp, it starts to rain again. Because the trucks don't have a canvas top to cover us, it gets cold—maybe eighty degrees with the wind chill factor. A lot of the guys are visibly cold; their lips are turning purple, and their faces are pale, or ashen, depending upon the race they are. Some are actually shaking. Three hours later no one is talking; instead we are huddled down as low as we can go to avoid the wind—huddled body to body to keep warm. Eighty degrees is cold compared to 110-plus temp without any breeze.

The jungle grows so close to the edge of these back narrow roads that occasionally foliage strikes the truck's cab or the side wooden slats we lean against. Christ, I think, Charlie could be watching us go by. He could be laying out there ready to ambush us at any moment. A couple of guys claim to have seen Charlie at various times only to have him disappear with the wind. If we've killed any of them, we haven't found them. Their comrades are either dragging them off, or they disintegrate when a bullet hits them. Personally, I believe they have built a system of underground highways. It doesn't take a rocket scientist to figure that one out.

They occasionally snipe at us as we hump through the jungle and every time, *every single time*, we overpower them with our collective firepower. Later we sweep the area but never, not once, have we found anything they may have left behind, not even a spent bullet cartridge. Word has spread among us that A company uncovered small, well-camouflaged holes in the ground that lead to stored munitions and miscellaneous first aid supplies. The only thing we do with the holes once we discover them is to first send in a "tunnel rat" to obtain an Intel report—if he makes it back out. We then simply throw a number of grenades into the tunnel's opening and walk away. That's it. I guess it's too costly and cumbersome to bring in excavating equipment to uncover the entire complex. We, the infantry, are doing on a small scale what the B-52 bombers do or attempt to do on a large scale—cripple the enemy's transportation and hiding network and force him above ground, force him to stand up and fight us on our terms. So far though, it isn't working. As far as I am concerned, we aren't losing; we just aren't winning.

Without warning a thunderous explosion occurs some distance in front of us. The trucks are spread out in one-to-two-hundred-foot intervals. We jump, startled, ready at the trigger. Smoke billows from a truck far ahead of us. With the convoy stopped, we're ordered to take a defensive position alongside the road, five to ten feet into the tree line. It's quiet. I heard shouts and screams in the distance.

"What's up, man?" a guy next to me asks.

"How the hell should I know?" I respond. "Just be quiet and keep your eyes open. It could be a trap. And right now it's working. He's got us out of the trucks. Be cool man, be cool."

I hear a faint distant cry for medic. Immediately I spin on my knees toward the road. Lieutenant Redy is at the road's edge and motions for me to stay put. He puts his index finger to his lips for me to be quiet and not move. That's OK by me, Sir, I think. He's right; they're too far away. Besides, I'm sure they've got a medic up there. Word spreads quickly. The lead truck was hit by a landmine—one injury, it's Martin, Captain Martin, my buddy! The fucking SOB, I'm glad. Sad that it happened, but glad it is Martin. So much for him making my life unbearable . . .

Minutes later, a Medevac helicopter hovers over them. He can't land so they lower a stretcher. Martin must have been hit pretty badly. If he was ambulatory they'd lower the penetrator, as opposed to a stretcher where he has to lie in the prone position. Captain Martin is about the fifteenth one of us to get hit. The first was Dutch Coughner; he was the one who was hit by our own chopper's rockets. The brass has named the enlisted man's club in his honor. But we called it the Friendly Fire Club. Part of me wants to see that bastard Martin die; the other part prays he lives. Martin, the guy who wanted to break me "his way." Guess again, Buddy!

Within thirty minutes from the chopper's departure, we resume our trek back to base camp. This time we have chopper gunships buzzing past us every five minutes or so. One passes at break-neck speed, treetop level, and I remember Louie Blade, my buddy, one of the Three Musketeers. The chopper passes us, traveling from front to rear of the convoy. Just as the last truck passes the ambush sight, the pilot lets loose with at least a half dozen rockets. I hear them over the noise of the trucks' engines and the chopper's blades whipping at the air. The tail of the rockets glow red surrounded by a bluish-white flame. Kaboom! Over and over. The rockets hit the earth in such rapid succession I can't tell exactly how many were actually fired. Boy, am I glad they are on our side.

Back at base camp, the brass wants a "full field layout inspection"—in two hours. They have got to be kidding! Each of us is required to clean ourselves up, clean the equipment we just brought in from the jungle and lay it all out on our bunks for inspection by our company commander. In our case, because Martin is no longer in the picture, it'll be his XO, my buddy, Lieutenant Wronges, the guy who busted me to PFC. We expected to be let loose, relax, unwind, get drunk, whatever, and they pull some chicken shit inspection. What a bunch of BS!

Two hours later, we learn the real reason for the inspection. The assistant company commander and his entourage walk through our tents, stopping with full military precision at each man's bunk. Lieutenant Wronges, our first sergeant, along with Sergeant Flock, have a detail of military police that trail them with canvas duffel bags to take our ammunition from us. All of our ammunition is collected and will be stored under the care of the quartermaster. This can't be real. Christ, we're in a combat zone. We're infantry soldiers expected to kick Charlie's ass, and they're disarming us! What's going to happen if Charlie, or worse yet, the North Vietnamese, attack? What are we supposed to do? Get in line for ammo? This is crazy, absolutely crazy.

On a brighter note, at least the mess hall is up and running and serving hot meals. Man, does that sound good. We put our equipment away and make a beeline for chow. It has been at least a week since I ate hot chow. Hot chow! Because the cooks never go out on line, we put on the melodramatics about our time out on line while we're going through the chow line.

One of the cooks I befriended while at Fort Campbell is Willie Lane, a black guy from Detroit. He is what we call, a "homey," a guy who is from your own city or town. In the army we have a tendency to relate to a homey more than others, unless, of course, he is a jerk. Willie is cool. He listens to all the bullshit war stories and occasionally puts the guys in their places by saying, "Now, be nice to me. You want this food, don't you?" And of course, if the chow looks good, all of us will back down, begging Willie to not withhold food from our trays. "Sorry dude, you be the man, dude!" some say in capitulation.

Other comments include, "God love the cooks; you guys are the greatest."

Others, however, play John Wayne—tough, stoic, and condescending. "Well, look here, pilgrim," a guy tries his best to imitate John Wayne. "Let me tell ya, fella; it ain't fit for man nor beast out there. We'll do the fightin'; you just stick to keeping us fueled with this here grub. Ya got that, pilgrim?" Most laugh, including the cooks who always have a quick comeback. They pick someone who hasn't said a word and put food on his tray then stop, look at him and ask, "Who be the man, trooper?" Of course, every time the response better be, "You are the man, Sir." And we all laugh. A good laugh, a genuine laugh.

This evening, we celebrate life. We toast one another for having lived another day. But it's a little odd that no one is sorry Martin has taken a hit. In fact, most are glad he got hit and don't want him to return.

Boy, did I drink too much. I got so drunk I couldn't find the medical platoon's tent. After groping around our compound for what seemed like forever, I laid down on the ground where I fell asleep, or passed out. I vaguely remember the sandy soil of our compound, which felt warm, soft and inviting.

I awake to find myself in my bunk. How I got there I have no idea. Once I come to and clear my head, I am told someone was shot in a fight at the club some time after I left. How did they get the ammo? Oh, well, I think, At least it's not me.

I pour water over my head to bring me back to reality. My head and stomach are killing me. I try to recall the events of last night, but nothing registers. "Who was hit?" I ask.

Savinsky from Chicago and Pellemar from New York, both medics, respond, "Sergeant Billings, the quartermaster's platoon's sergeant."

"Not too serious though, just a through-and-through wound."

Dallas interjects, "You know that little dude from South Carolina—Jefferson, Lincoln Jefferson?"

"No."

"Well," he continues, "he lost his cool. Word has it Billings was digging into his shit. You know, he's the small dude from Hicksville, USA. Guess the Sergeant got what was coming to him alright."

"Yeah, but where did he get the ammo?"

"Beats me. Must have had some stashed somewhere."

I feel bad for both parties, especially Jefferson. Jail time in Vietnam does not count toward the time necessary to rotate back to the states. Then I'm forced to think about Flock and how he's constantly on my back. Christ. We're supposed to be on the same side, but invariably race causes conflict; Jefferson is black, Sergeant Billings, white.

"I hope Flock doesn't get to me as bad as Billings got to Jefferson," I say.

"You got that right," chimed Chiefoot.

Though blacks outnumber whites in my platoon, we all get along pretty well. I think it is because we know our role in war, and mentally we are a cut above the average infantryman. Still, some of my white brothers often go out of their way to cause trouble. So, too, do blacks. It is a dangerous marriage of street toughs brought together under the guise of being a team.

Reporting to the aid station later, I learn that Captain Martin took some shrapnel to the face, neck, and right side. He was traveling in an empty truck that lead our convoy, and Charlie decided to nail him instead of the trailing trucks loaded with men. It doesn't make a whole lot of sense, but then, nothing makes any sense in this war.

AUGUST 27 1966

I am chosen to go out with A company's second platoon on ambush patrol. Great. An ambush patrol! We load up in "deuce and a half" trucks for the trip through No Man's Land.

We depart the compound at 1900 hours and reach our demarcation point ninety minutes later. We suspect Intel has a bead on Charlie's movements and wants us to throw him a surprise party. Nobody has told us this; hell they never tell us a damn thing. We, the low life grunts, simply have to put it together. We know it can't be for the exercise or training; those days are gone.

We wade into the jungle at the tail end of dusk, just barely able to see. I am in the middle of the pack of thirty guys, the radio operator to my rear, the lieutenant to his rear. Sergeant Lims floats among us from front to rear at random. I have known Sergeant Lims since West Point. I like him. He is a soldier's soldier—a square-jawed, freckle-faced, John Wayne-type friendly guy. The platoon leader, Lieutenant Pilgrim, on the other hand, is a prick. He is one of those West Point officers who think they know everything, and that everyone else, other than fellow West Pointers, are dumb shits.

On a break, I hear Pilgrim speaking on the radio in a muffled tone, trying to keep his voice down. From bits and pieces of his discussion with whoever is on the other end, I gather that night rocket attacks have increased at the far end of the air base north of us, and we've been sent out here for some payback.

The jungle has taken on a look I have not seen before. Not that I can see anything; it is dark. There is no moon out tonight. Something seems different. It's as if I can sense Charlie's near. The air smells different. We wade into a knee-deep swamp, moving as if in slow motion, to keep the noise of our movements down. Jeez, I think as I wade into the swamp, no one in his right mind should be out here. If he's here, he's truly an animal.

The bugs are thick; one bites and I jerk my head so violently that I damn near knock my helmet off. After that, I blow at the bugs that venture too close to my face. Shit, this is crazy. Alright, where are the movie cameras? Surely Hollywood is filming this. Then I dismiss the thought as being about as absurd as being here in the first place. Hollywood could never capture this setting . . . not a chance.

The leeches are having a field day. At certain angles I can see them swimming toward me. We are now up to our chests in the swamp. All ammo that can be held in hand and our rifles is carried over our heads. Lims is standing in the deepest part of the swamp, reassuring all of us as we pass him. He calms those of us who are on the edge of panic. He whispers to me as I pass him, "How you doing, Doc?" I nod at him without saying a word. Because his face is inches from mine, he sees I'm under control. "Good Man, Doc, take your time. It gets a little better up ahead." His words are well spent. I feel better after hearing them.

My mind flashes John Wayne war movies. I get angry. Hell, nothing could possibly capture this shit. How could they possibly capture what I'm feeling or what it's really like? I'm chest deep in doo doo, cold, being eaten alive by bugs and being sucked on by creatures from below. I jerk, feeling the leeches finding their mark. "Survive,

Harry." It's that little voice from within. "You'll be just fine. Keep your cool, big guy."

Once out of the swamp we stop, take off our gear as quietly as possible and look for leeches. I squirt repellent all over myself, rubbing it into my exposed skin and over my uniform. Screw it. I'll wait until it's light to strip down and look for them. They won't kill me for the eight hours or so until daylight. As I begin to dry off, I have an incessant itching in my crotch. In fact, I've had it now for more than a month. Don't know what the hell it is, maybe jungle rot. It seems as though I'm always wet, either from the rain, sweat or a swamp.

At about 2200 hours we reach the point where we will lie in ambush. We are at the jungle's edge that overlooks a rice paddy. A rise in the terrain affords us a natural barrier from the field of fire should we encounter Charlie. That is comforting, but the lower halves of our bodies are submerged in swamp water. Incredible. I'm going to stay here all night lying in water! The lieutenant is near me, so I crawl to him and ask, "Sir, are we going to stay here all night?"

At nearly a whisper he snarls, "Got a better idea, Private? Get back to your position." Hell, yeah, I have a better idea. A Holiday Inn would feel pretty good about now.

I've got to record this shit in my diary. I unwrap my diary from the layers of plastic it is contained in. I can just barely see what I'm writing. I doubt it'll come out legible. I write that we're out on an ambush patrol to strike whoever crosses by on their way to rocket the air base. Hope they don't come by.

It's cold. I'm out of mosquito repellent; I used it on the guys to help them get the leeches off. A guy from the artillery battery who is with us is calling our position in to his people. Minutes later shells explode just one hundred feet from our position. A mound of earth is protecting us from the flying shell fragments. Small pieces of shrapnel have a high whine. The larger ones have a deeper buzzing tone. They sound like a giant bumblebees as they rip past us, and when a piece of schrapnel hits the tree trunks, it makes a low, smacking-type noise. Christ, I hope they don't get any closer to us. I hope this patrol turns out to be just another routine bullshit mission; I hope they all turn out that way—routine and bullshit.

Chapter 9

AN ENCOUNTER WITH THE NVA

ACK AT BASE camp another shooting has taken place. A young guy I don't know snapped, shooting two guys—Squad Leader Sergeant Franks and a private, both of A company. I wonder what possessed him to shoot them? And where in the hell did he get the ammo? Hell, Franks is cool, and that private isn't even in the same company as the shooter. Word has it they'll both return. They both got lucky. Flesh wounds, no major damage to bone or artery. That is about as close to a million-dollar wound as you can come without getting seriously hurt.

Another mission is in the works. Rumor has it we're going to Da Nang. But first, Flock orders me again out to the field. I am supposed to hop aboard a chopper that will land alongside our compound. Because our tent is adjacent to the road where the chopper is going to land, we pull the sides of our tent down. Within minutes the temperature soars to what feels like 160 degrees. I grab my stuff and report to the quartermaster for ammo. Then I walk to the road and sit, waiting for my ride to the boonies. I am pleased, however, as I learned I am going out again to meet up with Sergeant Lims' platoon, A company's second platoon.

They have been out there now for about five days. I will replace my buddy, Steve Best. Medics rotate more often out of the field than infantrymen. Platoons are comprised of four squads. Three are rifle

squads and one is a weapons squad. Weapons squads are comprised
of guys who are responsible for carrying the M-60 machine-gun and
the thousands of rounds of ammo it will consume should we come
under fire, not to mention the numerous parts that may be required to
repair it. The weapons squad has two M-60 machine-guns, one at
ready, one in reserve. The men who do not carry the M-60 at ready
in the weapons squad are mules who carry the ammunition that make
the M-60 the effective, awe-inspiring weapon it is. In a firefight, the
M-60 can consume thousands upon thousands of rounds of ammo.
By the way, those mules have an official title—Ammo
Bearers/Riflemen.

I look forward to getting away from Flock. God, he reminds me of
my father. What an asshole. He's now resorted to having me doing
pushups if he sees a pocket unbuttoned. Now that's bullshit. We're in
a war, and he has me doing pushups. I wish he'd get off my case.

Once aboard the chopper, ten of us are en route to the war again.
We are flying unusually high over the landscape. What a beautiful
sight it is. As we approach the landing zone (the LZ), I check my
weapon and nod to the door gunner that I'm cool. Others in the
chopper do the same. We are landing in a clearing shaped like a big,
oblong football. Companies A, B, and C have taken up defensive
positions on the football's perimeter. They have been out here running
patrols for the last five days. I have no idea how long I'll be here.

Lower, lower, there. I get the signal to jump. Once out of the
chopper, we keep low to the ground and don't move. Generally, we
stay in this position until the chopper leaves and we can hear. If you
can't hear anything, you won't even know if Charlie is shooting at you.
The door gunner listens intently to something on his frequency.
Consternation is written all over his face. He motions for me to come
to him and yells in my ear. "We're taking small arms fire." His voice
cracks with emotion. Although I haven't heard or seen a thing, I
believe him. Why doesn't he fire his M-60?, I wonder. Then I realize
that he can't because he might hit those on line. Shit, we can't defend
ourselves at this position either; we have to rely on the guys on the line
to suppress those sons of bitches.

Once the chopper leaves and things quiet down somewhat,
someone asks for my designated company. When I inform him A

Company, he points in a general direction, and I am off to war. I am anxious to see Steve. I know he will be happy to not only see me, but also happy to be relieved as well. One of the companies is in a heavy firefight. I hear the buzzing of bullets passing overhead as I slowly creep toward A company.

When I finally find Steve, while still lying in the prone position, we exchange handshakes and smiles. He looks exhausted. He also looks like he is losing weight, too. I shout over the noise of gunfire, while still shaking his hand, "Ass Kick One to Ass Kick Two. You are hereby officially relieved. Your chopper will be here in one hour."

Instead of laughing, he snaps back with objection, "What the hell do you mean Ass Kick, I can take this shit, this ain't about nothing and, besides who made you number one?"

A loud explosion interrupts us. We instinctively roll and cover our heads and faces. I laugh a response, "I'm senior to you, asshole. That makes me number one in my book."

He shakes his head in submission, smiles and says, "Thanks, man, I need some relief; I've been humping every day, five thousand meter squad patrols since I've been here. I sure as hell need some shut-eye—some relaxation. Base camp with Flock sounds good right now, though I'm sure when I get there I'll think otherwise."

When the firing ceases, we stand up along with the others and embrace each other with a manly hug. We're comrades in arms, comrades for nearly two years. Steve looks me in the eye and asks, "How did you like that welcome from the NVA?"

Trying to play the role, I respond, "Didn't hear a thing." I'm still smiling when it sinks in, *"What the hell do you mean NVA?"* I'm shocked to hear it is the North Vietnamese Army. Real, honest to God, army soldiers. "Holy shit. How do you know, Steve?" I study him to find a hint that he is lying to me.

He likes my shocked response. He has the upper hand now; he's been doing battle with a regular army, an army trained and drilled as we have been. Holy shit!

I have feared an encounter with the NVA though I have always kept it to myself. "How much contact have you had, Steve?" I ask.

He responds, "Not much, nothing to speak of while out on patrol, just a couple of sniping incidents. Most of the contact has been right here." He points to the ground. "They've been testing us daily, but we've held them back without too much difficulty. Couple of guys wounded here and there, nothing worth talking about."

He says it so casually, as if we were talking about hotrod automobiles back on the "block." Within minutes, Steve gathers his equipment, exchanges small talk with me and strikes out in the direction of the chopper's landing zone.

Once he is gone, I turn to a couple of guys to ask if they have any proof that we are up against NVA. Frank Beeckman, a machine-gunner, is the first to respond, "Yeah, we've got a body count of twelve. They're wearing their green khaki fatigues with various insignia sewn on and wear helmets with the red star." I try not to show it, but I am really scared.

Lims visits me at nightfall, shaking my hand and welcoming me back to his platoon. "Doc," he says, "they're really out there, son. This is the big league game we've trained for. Tomorrow we are going out again on a predetermined route to try to get them to engage us. Are you up to the challenge, trooper?" I look him in the eye and say, "I'm as ready as I'll ever be, Sarge. What are we up against?"

His voice is steady, deliberate, and professional. "Intel reports indicate two North Vietnamese regiments, the 272nd and 273rd NVA Regiments, about 1,600 strong." Lims and I like each other. His little pep talk about going out on patrol tomorrow reminds me of the first one he gave me back at West Point. Of course, the big difference is, back then we were practicing; now we're putting it all on the line, and I'm scared shitless.

At the crack of dawn, A company's second platoon wades into the jungle. Thirty-two men burdened down with only ammunition, one box of C rations and water. Our rucksacks are stripped of the usual several pair of socks, ponchos, extra C rations, and other miscellaneous equipment. All that's required are the bare essentials necessary to sustain an extended encounter with the NVA.

Everyone carries nearly three times the required 700 rounds of ammo in addition to four to six grenades that hang from various places on their rucksack webbing. We are loaded for bear; however, the bear we are hunting has far more than just weight and teeth. Well, I think, let's get this shit over with.

We slowly pierce the dense foliage of the jungle. Each man walks cautiously while looking around, stepping forward with deft movements. Hand gestures serve as the only form of communication. Fist in the air means stop; hand held with palm to the earth means get down. Fingers serve to indicate how long until the next break, where we'll sit in silence, resting to regain strength, which rapidly diminishes while humping the jungle. All along and with each step forward, fear and fatigue wreak havoc on our nerves as well as our bodies. Sweat oozes from every pore, soaking our uniforms; in some cases, once the uniforms have dried, they turn white from the salt in our bodies.

Without warning, machine-gun fire erupts in front of me. Foliage is raining down, stripping the trees as bullets seek their intended target. Immediately the platoon returns fire. The roar of gunfire is near deafening. "Medic!" someone shouts. "Doc! Where's the medic?" His plea is barely heard over the sounds of the firefight. My heart is beating against my chest. It's difficult to breathe, but I crawl forward, praying that I won't be spotted by the NVA.

As I near the radio operator, the lieutenant is yelling into the telephone-type handset. Above the noise of battle, I can just make out that he's calling for fire support. Somewhere miles away an artillery battery is springing into action. The lieutenant barks the grid coordinates for them to aim their huge tank-size howitzers. Lieutenant Pilgrim screams again into the mike, "Goddamn it, let's get some support out here now! They've got us pinned down; we can't move and we can't see them. Estimate enemy position to be less than two hundred feet north by northwest of our position. Do you copy? Over."

Still crawling in the direction of the cry for medic, I glance to where I think the fire is coming from. Jesus, the jungle is disintegrating. Usually the sunlight filters through the dense foliage, creating strange patterns on the jungle floor. Now the sky is plainly visible without foliage obstructing it. Because of my infantry training, I know some artillery lieutenant is shouting, "Alpha Battery only, fire one." When fired, there's an explosion with such magnitude that it sucks the wind out of those near the howitzer. "One off!" yells the sergeant as his crew works feverishly to reload the howitzer with a projectile weighing approximately one hundred pounds.

"Delta Battery only, fire one." Another explosion rips through the air. The shock wave blows dirt that forms a cloud of dust. "Delta

Battery, one off, Sir." The Lieutenant in charge of the artillery battery issues another command. "Battery's Bravo, Charlie and Echo, dial in previously stated coordinates and stand by to fire." Each responds in a calm, professional manner via radio contact with their officers. Lieutenant Pilgrim puts aside the microphone and screams to us, "Incoming! Incoming! Heads up men!"

I finally reach the guy that is hit. He isn't moving. He is motionless, lying facedown. Another guy nearby screams, "He's dead, Doc. He's fucking dead!" I squirm out of my rucksack while prone, open it, and grab a handful of four-by-four gauze pads and a roll of gauze. I dismiss his statement. It was probably said out of shock and the fear of coming under heavy fire. What the hell does he know about death? I struggle to turn the guy over to get a look at his wounds. It is difficult because he still has on his rucksack. A bullet buzzes past. Whoa. That was awfully close. I position myself to the guy's left; my body's on the incoming side of enemy fire. I pull hard on his right shoulder to roll him face up. Holy Shit!

He took a multitude of hits right through the neck and face. I can't even recognize him. Blood covers open, jagged wounds. The shot group is confined to an area no larger than a softball. I recoil at the sight and glance at the nametag sewn on his fatigue shirt. "Vasquez." Someone shouts over the gunfire, "How is he, Doc? How's Vasquez?"

"He's dead," I shout back. "Just keep firing, but watch your ammo." Leaving Vasquez , I scrambled for better cover.

Suddenly without warning, an explosion strikes, sucking the air from my lungs and causing tremendous pressure and pain in my ears. I feel my body rise and fall when a second one hits. My ears are ringing. I try opening my jaw wide to clear them, to get them to pop and feel an itching in my internal organs. What the hell was that? Boy, was that ever close!

The artillery lieutenant tweaks his battery's aim, giving new coordinates and yells, "All batteries, fire one each. For effect!" Simultaneously, all five guns fire—each of them sighting different degrees of latitude and longitude. As they fire, it obscures the vision of those providing support for us out in the jungle. I crawl back to where I think the lieutenant is. Halfway there, five explosions occur within three seconds. My body bounces with the shock wave. I find it difficult to breathe; it feels like someone just punched me in the stomach. I lie motionless, attempting to regain my senses and my breath, hoping no one needs help. "Medic! Medic! Over here! Charles is hit!" Rayford Charles? I wonder. I've known Charles for about a year, but we aren't tight.

Small arms fire has stopped, but my ears are still ringing. I feel a little dizzy. Hang on, Spencer, I tell myself, Hang on. I make my way down the line of men, and as I do, each of them offers words of concern and encouragement. Meanwhile, the cry for medic doesn't stop. I get a little angry. Christ, if Charlie's still out there, he'll know the only one moving to their shouts is me, the medic. "Shut the fuck up, damn it! I'm coming!" I scream. I crawl past Lims, and he crawls right behind me.

Damn, he doesn't have to do that, though I admire him all the more for doing so. I always knew he had concern for his men, but now he is putting his life on the line by following me—it gives the NVA two targets to shoot. His moving right behind me just increased my chances of not getting hit by fifty percent, plus, I suspect, he wants to see for himself the condition of Charles. Sergeant Lims—what a guy!

Charles' wounds turn to be the result of "friendly fire." The howitzers not only hit the enemy, but Charles as well. He is bleeding profusely from the shoulder area. A large piece of shrapnel tore off upon impact and headed right toward him at ground level. His clavicle bone is shattered, and I can see a golf ball-size, shiny piece of gray metal smoldering, lodged within him. God, burning flesh stinks. Charles is in a lot of pain and weeping in between screams that it burns. I reassure him that he will be OK, that his wound is not life threatening and that his ticket home has just been punched.

He calms down some after his wound is dressed and I give him an injection of morphine. Afterward, I tell Lims that I believe Charles is ambulatory, but we have to get back to BSOP as soon as possible. Lims nods and crawls back toward the lieutenant. A sweep of the area will be taken to ascertain how many, if any, enemy lie dead. Success in this war is measured not in terms of who controls which spot of land, but by the number of enemy killed. The brass needed numbers. Lieutenant Pilgrim forms a plan to check out the area to get those numbers.

The platoon makes a V-formation, moving in pairs at his verbal commands. I am told to stay put and watch out for Charles. After minutes of silence, I hear several shots fired, but only single shots as the men roam over the area where they try to find what is left of the NVA. When all is said and done, fourteen North Vietnamese soldiers were killed. Still with Charles, I strain to listen to our guys. Some are clearly jubilant, letting out cries of victory. Lims, however, shouts at them, attempting to control those who get a high seeing dead bodies!

He has to be careful. Guys like those (whom we dub "Crazies") are a tough group to deal with. Those types of guys are feared not only by the enemy, but by us as well. They are contemporaries to VC Sappers. But our guys won't go that far; they simply get off in the heat of battle. Crazies among us scare us. The army rewards them with medals, but we all know better.

On the primordial edge of existence, we know the pecking order of the survival chain. We give those guys all the space we can because their moods can turn at the drop of a hat. On small-sized patrols such as a squad or a platoon, the law is nonexistent. The common factor holding us together is our desire to live. A couple of the Crazies argue a little with Sergeant Lims. They want a trophy—an ear from one of the dead. Lims talks them into taking a helmet and a machete instead. Reluctantly, they give in to Lims' insistence to conduct themselves in a professional manner. Lieutenant Pilgrim is among them, but as I lay here listening to them argue, I don't hear him raise his voice or interfere with Lims' negotiations with the pair; maybe he knows better than to do so.

Satisfied that this one encounter is enough for one day, the lieutenant, upon radio contact with BSOP, orders us to return. Word spreads quickly that he reported twenty-two enemy dead, not the actual fourteen counted. Most of us don't care what he reported, numbers mean nothing to us. Tonight, back at BSOP, I feel less apprehensive about contact with the NVA; however, I pray it is my first and last encounter with them.

For five more days I hump the jungle, but don't make any further contact with Charlie or the NVA. Other company's platoons make contact almost daily. I have skated by unaffected so far, that is, until all three companies attempt to leave via our taxi—the beautiful beast we call *the chopper*.

September 10 1966

Three companies strike out into columns of two, all parallel to one another, for a total of six columns. America's finest, an entire infantry battalion, walks through the jungle, looking to make contact with the NVA. Just before we went out, I learned that we are heading back to the same landing zone (LZ) where we had disembarked coming to this operation. We were shocked because we know it's not supposed to work this way. Charlie or the NVA almost always booby-trap old landing zones, or, if they don't booby-trap them, they lie in wait to pick us off one by one as we make our way to the choppers. They will withhold shooting until the choppers, somewhere around ten, land at the same time, and then shoot because our backs are turned and the noise of the choppers in close proximity drowns out the sounds of their weapons firing. Therefore, we won't know what direction to return fire or even if we're being shot at. As the saying goes, you never hear the shot that kills you.

There is also some confusion on the LZ because we have pre-assigned choppers to get into. It isn't a mad dash and jump into just any chopper. If, for whatever reason, the chopper is not in its proper formation when landing, we have to find it; ten choppers landing simultaneously take up a lot of ground. If our chopper isn't where we believe it to be, we have to run around dodging chopper blades. When they nose-over upon take off, their blades could dice anybody not paying attention.

As usual, we start off at dawn. I am told the LZ is eight hours from us, that is if we hustle and if we don't make contact with the enemy. That is too many ifs for me. As we walk, stealth is not part of the picture. We tear at the jungle in an effort to make the ETA to the LZ. There are 120 men to a company, three companies; let's see, that's 360 guys crashing through the jungle. Gunships buzz past us every ten to twenty minutes. Knowing they are close by to support us should we make contact provides me a degree of comfort. The NVA's 272nd and 273rd regiments would be nuts to attack. Most of us think the same. Guys are talking while walking, and the sergeants and platoon leaders don't tell them to shut up. Now, that's different. We arrive at the LZ without incident in seven and a half hours. It's 1300 hours. Because we did not stop to eat, I'm starving and running out of energy.

As we near the LZ, each company fans out, encompassing approximately half of a large oval clearing surrounded by dense jungle. Each company spreads out at the jungle's edge, taking up a defensive position. I scan the clearing. Sure enough, it's the same clearing where I relieved Steve Best just a few days earlier. We are told the first company to leave will be C Company, followed by my company, A Company, and then Bravo Company. Extraction begins at 1400 hours. I sit down, exhausted, with the others as I whittle on a fallen tree trunk.

Minutes later a firefight breaks out east of our position. Bravo Company is involved, but they are too far for us to join in, so we stay put. It's their war now. As seconds pass, we begin to get a little concerned. Despite the collective firepower of Bravo Company, the firefight intensifies.

Within a few minutes we hear the distant thunder of approaching choppers. It is a comforting sound to know they are on our side. The first one to come into view is Iron Mike's chopper, our battalion commander. As he flies by in the direction of Bravo Company, he is on the aircraft's loud speaker stating, "Drive on, men. Drive on." Iron Mike's chopper is closely followed by three heavily-armed Huey gunships that are laying down hell fire on the enemy's position. What an impressive display of firepower. That'll teach them to screw with us. The gunships make three passes each, but the enemy is still out there; they're still firing with full force. Jesus!

Lieutenant Pilgrim is listening intently to the radio, monitoring radio exchanges of Bravo Company's platoons to learn what they are up against. Like a narrator calling out plays of a football game, he hollers the developments to all within hearing range. "Bravo Company's engaged with a North Vietnamese outfit; they think it's the 272nd NVA Regiment." He has concern written all over his face.

Suddenly, out of nowhere, we come under fire. Jesus! I roll behind the tree trunk that I was carving my name into. They've got to be crazy to attack a battalion! That is, unless they have more men out there than we do. In-between bursts of fire, I ask Lieutenant Pilgrim, "How many men are in a North Vietnamese regiment?"

He's preoccupied, screaming at the guys and telling them which direction the shots are coming from, and snaps a response, "Anywhere from 600 to a 1000!" and resumes directing the men fanned out in front of us.

It sounds as if we are getting hit pretty hard when suddenly air force F-100 Super Sabers strafe the jungle with cluster bombs. As the bombs drop, small fins pop out of them. Each bomb detonates at a different altitude as they fall toward the earth. It's an amazing sight and sound—an awesome display of power. Another jet drops napalm. Oh, my God! Upon impact the jungle ignites into a ball of fire, perhaps as long as the length of two football fields. Wow! I almost feel sorry for the enemy. Holy shit! Am I glad they don't have anything like that to throw at us! If they did, we'd really be in deep shit!

As the sounds of the jets fade, we notice most of the firing has stopped. I then hear a faint cry, "Incoming fire mission!" repeated several times. That means artillery is next. Somebody's planned this one pretty well. Normally, we have to wait about ten to thirty minutes before any form of air or artillery support begins. The fire support comes on the heels of each other—first gunships, then the jets, and now artillery—all within five minutes of each other. I am impressed.

Artillery rains down, barrage after barrage, for about ten minutes without let up. Man, we are kicking ass, but I have a growing sense of fear. Those guys are not done yet. They're still out there firing as the first wave of choppers approaches. The sound of a Huey helicopter is an unmistakable one. Ten of them, from this distance, sound like rolling thunder—like a thunderstorm on the horizon. There are 120 men from Charlie Company poised to move out and meet the choppers when they land. There are ten men to a chopper, ten choppers to a wave. Only twenty guys will be left to jump aboard the second wave of choppers, and then it's our turn.

The lead helicopter pilot, in the ten-chopper formation, breaks radio silence just before reaching the tree line of the LZ. His voice emits from a common air frequency used by his squadron. It is a voice that is both professional and calm. "Heads ups, cowboys, we are landing *hot*." The pilots acknowledge their Aircraft Commander in numerical sequence. "Two Niner Zero, copy; Two Niner One got it, Two Niner Two, Roger," etc.

Suddenly and without fanfare, one of the choppers is hit. It had just cleared the tree line when an RPG (Rocket Propelled Grenade) hit just above the head of the copilot's position, striking the side of the engine. "Two Niner Niner's hit, I repeat Two Niner Niner is hit; we are going down. Do you copy, Cowboy Hunter?"

Still calm and professional, the Squadron Commander in the lead chopper responds, "Copy, Two Niner Niner." He then calls to the gunships accompanying them. "Cowboy Gunners, did you copy Two Niner Niner's transmission? Over."

The lead gunship's pilot responds, "Copy that Cowboy Hunter, we've got him in sight. We got him covered. Over."

Cowboy Hunter simply keys his mike and says, "Roger Cowboy Gunner . . ."

The firefight directly in front of me intensifies as the choppers land and the men of Charlie Company scramble to board their assigned choppers. Pilgrim is back on the radio yelling at the top of his lungs. I move toward him to hear what he's saying, hugging the earth as I go.

When I get within a couple of feet of him, I hear him calling for air support to our immediate south, "They're just one hundred feet south of my position, goddamn it." Jeez, I've never seen him this shaken up before. Someone is really getting an ear full. "Papa Lima Alpha Sierra Papa, this is Cowboy Gunner Three Zero Zero, identify strike position with red smoke over." Pilgrim screams into the mike. "Look, goddamn it, they're just a fucking stone's throw from my position. We're pinned down; Charlie Company is taking hits as they evacuate. Now, just do it goddamn it! Over!"

Cowboy Two Niner Niner hits the ground. It bounces twice before its tail section breaks off. Good, I think, those glory boys are now going to get a taste of what it is like to be on the ground. Christ, look at them! Their fatigues are greener than a pasture. All aboard Two Niner Niner escape without injury. They are really lucky. The gunship is hovering over the downed chopper.

"Papa Lima Alpha Sierra Papa, be advised I cannot provide coverage that close without ID marker. Show red smoke for coverage area. Over."

Pilgrim throws a fit. He cusses, speaking to no one in particular, then screams for a squad leader, any squad leader, to throw a canister of red smoke toward the enemy. Given the noise level, no one but I can hear him. It's as if I'm just a spectator. I'm not firing at the enemy because the guys are directly in my line of fire. I'm content to stay near the lieutenant. Bullets fly just over me; they make a popping sound as they pass by.

Pilgrim is livid. He tears at his rucksack, searching for a canister of red smoke. When he finds it, he jumps up, screaming, "OK, you fuckers! I'll give you fucking smoke!" and bolts straight toward the enemy—jumping and stumbling over those out on the line. I can't believe my eyes. The son of a bitch doesn't stop where the guys are sprawled out firing, instead, he continues running into the jungle. What the hell is he doing? He was close enough to throw it when he was even with the men lying on the ground. Where the hell does he think he's going? "I'll give you fucking smoke, you son of a bitch!" Pilgrim screams when suddenly, he's in front of a North Vietnamese soldier crouched in the shooter's stance. They make eye contact, both startled and scared out of their minds.

The young Vietnamese soldier turns to shoot, but Pilgrim beats him to the punch, firing three rounds in rapid succession; he then throws the canister. I lose sight of Pilgrim momentarily as he penetrates the jungle's edge. But just as suddenly, he reappears, white as a ghost, chalky white, and dry skinned. Shit! He's either been hit, or he's in shock. I scream, "Are you all right, Lieutenant?" I can't hear his response, but I think he's OK. He nods without looking at me.

I think I heard someone calling for a medic. Straining to hear above the roar of Dante's Inferno, I hear it again. Oh, shit! Here I go. I jump forward, sliding as close as is possible over the fallen tree. "Who called for a medic?" One of the men rolls on his side and points to his left. He says something, but I can't hear him.

As I crawl with my .45 and small aid kit in hand, the first of the choppers to land flies right over us. Then another, and another. In between them, the gunship opens fire with rockets that hit directly in front of the men, nearly hitting them, as they dance toward the enemy. More choppers fly overhead, and the guys begin to settle into a familiar firing sequence. Left to right, middle to left and right to center. The guys are responding to their training: *Pin the enemy with an offset sequence firing pattern.* Yeah, baby.

I can't contain myself and scream like a fan at a football game, "Airborne!" No one responds verbally; they respond like a smooth running machine with their weapons. Kaabooom! Kaabooom! Two guys take a chance getting up on their knees to throw grenades. The air vibrates slightly from explosions, then I clearly hear someone scream, "Medic."

"I'm here," I shout. Where is he? My eyes sweep the terrain trying to find him.

One guy stops firing, motions for me to come his way, and pulls the injured guy toward me. I roll over a few times and head in his direction to help get the guy out of the line of fire. When I get to him I feel for a pulse on his neck, but I am shaking so badly I can't feel a damn thing. "Medic! Medic!" It's coming from the other side of the line. I shake the guy closest to me, telling him to spread the word down the line that I'll be right there. I turn my attention back to my patient. I rip his fatigue shirt open, exposing his chest, and put my ear flat to his skin. I can't tell if he has a heartbeat; it's too damn noisy with the firefight in progress. I stick my cheek next to his open mouth and nose to feel if he is breathing. Aw, shit, nothing. I raise his closed eyelid. Shit. Fixed and dilated, both of them. He's dead.

"Shit!" I scream to no one in particular. Shit! I move toward the other cry for medic as the firefight slows down. Good sign. I can do without this shit. Come on you fucking NVA, don't you know when you're licked? When I get to the other guy, he too, is dead. "Dee dee mao, fuckers! Get the hell out of here!" I scream.

The firing stops. Sergeant Lims begins to bark commands. "Cease fire! Cease fire, second platoon! Stop, will ya?" The men slowly stop firing, one at a time. With the choppers gone and the firefight over, it is quiet, as in deaf quiet. Pilgrim is on the radio when Bravo Company comes under fire again. Holy mackerel! Those bastards are still alive! How the hell could they have survived all that shelling and napalm? Even though the jungle is still on fire, they're still out there. Man, they're a tough bunch.

An hour passes before the next wave of rolling thunder is heard off in the distance. The choppers, our ticket to safety, are returning. Pilgrim shouts, "Second platoon, get ready to evacuate upon my command. First squad, take the chopper marked C for Charlie."

"Got it, Lou." Pilgrim continues assigning squads to choppers and gives one last command, "Squad leaders, take your dead with you. And that's a direct order."

Our excitement and anticipation grows at the sound of the approaching choppers. "Sergeant Lims, Hoornstra (the radio operator), and Spencer, follow me." states Pilgrim. "We'll be the last to board and provide cover fire as the squads run for the choppers. Our chopper is G as in Gulf. Understand?" We all respond in the affirmative. Louder and louder the thunder grows. Closer, come on guys, let's get here. Time feels as if it's standing still. Suddenly two gunships cross overhead, firing rockets from pods hanging out on both sides of their aircraft. Good, that ought to hold them down for a while. But for how long? Will I make it? Will any of us make it? Will someone else get hit? A million scenarios flash through my mind.

The thunder begins to rise to such a level that the sounds of Bravo Company's firefight are drowned out. I see the first chopper, then the second. Come on, guys, land. Let's go; I want to get the hell out of here. "Go! Go! Go!" shouts Pilgrim. As the other men make a mad dash for the choppers, the four of us begin firing into the jungle to suppress the NVA, not giving them the opportunity to stick their heads up and draw a bead on our guys. After what seems like several minutes, too many, Pilgrim finally shouts, "Let's go! Men! Now!"

We all stand, bent over at the waist, and sprint for our assigned chopper. While running, the weight of my rucksack shifts from side to side, nearly causing me to fall. As we approach the choppers, some are already beginning to take off. Lims screams, "Watch out, get down!"

The chopper directly in front of us noses over, its blades dangerously close to hitting us. Wow, that was close. I feel as though I'm playing football, and I'm the one carrying the ball. I scan each chopper's markers as I near them, looking for chopper G. There's D. The chopper we are running past slides sideways while attempting to get airborne, and it is headed our way. "Watch out," Hoornstra yells.

There it is. I see it. I feel a rush of excitement, fear, and terror. The chopper is still about one hundred feet away. Increasing my speed, I feel the strain on my legs. Don't give out on me now, legs. Closer, closer, come on. Lims is the first to reach the chopper. He turns back and waves for us to hurry. "OK, Sarge, I'm coming."

Before we get into the chopper, Lims stops and yells for us to clear our weapons. Many accidental shootings have taken place because guys forgot to clear their weapons. We've heard stories that a round left in a hot chamber could "cook," thereby exploding, just as if the trigger had been pulled.

In our haste to get to the choppers, everyone except Lims has forgotten to clear his weapon. I rip the rod back that holds the bullet in the bore, and a bullet spills out onto the chopper's floor. I jump into the chopper. The pilot has his engine at such a high rpm that we are airborne seconds after boarding. We go airborne so quickly the g-forces pin me to the floor of the chopper.

I chance a look out to the side of the aircraft and spot an enemy soldier taking aim right at me. Simultaneously, the door gunner spots him and lets out a burst from his M-60 machine-gun. I jerk back, attempting to get out of the line of fire, and close my eyes. Oh, God, please watch over me. Get us out of here safe, please.

We clear the LZ safely, and within a few minutes we all loosen up and begin smiling. The flowing adrenaline still pulsates within each of us, causing us to act giddy and laugh at anything anyone says. Lims, showing unusual emotion, his eyes wide, screams, "Boy! That was close! Wow!"

Finally, we unwind and relax for the thirty-minute flight back to base camp. I am so relaxed that I move to the chopper's edge and let my feet dangle over the side. Thank you, God. Thank you very much. I let my mind drift to a better place and a better time.

Nearing our base camp, we fly over the air force base complex. I look down to see guys throwing a football to each other as if they were on a playground back home. Others are in bathing suits sunning themselves.

Don't they know there's a war out there? Look at them. They have absolutely no idea of what I've just been through. Will anyone ever have any idea of what we've been through? Then little voice inside asks, "Does it really matter, Spencer?"

A couple of days later, a battalion formation is held to conduct services for our fallen comrades. The symbol of each man who was killed is an M-14 rifle with bayonet attached driven into the ground, bayonet first, with a helmet on the butt of the weapon and a pair of boots alongside. This is a solemn occasion for our platoon. Two of the six rifles, steel pots, and boots are for Willie Sykes and Benny

Gerrilleo, fellow medics. However, we don't allow ourselves to dwell on their untimely deaths. Willie's statement comes to mind, "Better any one of them than me." His statement doesn't seem so cold anymore.

During battalion formation, those individuals who demonstrated heroism while under enemy fire are honored and recognized by either receiving a Purple Heart for being wounded in action or Bronze Star for valor in action. Iron Mike also takes this opportunity to let us know that on our next mission we will be sent to Da Nang to help the marines.

The marines are pushing north and need troops to guard their perimeter as well as the high points on the mountaintops overlooking their base camp. But before we trek up north, we have one short mission entitled Operation Atlantic City, which begins tomorrow, September 13, and runs through the 22.

We are dismissed at 1100 hours, so, with some free time, I decide to look up Louie Blade, my fellow musketeer. I learn his aviation unit is but a short fifteen-minute ride away. I am anxious to talk with him and exchange stories about our recent experiences. I also want to talk to him about the possibility of transferring to his unit. I feel that my chances for survival are better in an aviation unit. At least I'd stay cleaner. That appeals to me.

After several stops to ask for directions to the Cowboy's Aviation Unit, I find myself walking up to Louie's tent. I know he'll be both surprised and happy to see me. One of the other things I want to know is if he knows what happened to Terry Taller, the other musketeer. Entering his tent, I am surprised to see how ill-kept it is. Compared to my platoon's tent, this is a pigsty. All the guys are sleeping. Everyone still asleep at this hour? I like what I am seeing even more.

I wake a guy to ask him where Louie sleeps. He appears irritated at my waking him. He shakes his head, trying to come to his senses at seeing a stranger in his tent. "Sorry," I say, "but I'm looking for a friend of mine. Louie Blade." To make him realize how important it is that I find Louie, I volunteer more information. "Hey, guy, Louie and I went all the way from basic training through jump school together. Know which bunk he sleeps in?"

The guy lowers his eyebrows, staring at me the whole time I am speaking to him and responds, "Look, buddy, I don't know who you are or where you are from, but Louie is dead."

"Dead? No! Look, maybe you didn't hear me. I asked for Louis Blade; maybe you got him mixed up with someone else."

The guy's lying on his stomach and puts his face back down as if he wants to go back to sleep. I walk around his upper bunk to face him. With his face on his pillow, he says it again, only this time in a softer tone, "His ship took an RPG the other day. All on board died. Louie took it right in the head. Completely decapitated him." I recoil in shock but try not to show it. I softly acknowledge him, only half believing him, and apologize for waking him.

He knows I took it hard. As I walk toward the door, he picks up his head again and says, "I liked Louie too, guy." I look at him for any sign that he might be pulling my leg, but there isn't one. My world is full of nothing but hatred, fear, fatigue, and death. I consciously try to invoke the airborne beat and slogans, but nothing follows. I feel empty, alone, and scared. Who's next? What is my fate? Just as there is no beat, there is no response.

While driving back to my base camp, one thing comes to mind: I have changed my mind about transferring to an aviation unit. Louie extended his time in Vietnam when he could have gone back to the states. His year in-country was up last April. I know that because, after leaving his tent, I stopped by his company headquarter's tent. Louie's first sergeant told me that, apparently, Louie had extended his tour six months in an effort to get out of the army six months early. Damn it, Louie, I'm going to miss you. Goodbye, my musketeer. Goodbye. Out of sight. Out of mind. "Just turn it off, Spencer. Turn it off," states that voice from within.

That night, feeling lower than whale shit on the bottom of the ocean, I decide to go to town with the brothers. We are going to toast our fallen brothers: Willie Sykes, Benny Gerrilleo, and Louie.

Even in Vietnam segregation is obvious. Half-black Vietnamese are ostracized from those who are pure blood Vietnamese and/or even from those who are half-white. Leon Dallas, Chiefoot, Marvin Beatty and I seek out the establishments that cater to blacks. Once past the base's compound gates, we hail a Lambretta scooter taxi. Dallas flips the driver a couple of "green backs," which we aren't supposed to do.

We are paid in script, a negotiated instrument the Vietnamese honor. The driver, in return, gives him a pack of cigarettes.

Thinking we can get cigarettes cheaper at our base camp's exchange store, I offer to share my cigarettes with Dallas. The three of them look at me sheepishly and laugh, "They ain't cigarettes, Spencer," and give each other a slap of five. Chiefoot, however, takes me into their confidence. He leans toward me and says, "It's a Mary Jane, Spence." They all laugh at my not knowing what he means. They get a good laugh. Afterwards, Dallas, sensing I still don't have a clue, states, "It's marijuana, Harry. Relax, man, I'll teach you. You'll like it, man, trust me." I nod OK.

As we drive on through the main dirt road of Bien Hoa, the brothers light one up. I sense they'll look out for me. At this moment I want badly to trust someone. After they carefully detail what I should do, I inhale on the joint, filling my lungs with smoke, and hold my breath. Because I am in excellent shape and have been all of my life, I can hold my breath twice as long as any of them. They limit my toking on the joint to three times, informing me the THC content of the drug is far superior than anything back in the states—whatever the hell that means. After the third toke, Beatty says, "That's enough now. Just kick back, relax, and let the buzz mellow you out, brother." An internal vibration starts first within my lungs, then works its way toward my face, and then my head. Wow! This shit is cool.

I was depressed before I sucked on the joint, but now all is right by the world. My heart accelerates, but I am not anxious. I feel mellow, joyful, happy, and content. Everything seems to be moving in slow motion. Inhibitions absent, I look out the side of the taxi and take in the sights, enjoying everything and everyone I see. The brothers leave me alone, speaking among themselves, and every now and then ask, "How you doing, Spencer?" Feeling every muscle it takes to speak, I smile and say, "Fine brooothhhers, I'm cool." They laugh at seeing me so stoned, knowing it is the first time I have smoked a "Mary Jane."

We pull up to a bar and stroll in as if we had been there a hundred times. Sounds of soul music fill the air. "Duke Of Earl" is playing as we walk through the door and talk the talk to the locals. I feel like I know everyone. It is a comforting feeling I will never forget, nor do I want to. The four of us, after working the crowd, find a make-shift booth big enough for eight.

A young Vietnamese girl, maybe sixteen to seventeen years of age—I can't really tell—approaches our table and asks what we want to drink in very hard-to-understand, broken English. Because I am the only white person in the bar, she focuses her attention on me more than the others. "You cherry boy?" she asks.

It is hard to understand her enunciation of our language. I thought she guessed my name and respond. "Yes, my name is Harry."

She giggles, thinking I am admitting that I am a virgin. She then speaks to those standing at the bar and they too laugh.

Just then a sweet young thing slips beside me, speaking in her tongue, and she puts her hand on my crotch. She cooes, "You cherry, boy?"

Again I am bemused, thinking the guys told everyone my name, and respond. "Yes, my name is Harry."

Her eyes widen as her grip finds its mark. I may be a little slow because I'm buzzed out of my mind, but I still know what she wants. However, due to the intoxicating effects of the marijuana, I am not the slightest bit interested in having sex. The buzz I am feeling is everything I can handle.

When she realizes I am not responding to her crotch massage, she becomes angry, saying something obviously not very complimentary in Vietnamese. She stands up from the booth, turns around and lets out a blood-curdling scream. I grab her and push her aside, thinking it may have been a rat that scared the living shit out of her.

A grenade rolls across the floor toward us. The handle is not attached so I know it is live and about to detonate. Dallas and Chiefoot, sitting on the opposite side of the booth, run for cover. Everyone in the bar is running for cover, but I am so damn buzzed I just sit there looking at it. Staring, waiting for it to explode. So, this is how it ends, I think. Beatty's sitting next to me, yelling, and realizes I'm not going to run, so he stands up on his chair and jumps onto and over the tops of several tables to get away from the impending blast. Still, I just stare at the grenade, not moving—waiting—but it doesn't go off. So I start to laugh. I step right over it, laughing harder with each step I take out of the bar.

Once outside, I can barely breathe from laughing so hard. Everyone, including Dallas, Chiefoot, and Beatty, look at me like I am crazy, which makes me laugh even harder. Chiefoot, eyes wide with bewilderment, grabs my shoulders and shakes me in an attempt to have me regain my senses. "Jesus Christ, Spencer, what the fuck's wrong with you? You could have been killed you stupid son of a bitch!" I look him in the eye and ask how he knew my mother. "That's it," Dallas yells, "Spencer's new name is ICE."

"How about stupid?" Beatty responds.

Civilians who gathered around us look at me as if I came from Mars. I point to the wings sewn on my fatigues and say, "Aeeroborne! They can't kill us; we're aerroborne!"

The brothers are not as wasted as I am. Dallas grabs me by the shirt and pulls me along behind them, saying, "I'll give you aeeroborne. You dumb shit. Let's get the hell out of here."

The next morning, we fly out to God knows where. An army plane known as a Caribou is the ticket out this time. Caribous are STOL aircraft (Short Take Off and Landing capabilities). I'm assigned as a backup medic. We're out in the jungle, but not on line going out on patrols. The mud airstrip is a few feet from our position. As usual, it's raining.

Flock has me digging again. This time, our "graves" are to be two feet wide, two feet deep, and six feet long. He doesn't want anyone to help me, so he assigns the others some other crap. Later, six of us build a makeshift tent by combining our ponchos. The ground is soaking wet and muddy, but at least the rain won't beat on us from atop. Meanwhile, the mosquitoes are having a feast, and we're the main entrée.

Next morning, Flock orders me out on line to take Steve Best's place. Steve has contracted malaria. This time I'm assigned to Alpha company's third platoon. I don't know any of the guys. That's cool. As is customary, I report to the platoon sergeant. He isn't in a very friendly mood. He acknowledges my presence and tells me to chill out, pointing to a large boulder. The sun is out, but I am still cold. I damn near froze to death last night. It got down to about seventy degrees. You'd be surprised how cold it feels lying in the mud at night in seventy-degree weather. The warmth of the sun and the heat of the boulder cause me to fall asleep.

Three and a half hours later, I wake up and learn that my platoon has moved out on patrol without me. Oh, my God! How can they go out there without a medic? Oh shit, oh shit! Flock's gonna have me by the short hairs. I walk over to Sergeant Lims' platoon, the second platoon, to speak to their medic. "Hey, Sarge, where's your medic? I need to speak to him."

Lims looks startled. "You're our medic, Spence. What are you talking about?"

I am really confused at this point. "No," I say. "Sarge, I came out here to relieve Steve Best. He's got malaria; he is assigned to the third platoon."

Lims smiles and says that I must have my wires crossed. "Best is assigned to me. Relax, will ya? What are you so uptight about anyway?"

I let out a sigh. "Are you sure, Sergeant Lims? I was told that Best is assigned to the third platoon this time out."

"Relax, Harry," Lims states. "You're in the right place, boy."

He says it so reassuringly that it lifts a tremendous guilt bag from my conscience. I am, however, wired. I shake, but try to conceal my emotions. Off in the distance, I hear muffled explosions. Lieutenant Pilgrim, listening to the radio, tells Sergeant Lims that it's the third platoon and that they walked right into an ambush. I walk away, turning towards the sounds off in the distance, thinking, who is the medic? How is he doing? Has he been hit?

The firefight can be heard, but barely. They are out about two miles. Ten minutes later, everything falls silent. The fight is over. I walk back to Pilgrim and ask if he knows who, if anyone, got hit. He doesn't answer, just shakes his head no. Thirty minutes later word filters back to us. A squad leader was killed who had seven days to go until his discharge. Seven fucking days! Lord, not me, please. If I've got to get it, make it sooner rather than later.

Seven days. I can hear Iron Mike, our battalion commander now. "Men, they made the supreme sacrifice. You should be proud to have known them." What did they acquire for their sacrifice? What the hell are we fighting for? Then I catch myself. Don't think like that, Spence. Don't. Forget it. How many days do you have left? Two hundred and eighty five days and counting. I am getting there, all right, just not as fast as I want to.

Four hours pass when Alpha Company's third platoon returns from patrol. I run out to meet them, anxious to talk to their assigned medic and learn about their encounter. The men look worn out as they labor under the weight of their rucksacks. They are all quiet. No one says a thing as they pass us. I spot Gino Washington and run to greet him. His fatigues are so soaked with perspiration he looks like he just came out of a shower with his clothes on.

"Hey, Wash," I ask, "what happened out there? You OK?"

His eyes dart fleetingly, catching mine, and he responds, "Everything that could go wrong did go wrong." He is highly agitated. "They hit us with everything but the kitchen sink—RPG's, machine-guns, and satchel charges. They hit us on three sides, alternating their attack. Just when we would try to run in the opposite direction of the fire, we were hit in the direction we ran. Six KIAs, four wounded. I couldn't help them. I couldn't even get to them under that fire."

He's shaking his head in grief as he walks, and I slip my arm over his shoulder, squeezing him toward me. "Hey, brother, it'll be fine. Be cool, don't take it so personally."

He glances at me, tears welling up. "Spence, I couldn't get to them. They were screaming for me, but I couldn't get to them. They had us pinned down. The only thing that saved our asses was the gunships. Without them none of us would be here now."

"Yeah, but look, Wash, it's over. Forget it. Get it out of your head, or it'll kill you. Do you hear me?"

We continue walking, and without looking at me, he asks in a solemn tone, "Did you hear about Sergeant Marcoux?"

"Claude Marcoux," I gasp in shock. Up until this moment I didn't have a name attached to the guy who was killed seven days before his discharge. "Yeah," I respond in a soft voice, "I heard." But I don't say another word about him. Washington has sustained enough trauma for one day. I don't need to exacerbate his emotional state of mind.

"He had seven fucking days to go, man. Just seven fucking days and he was killed." Then with a rage he can't contain, he screams, "Seven fucking days! That's it! And he could have been a civilian! Goddamn it to hell!" Wash kicks at the ground in disgust.

I look up ahead of us and spot Specialist Willie Runner, one of the medical platoon's squad leaders. I guess he has already heard how bad things were for Gino Washington and is waiting to debrief him.

As we came up to Runner, I simply nod at him and continue back toward the second platoon's location. Washington will have those demons on his back for the rest of his life if he doesn't come to terms with the realities of our role in combat. The "what ifs" will kill you if you don't control them. Put it out of your mind, Gino. Bury it, forget it, buddy. If it doesn't serve a positive, it'll serve to haunt you the rest of your life. Throw it out, man. Forget it, forget if you can.

Later that day I learn the second platoon is slated to go out and follow the same route the third platoon took. It's not meant to take any ground and secure it. It's simply meant to engage the enemy. Iron Mike wants to know how many of the enemy were killed in that fire-fight. Reports from the gunships' pilots indicate upwards of twenty enemy soldiers were killed. The third platoon's officer didn't stick around to do a body count. He did, in my mind, the right thing by getting the hell out of there, but our battalion commander wants veri-fication, a body count.

At dusk this evening, everyone in the second platoon is cleaning their weapons, even cleaning and oiling bullets. Reports continue to flow that our M-16's jam in the heat of a firefight, especially when they get hot. My M-16 hasn't jammed, but I've never really over-heated it. I have been lucky so far on that account. Sitting together in a circle, ten or twelve of us check and double check all our gear. Nerves are running high.

A lot of the guys are edgy, speaking angrily about any subject anyone brings up. The general state of consciousness is—who is next? Each thinks it won't be him; it's always the other guy that's going to get hit. Sergeant Lims is making his nightly rounds, checking on each man and his state of readiness. He walks up to our group last, making small talk designed to gauge our fitness for tomorrow's patrol. He closes his talk by stating, "Remember, fellas, we are our nation's finest. We have practiced for years for this. This is not some kind of game out here. If anyone can face the enemy on his turf, we can, and don't you ever forget that. You got that, troops? Airborne!"

The group's response to his prompt is weak, "All the way, Sarge."

"Yeah, Sarge, we're bad, but we can't fight what we can't see.

Why don't those bastards show their faces? Just once, I'd like to see him eyeball to eyeball. That's all I'm asking, Sarge. I mean, if I've got to take a hit, I'd like to know who, what, and where it's coming from."

Lims is in a crouched position. He drops his head and looks at the ground. He doesn't have a comeback. The army didn't prepare him to deal with such questions. Still staring at the ground, he begins shaking his head while the guy finishes and then responds. His voice is soft then grows loud and stern: "Look, I know what you mean, and what you're getting at! I didn't expect this shit either, but we've got a job to do." His voice growing louder still. "And, by God, we will do it! *Do you understand me, trooper?*"

We have never seen Lims so adamant and so stern. But the trooper doesn't back down. Instead he fires back, his voice rising to the level of Lims,' "Yea, Sergeant Lims, I understand! I understand that we're getting picked off, one by one, attempting to give the colonel a body count to bolster his career by a *fucking enemy we can't see!* But what I don't understand is why we are told not to fire unless fired upon! Why do they take away our ammunition when returning to base camp? And *why* in the fuck are we here? We don't take any ground and hold it! We just go out on patrol and let him shoot first! *What kind of fucking war is this?* These gooks could care less who runs their fucking country! Hell, I could care less who runs this country! All I want, Sergeant, is to go home in one fucking piece! But the rules of engagement have the odds stacked against me! Now Sergeant Lims, *do you understand me?*"

We are all in a state of shock. No one has ever said more succinctly what we are thinking and feeling. Silence permeates the air. We are waiting for the hammer to drop when, lo and behold, Lims stands up with his hands on his hips, nodding his head. He is searching for the right words. Finally he responds, "Yes, trooper, I understand you. Your point is well taken." Then pointing at all of us, he closes with, "*And,* I understand that there will be a *full field inspection* at 0500 hours tomorrow!" He walks over and jabs his finger into the guy who spoke up and asks, "*Do you understand me, Private?*" He then turns and walks briskly away, leaving us to prepare for the inspection.

One of the guys in the group speaks up, "Way to go, Lacey. Thanks a lot." Someone else interjects, "Cool it, man, Lacey's right. Back off, man." "Whatever," the guy retorts. "What fucking ever."

The inspection turns out to be another typical army joke. Sergeant Lims along with Lieutenant Pilgrim walk up to each man, take a quick look at his rifle, and ask how much ammo and water he is carrying. They don't bother with me, only saying, "You ready, Doc?" I respond to Pilgrim with cock assurance. "Ready as ever, Sir. Let's get this shit over with."

We wade into the jungle, passing the guys assigned to guard the perimeter. As we hump through the jungle, my crotch is itching terribly. Damn, what the hell itches so badly? I try to ignore the itching and concentrate instead on the guy ahead of me, watching his movements carefully. Because our leaders never want us to take the beaten path through the jungle, we forge a new one. The thick under-brush tears at my uniform and rucksack.

A "wait a minute" vine snags my rucksack, jerking me back. I pull my upper body forward, bending at the waist to rip loose from its grasp and fall flat on my face. Shit. I struggle back to my feet. The guy behind me grabs the bar at the top of my rucksack, yanking me backward to an upright position. I immediately turn, thinking the fucking vine is after me, only to see him smiling in silence at my clum-siness. I return his smile and trudge on. The area where the third platoon got hit is another three hours from us. By mid-morning and, after four hours of ripping through the jungle, we come to some rice paddies at jungle's edge.

We take a break while Lieutenant Pilgrim has a powwow with his squad leaders. Listening in on the group's periphery, I glean enough to learn that our destination is the tree line on the far side of the rice paddies—a good half mile walk through open fields, exposed and vulnerable. Not good. Not a very bright move, I think. But following the jungle to get to that point will take at least another six hours. I tune out what is going on in the meeting between the squad leaders and Lieutenant Pilgrim. They are in hot debate. They are trying to dissuade Pilgrim from marching straight out in to the open rice paddies.

I drift, turning inward. I am afraid that I am doing just what I have feared—growing guilty that I am surviving when others have not. I cannot stop the forbidden thought that I want to get wounded. Perverse as it is, I want to take something back with me to physically prove that I have been to war. I struggle with that growing thought.

Pilgrim's voice rises above the others: "I don't care what you men think, goddamn it! This is not a democracy. We will do it my way! That's an order." Lims now walks to the guy who is assigned the point position and instructs him exactly where he wants him to lead us to. He turns, snaps his fingers, and we all respond. In a staggered column of twos we begin the trek across open rice paddies. Vietnamese women are bent over in the water. I think that they're either harvesting or planting rice.

The platoon walks on mounds of earth that separate one rice paddy from one another. Boy, we make excellent targets for Charlie or the NVA to practice on. Halfway across the rice paddy, an AK 47 opens up on us. The water in the rice paddy jumps up as the bullets hit, working their way toward us.

Charlie's first salvo is short and too far to the left. We take cover behind a mound of earth. Lims yells, "Anybody see where it came from?"

I respond, "Yeah, Sarge. Exactly where we came from." We just lie there, not returning fire, hoping to catch a glimpse of whoever that son of bitch is. Five minutes goes by. Ten minutes. Lieutenant Pilgrim, who has been on the radio most of that time, orders us to return to where we came from—right back to where the shots originated.

Very reluctantly, we get to our feet. With great trepidation, arms at the ready, we begin to go back after whoever has followed us out here. This time we're not using the mound of earth for the trip back; we venture right through the muddy rice paddy. We're knee deep in water and mud. Now this makes a lot of sense, I think.

Without warning, a shot rings out from our rear, striking one of the men. "Medic!" someone cries out. "Medic!" A guy is down in the water, lying in the prone, helmet off, and water up to his chest. I run toward him, and another shot is fired, hitting the water just to my right. I lunge forward like a swimmer, diving into the water. Meanwhile, the men open fire. Half the platoon is shooting in the direction where we came, half in the direction of where we were headed.

Here's another fine mess you've got yourself into, Spence, I think. I am drenched and submerged in mud, trapped in the middle of a rice paddy with a man one hundred feet away from me exposed out in the open. I pray nothing else goes wrong. Gino Washington's words of yesterday pop into my head, "Everything went wrong." Oh, no. Not me, not now. I crawl toward the guy under the cover of fire the guys provide.

One of the guys yells, "Hurry, Doc, get him, and let's get the fuck outta here," and resumes shooting. Lims screams, "Harry, if he can walk, patch him up later. We've got to get out of here!" I hold up my hand as I crawl as a way of acknowledging his command. When I am close enough, I ask the guy where he is hit. He doesn't appear to be in too much pain. "The shoulder, Doc. My right shoulder. Knocked the fucking wind out of me."

Blood has discolored the surrounding muddy water, turning it a purple/black color. I ask if he can walk. "Not with this rucksack on, I can't. I already tried to move with it on. The strap of my rucksack cuts right into it. I'll just leave it right here." I help him wiggle out of the webbing and push it away as we both stand up. Jesus, I think, the weight of my own rucksack has increased with all the water that has seeped into it.

"We're coming, Sarge!" I scream, stumbling forward, trying to help the guy walk to a mound of earth so we can take cover. He is going into shock. His face is as white as a ghost, and, by contrast, his lips are bright red. The men are doing an excellent job laying down a field of cover for us. I can't hear whether Charlie is firing back or not; the noise of our weapons blocks out any sounds of returning fire, if there is any. I lay the guy down.

Lims crawls over to check on us. "Is he hit bad, Harry?"

"I'm not too sure, I have to examine him closer. It doesn't appear that the bullet went all the way through, though it may have ricocheted, causing internal damage."

The guy starts to moan. The reality of what has happened to him and the pain have surfaced. I inject him with morphine, apply a pressure dressing and wrap his torso while strapping and immobilizing his arm.

The firing slows to the point that I can tell Lims that we have to have him evacuated. "Sarge, get me a Dust-Off with a One Bravo priority. (Alpha priority is life and death. Bravo denotes a lesser priority.) His wound is potentially life threatening, but he is currently stable." First we have to get out of the open and take refuge in the jungle. Lieutenant Pilgrim orders two squads to run a flanking maneuver while the rest of us move straight toward the area where we came from, approximately a football field away. Lims tells one of the men to pick up the wounded guy's rucksack as we make our way back. He is behind me and when I turn slightly to face him I hear him mumble, "Fuck that rucksack."

Once back in the jungle foliage, the platoon maneuvers to secure the immediate area. We then begin to clean our weapons. A lot of them jammed when we were returning fire in the rice paddies. Some are so jammed the guys have to take their cleaning rods out and ram them down the barrel to extract the expended cartridge casing. Within forty-five minutes, a chopper is hovering over us. The injured guy is strong enough to go out on the penetrator as opposed to a stretcher. Four and half hours later, we're back at BSOP and dirtier than shit. The adrenaline rush coupled with humping the jungle has exhausted us. Bob Lacey's words to Lims last night turned out to be prophetic. Charlie got another one of us all right. The irony is that it was Lacey himself who took the hit!

Chapter 10

COMMUNICATING WITH CHARLIE

TWO DAYS LATER, I find myself on what we dub a "Death Patrol," a squad comprised of just twelve guys humping the boonies all day. At nightfall, we will take up defensive positions to ambush "the most deadly game" . . . if he enters our killing zone.

All day we move in stealth, slowly and cautiously, no talking and no smoking. If we have to take a dump, we dig a hole and bury it immediately, camouflaging it. We eat c-rations, also burying the empty cans. We don't want any smells or rattling cans to give us away. Our individual inventory of equipment is light on personal stuff, heavy on ammo and water.

Twelve guys collectively doesn't scare Charlie. If we are ever going to get killed or captured, the odds are it will happen on a squad patrol. Flock took great pleasure informing me I had drawn the short stick. He flew to BSOP from our base camp back at Bien Hoa just to deliver the news himself and said, "Spencer, I'm going to give you the opportunity to become a real hero. Report to Bravo company's second platoon and look up Sergeant Garcia, the platoon sergeant."

Sergeant Garcia—the same sergeant I pulled perimeter guard with when I shot that monkey. Not bad, he seemed to be a nice two-faced guy. Bravo Company's first sergeant sucks because he chewed me out for shooting, but I can live with Garcia and his men. Still, I don't like the idea of a squad patrol. Anxious, I forge in the direction of Bravo company. Let's just get this shit over with. I pray, "Please, dear Lord, watch out for all of us today. I don't want to do this, but I don't have much of a choice in the matter."

I let my mind drift to Beatrice. A smile spreads across my face and I recall the very first time I saw her face—those almond, slanted eyes, her turned up nose, and her initial snobby posturing. I received another letter from her. She's going in to her third year at the University of Michigan with plans to go on to law school. Christ, how can I compete with that?

I'm from the inner city of Detroit. She moved to the suburbs a year after we met. To a large degree, she has become someone I don't know. Ha, at this rate, I might become her gardener. Still, I can't help but think about her.

"Hey, Spence, over here! Let's go man. We're moving out!" shouts Bill Spears from Bravo's second platoon. I change to a half-step trot, my rucksack swinging from side to side with each step. Garcia's platoon is already loading into a chopper that has yet to start its turbine engine. It will serve as our limo to war's edge, taking us out to the predetermined point for our date with Charlie.

Once there, we continue humping all day in silence through the rain. At dusk, we lay out four Claymore mines, establish our fields of fire, and settle down for a long, and hopefully, uneventful evening. We set up alongside a well-beaten path that someone has obviously been using. Each of us lays out in front of himself upwards of twenty magazines of M-16 ammo along with two grenades. If the shit hits the fan in the dark, you don't want to be trying to figure out where the hell your ammo is.

Later, right on cue, it begins to rain even harder, and the fucking mosquitoes are having a grand old time with our wet bodies, with an occasional leech thrown in every now and then for good measure. While lying in wait, we don't have the luxury of swatting the mosquitoes or moving around to check for leeches. We're are at the mercy of their unrelenting attacks until morning.

Leeches won't kill us, but that sucking sensation, especially if they number more than ten, unnerves us. If they're on you for ten hours, they grow from a skinny two-inch worm to a fat five-inch night crawler, filled, of course, with our own blood.

At 0100 hours it is my turn. I have managed to nod off and on until now. The guy next to me simply pushes me to wake me and hands me the generator that is connected to the claymore assigned to my sector of four guys. The platoon is split up in three sections of four. Each group has its own claymore. The exception is the squad leader; he has his own claymore and doesn't pass it along to anyone.

If someone begins to snore, we tap the guy next to us, and, because we are body to body, tell him to pass it down until the guy who is snoring is awakened. Once awake, I realize how badly the mosquitos have bitten me. The side of my face is hot and swollen. I touch my face and wince to see if I can move my cheek. Shit, the mosquitos did a pretty good job. The swollen area of my face barely moves.

On a positive note, I can't feel too many leeches on me. I put my hand in front of my face. It is so dark that I can't see beyond twelve inches. Man, it's really dark. When I glance at my watch it is only 0145 hours. The rain is coming down so hard that I can't hear any enemy movement, if there is any. Then again, maybe Charlie can't hear us either.

With one hand on the generator and one hand on my M-16, I lie on my stomach with my chin on my small aid kit to support my head and stare out into nothing—total darkness. Suddenly I think I feel something pull on the generator. What? What the hell is that? Is it my imagination? Goddamn it! Did something pull on the wire leading to the generator in my fucking hand? No can't be! It's gotta be my . . . *goddamnit!*

Something or someone is pulling on the fucking wire! I'm loosely holding the generator, staring at it when I both see and feel it move. *Holy shit!* It's not my imagination. I keep staring, not moving, looking out to spot them. But the claymore is fifty feet from our location. I can't see a damn thing. I slowly, so very slowly, take off my steel pot. The rain beating on it may have blocked out any sounds I should have heard. The rain increases in volume, running down my face and into my eyes, forcing me to blink to clear my vision.

Involuntarily my heart pounds against my chest. I'm gasping for air. I try to contain my heaving for air for fear that Charlie might hear me. If I wake the guys, it might start a panic. Wait . . . wait. Then I feel three distinct tugs on the line. Oh, yeah, you fucker. I cautiously return with three pulls of my own, and the line falls slack. Nothing. I wait and wait.

Thirty seconds goes by and the son of bitch does it again. I smile. Well, I'll be dammed! I'm talking to him, and he's talking to me. A little game of tug of war with that son of a bitch. Incredible! I slowly shake my head in disbelief; he's trying to goad me into blowing the fucking Claymore! The son of a bitch has already turned it around on me and wants me to panic and squeeze the generator! No way, Jose! I want to scream, "Checkmate, motherfucker!" But instead I just smile in the fascination of what I am experiencing. Gotcha dude. Now what are you going to do? Cause I ain't going to do shit until you do, fucker.

The game goes on for about twenty minutes, back and forth. Then just as quietly and suddenly as it began, it stops. At 0300 hours I wake the guy next to me to put him on watch. I decide not to tell him anything I've experienced, other than to tell him I think I heard movement to keep him on his toes. I pull a wire loose; it's one of the two wires that are connected to the Claymore, and put my chin back onto my small aid kit, staring until I hypnotize myself to sleep.

The stopwatch in my head wakes me at 0500 hours. I wake knowing the guy right next to me will still have the watch and that he might discover the disconnected wire and reattach it, possibly detonating it and killing us. I whisper to him to let him know I am up, also gesturing with my head for him to lean closer to me, "Psstt! Hey, look, man, don't panic, but I disconnected the Claymore before I gave it to you." His head jerks; he looks at the generator in disbelief. "Don't panic," I say, "but I believe Charlie turned it around on me." His eyes grow wide, but his brow narrows; he only half believes me. "Look, guy, he pulled on it a couple of dozen times, trying to get me to respond." I then smile broadly and say, "But I didn't bite the bait, man. Now just be cool, we'll check it when the others are up." He nods his head, still in that half-believing mode.

After hearing my story, the squad leader's first reaction is to say, in a hushed tone, "Spencer, you're so full of shit! You've got an imagination bigger than shit. Stay put." He turns to one of his trusted men saying, "Boliss, you come with me. The rest of you guys relax." The two men go out to check the Claymore. A minute later, the squad leader trudges back, not caring how much noise he is making. The Claymore is in his hand when he says, "Doc, you're one good man. The son of bitch turned it on us bigger than shit. I wouldn't have believed it if I hadn't seen it with my own two eyes! Good job, man. Five minutes men, and we're outta here."

When we finally get underway, heading back to our pickup point, my crotch is itching terribly. Goddamn jungle rot. It's easy to get jungle rot, a general break down of skin tissue, from being dirty and wet over a prolonged period of time. Despite taking antibiotics and applying antibiotic ointment, my condition is getting worse.

Chapter 11

HOA KHAN CHILDREN'S HOSPITAL—DA NANG

DISEMBARKING FROM THE C-130 aircraft at Da Nang's airstrip, I am struck by the scenic mountains and ocean. The marines constructed a sign right into the side of a mountain: "Home of the Third Marine Division." I am impressed by most of what I see—that is, until we get up close and personal with members of the United States Marine Corps.

As we pull into their compound via the familiar five-ton cattle trucks, the marines jeer us as if we are the bad guys. We just assume they are jealous. After all, anyone can become a marine, but it takes much more to become a paratrooper. "Screw 'em" is the general consensus among us. They are nothing more to us than a glorified army wearing a different uniform. Our chests increase in volume the closer we get to them, and they know it. When we don't wear our steel pots, we wear our baseball caps with wings sown into them; paratrooper wings are also sewn on our fatigue shirts as well, just above the U.S. Army insignia on our left breast. Is there a rivalry? Ooohh, yeah, you betcha!

Once we receive our marching orders, so to speak, and parameters of jurisdiction, we are told to stay away from the marines enlisted men's club. Tensions are running high. The marines are upset that army paratroopers are coming to help them. What they don't know is the crazies among us take that admonition to "stay clear of them" as an invitation to kick some ass.

So, after we settle into our temporary tents, a group of about twenty crazies makes a beeline for the marines enlisted men's club. Leon Dallas has been monitoring the crazies as they fanned themselves into some bullshit state of mind. Dallas tries to entice a few medics to go along under the guise that someone may require medical attention. But only three of us strap on our small first-aid kits and trail the main group of would-be trouble makers headed toward a rendezvous with destiny.

Shit. What the hell am I doing here? I think as I walk between Dallas, who stands about 6'1" and is 210 plus pounds of solid muscle, and Specialist Willie Runner, another stout tough guy. Then there's me. I am 6' and my weight is down to about 150 pounds, having lost fifteen pounds since being in country. I'll get creamed! Nonetheless, I follow like a sheep being led to slaughter. Dallas doesn't help matters. Even though Runner outranks him, Dallas takes the lead, saying, "Runner, you cover my back. Spencer, you cover Willie's back."

"Got it," I say with false bravado. Runner simply says, "Cool." The closer we got to the club, the broader our chests puff out and our guts suck in—a guy thing.

As we approach the marines enlisted men's club, the group of twenty or so crazies has stopped and is waiting for us. They have come up with a plan. Knowing that tough guys know other tough guys, one of them speaks to Dallas. "Looky here, you being medics and all, ya'll go in first, and, if they give you some shit, know brothers, we's be right behind you. But we'll stay out here first for a couple of minutes. And if we hear anything happening," his face glows, "Air fucking borne brother."

Runner retorts, "All the way, brothers."

Dallas looks at Runner and me for feedback. I shrug with indifference, but Runner takes the challenge, saying, "No fucking problem, brothers, let's do it." Speaking to himself as Dallas throws open the door to the club, Runner then adds, "Fuck these motherfuckers; marines ain't about nothing."

Music blares, white music. I am the last one in, letting the door close itself behind me. But Dallas stops just a couple of feet inside the doorway, putting his hands on his hips. The words in the song playing in the background get my attention for just a second. "Lightning striking again and again and again" fill the tensed air among the marines and the three of us paratroopers who dared to enter their little Boys Club.

There are about 150 guys crammed into a room which, had the fire marshal been present, would have been closed due to overcrowding. Slowly all eyes fall upon us. A paratrooper's uniform is decidedly different than a marine's. Within seconds, someone pulls the plug on the music. Oops! They're taking the bait. But Christ, they outnumber us by at least four to one, and that includes the brothers outside. Seventy-five percent of those in the club are white; the rest are either Hispanic or black. The guys outside are seventy-five percent black. "Hey!" someone shouts, "What two things fall out of the sky?"

Before any of them can respond, in unison Leon Dallas and Willie Runner, as if they have practiced for this encounter, yell, "Baby makers and bad-ass motherfuckers!" I gulp in disbelief. If ever I heard a better response to a challenge, I can't recall it. Their timing is absolute perfection. The entire crowd is dead silent. I stand there dumbfounded, waiting for the charge of the Third Marine Division. Five to ten seconds pass before someone in the crowd of marines let out a loud "Whoa!"

The three of us tense. Shit, I'm ready to scream for reinforcements when they all start laughing. Two marines closest to us stand up and stick their hands out as a peace offering to welcome us. Dallas doesn't move though, but I do. "How ya doing? Nice to see ya!" and the ice is broken. We didn't spend a dime the whole evening and got pleasantly drunk.

They sing their marine hymn; we sing our *Gory Gory, What A Hell Of A Way To Die* jump song. Strange bedfellows became one as the evening wears on. They respect us for being paratroopers while we pretend to respect them. Or maybe we both pretend to like and respect each other. Who knows, but before the night ends, the inevitable happens—a marine and a paratrooper get into it. Who won? Who cares!

The marines are as gung ho or brainwashed as we are. To sum up that evening, I'd say it reminded me of dumb and dumber, swapping war stories and tales of the local prostitutes. A lot of bullshit, not much substance.

Within twenty-four hours, all infantry companies, along with their respective platoons, are split up and assigned to various defensive positions surrounding the Third Marine Division garrison. The medics not assigned to those out on the line are told to report to Hoa Kahn Children's Hospital, located on the periphery of the base. I got lucky. We drew straws for assignments; I am to work in the hospital, basically as a ward nurse.

Before reporting to the hospital, mail call produces a pleasant surprise. Beatrice has written me another letter. A letter from anyone is like receiving a gift. Getting one from Beatrice is a blessing. To my delight, we are growing closer again. Her tone in her last three letters has been more supportive despite the fact that she feels this war sucks. At college, I assume, she's analyzed the whys and wherefores and debated with other students and the faculty the moral and legal implications of the war. She is obviously worried for my safety. Shit. I'm worried for my safety.

At the close of her letter she asks if I plan to go on R & R (Rest and Relaxation, but in my case, I'd call the latter Recuperation). The gist of her letter, which is coyly couched, is that she might be able to meet me in Hawaii if I can hold out until spring break. I smile at her assertiveness, grin at the possibility, and laugh openly. Hell, yeah! I can wait 'til spring break, baby!

I've waited and watched her grow and develop, secretly convinced that I will one day marry her. I love her. Right from that first moment we met, I loved her. Throughout the years, despite her casually dating others, I was always with her, if only in my mind. Occasionally I would surprise her by driving out to her parents' home in Southfield, Michigan, while she'd be on a date or out with her girlfriends, and I'd just sit on her porch waiting for her. However, her father, a Southfield firefighter, and tough-guy type, thought I was nuts. But he admired and tolerated my intrusions, saying, "Boy, don't you have anything better to do with your time than to come here and sit, waiting for my daughter?" And then, smiling he'd add, "Haven't you ever heard of a telephone, young man?"

Since the ninth grade, Bea and I have never lost touch with each other, and if I have my way, we never will. Then my Catholic morals kick in, and I wonder if her dad knows she may come to meet me. Of course there is the aspect of sex. How in the hell am I going to cross that bridge? We've never had sex. I felt so much for her that I was afraid to go through with it when we necked at a local park back in high school.

And now, more than ever, I wouldn't want to get her pregnant, ruining her plans of college and law school. Me? With a beautiful girl like her? No, I won't do anything but the right thing.

As I walk in the direction of the children's hospital, F-4 Phantom jets take off from the distant airstrip. When they reach our location they are only 500 feet off the ground. This is the first time I have seen F-4s. They are an awesome sight and sound much more powerful than the F-100 Super Sabers or the F-5 Freedom Fighter aircraft I'd hear daily at Bien Hoa's air force base.

Continuing with the half-mile walk to the hospital, this being only the third day in Da Nang, I am still struck by the different sights. The majestic-looking mountains of the coastline transition smoothly into the ocean with a shoreline of beautiful white sand. It would be attractive and peaceful if it were any place but here. Fear never allows us to take in the natural beauty of this place because beauty connotes tranquility. The peace of nature is not for us. Survival comes first; scenery comes second. I can never relax in this country. I never know when or where I might get hit.

One thing does make me feel a little better, though; they have allowed us to keep our assigned ammo with the caveat that we account for all of it at inspection. No problem. If I've got to use it, I could care less about accounting for it. I wonder if they took ammo away from those who served in World War II or in Korea. I'll make it a point to ask someone.

The hospital work is interesting. It affords me an opportunity to sharpen what little medical skills I have. There are three Vietnamese nurses assigned to work with us and to act as our interpreters as needed, which is more often than not. The kids range from infancy to twelve years of age. Most suffer from malnutrition, infections of all sorts, skin rashes and tropical ulcers (large boils that look like the top of a volcano cut off, ranging from one to three inches in diameter). Malaria is also quite prevalent. Eventually I will see children die. I know that and try to prepare myself for it.

I overhear Doctor Pierce in consultation with a navy doctor, discussing the condition of the only twelve-year-old we have at the hospital. She has lymphatic leukemia and is terminally ill. We can't do anything but administer drugs to help her cope. The hospital is little more than a pole barn about twenty-by-forty feet with a steel-corrugated roof and screened walls. Slats of corrugated metal are spaced wide enough to see through them. The interior is spartan. A continuous wooden bench runs along the outer walls, which serves as a place for the children to sleep. It stands about waist-high with a one-by-twelve piece of wood screwed in to the end of it so the kids won't roll onto the floor.

A second bench, elevated one foot off the floor, houses the older kids and doesn't have this roll out safety slat of wood. Six of us medics work staggered ten-hour shifts—overlapping during the busy waking hours of the children.

Within a couple of days, the twelve-year-old begins to moan and cry, sometimes with total abandon. I am grateful I don't speak the language. The little girl bursts out and says something I just know is a prayer for mercy. Her inflections pretty much tell her plight. Although I try not to listen to her cries, I can't stop myself from being emotionally drawn in. After six hours of continuous cries, I ask a nurse, who goes by the American name of Sandy, what the girl is saying. I can't stand it any longer. I have to ask simply because I watched the nurses reactions as she wailed. They appeared too cold and distant. I didn't like that; it vexed my soul.

Because a good number of Vietnamese are Christians, and a sizeable percentage of those are Catholics, I feel I might be able to somehow reach her. "Sandy." I ask, "can you tell me what number 112 is saying?" (We give patients numbers as opposed to names due, I assume, to our inability to grasp their names.) I wanted to know if they are mistreating her, or if she just wants something I can give her to comfort her.

The older nurse, Nyguen, who is obviously the leader of the three, speaks up. "She's crying out to God to help her—to cure her and to take away her pain. She wants to go home to be with her family. She says that if God will do that for her, she'll be a good girl and become a nun."

My reaction is as if a knife has just pierced my heart. I feel like running away from this reality and crying out to God to stop this madness, all the madness of mankind. My mind races, thinking of all the injustices of this world: The punks on the street who rob the elderly, the sick, those who murder, the liars, the cheaters all over the world. My eyes well up with tears, and I run outside, feeling like I'm going to break down like a lost wolf puppy might, crying as if there is no tomorrow. I feel her fear, her sorrow, and look up to the heavens.

For the first time in my life, I raise the most profound and fundamental question all of mankind must at one time have asked. "God," I say softly. "Why, my Father, why? Before I die please, one day, tell me. Why does all the madness in this world exist? You are the Master Engineer, the Master Scientist. Why did you do it this way?" With one knee on the ground and one knee propped to support my forearms, I silently weep for mankind's shortcomings, and I weep for me. Hell, the last time I asked God for something I got the shit kicked out of me by my father. But in all sincerity, I wonder, how in the hell did I get myself into this mess? What could I have done differently to avoid being here? And that little voice we all have within us says, "Harry, you dumb shit, you should have stayed in school. You should have applied yourself instead of skating through high school, settling for C's. The teachers were there to help you, but instead of realizing they were your mentors, you saw them as the enemy."

I think about Beatrice. She applied herself. She took school very seriously. Somehow she saw that school was a road map and followed it, convinced it was a ticket to fulfillment and ultimate success and independence. I shake my head, disgusted with myself for being so stupid, for not realizing this back then. And then that voice calls out again, "It's not too late, Harry. You'll only be twenty years old when you get out of this place. You've got that G.I. Bill." I wipe the tears from my eyes. Yeah, I think, I can't beat the system. I've got to join it, embrace it. Grab what is out there for the taking.

I feel better about myself as my thoughts direct me to a path in life that I fought and dismissed in my younger, rebellious years. I know what I have to do. For the first time, I have a plan. After returning to my land, my country, I will never again take things for granted—not a light switch or the flush of the toilet. America is the greatest country on this earth! Sure, things could be better, but on a whole, it is still the land of great opportunity. No other country in mankind's history has ever held out such promise to its citizens. You stupid shit, I think to myself, smiling slightly. I stand up, straightening myself.

I feel better as I walk back into the hospital. I have a direction for the first time in my life that makes sense, and I feel motivated as I go about my work in the hospital. Now all I have to do is survive. Whoa. That thought brings me back with a screeching halt to the realities of war. Will I heed its lessons? Will we as a people learn that war is predicated upon a lie? The greatest lie ever told and rendered to mankind. Then the cynicism within me comes to the fore. What a way to control population!

The young girl dies a week later in mid-afternoon while the other children laugh and frolic about, oblivious to her passing. They have absolutely no concept of death as they crawl and run about as if nothing unusual had transpired. In fact, I didn't even know until I realized she wasn't crying as I readied an injection of Demerol. With syringe in hand, I take one look at her and know she is dead. She has that look—the color is gone from her face, replaced by an ashen gray hue. No perspiration, her skin is dry and cold to the touch. Her eyes are wide open, pupils fixed and dilated, staring at death as it came to claim her.

My reaction is immediate. I stare at her frail empty body, saying to her, saying to myself, "Goodbye, my little one. Rest in peace. You are now pain free." Then I glance upward, "God, look after her and comfort her. She has suffered a lot. Please, dear Lord, embrace her with all your splendor and love. Rest in peace Number 112, Amen." I feel helpless and empty, as if part of me died with her.

As the days turn into weeks, I fall in love with a little fella we call "Four Legs." Four Legs is so named because he came to us with a compound fracture of the left leg. He walks with "four legs"—two of his own and two crutches. His village was under siege by Charlie, and the marines had called for artillery support to roust Charlie from his village. Four Legs caught a chunk of shrapnel in his leg, shattering his femur. Friendly fire claimed another victim.

In his first few days with us, Four Legs is distant and aloof, but I sense that he likes me, though the nurses tell me he doesn't like Americans. I smile in his presence and tell him there are a good number of Americans I don't like either. Then I ask the third nurse, Kim, to tell him that if I were him, I wouldn't like Americans either. I can't blame the kid for feeling as he does.

When Kim tells him what I said, he bursts out, "You number ten thousand!" I am shocked to hear this little five-year-old, who looks to be as small as an American two-to-three-year-old, speaking English, even if it is barely understandable. I shoot him a glance. He is sitting on the floor, crutches at his side, his good leg bent; the bad leg is in a cast, straight out on the floor. Realizing I'm searching his face to make eye contact, he lowers his head. But his eyes look up, shadowed by his eyebrows, waiting for a negative response from me.

His body posture is both scared and defiant when I speak to him and use a Donald Duck enunciation to my words. As a kid, my father could imitate the sound of Donald Duck. I am pretty good at it, too. When I was younger, I thought I would be the next generation to do the voiceovers in Hollywood for the duck. That is all it takes! All the kids are totally fascinated at the sounds emanating from me. They surround me. Some hug me; some try to see if I have something in my mouth. I go along with them, opening my mouth wide as they peer into it searching, poking, looking for a device they are sure is somewhere in there.

Even the nurses can't contain themselves and laugh openly. They marvel at such a strange sound. What makes it so funny to them is that they can actually understand what I am saying. So in my best Donald Duck, looking at the nurses, I continue, "My name is Donald Duck. What is your name?" They cover their faces with their hands, laughing and giggling like little girls. The children laugh too, not just because I sound silly, but at the sight of the usually serious matrons laughing like one of them. Four Legs tries hard not to laugh, but I can tell he is hooked. Turning toward him, about to conclude my little show, I point to him and say with Donald Duck inflection, "And you! You, Four Legs, you number ten thousand." We begin a friendship that grows to such intensity I actually want to adopt him. We became the best of pals. Wherever I go in the hospital, he hobbles along behind me.

The marines have built an outdoor movie screen and small projection house not too far from the hospital. As a special treat from time to time we take as many kids as we can to a movie. Even though the kids can't understand a single word, they follow along, interpreting the movie and narrating the scenes among themselves. The children's giggles and laughter and their rapid chatter sometimes annoy the guys. Occasionally, one will yell, "Hey Doc, can't you get those kids to shut up a little? We're trying to hear, man." Then I make the physical gesture to the kids, putting my index finger to my lips, but never really back it up. I could care less if the men can't hear a word.

My movie is watching the kids enjoy themselves. More than likely, they have never seen a movie or television in their lives. Seeing them laugh while trying to be quiet and contain themselves not only makes me feel good, but it also takes their minds off their ailments or injuries.

After twenty-eight days of working at the hospital, my buddy, Sergeant Flock, informs me that I will be going out on Hill 358. Hill 358 overlooks the Da Nang Harbor from the distance of about eight miles. Walking up to me, grinning, he says, "Well, Spencer, your little vacation is over. You're now assigned to Alpha company's second platoon; you'll be replacing Sergeant Tom Brown." Tom is the medic who got my stripes when I was busted. He continues, "Take everything you have. You'll be out there for the remainder of this operation, running squad-sized patrols in the mountains." I quickly calculate I will be out there for about three weeks.

My heart sinks at the thought that I'll never see my little patient friends again. Flock snaps before turning away, "You'll move out in two days. At 1100 hours the day after tomorrow be at the compound LZ for your ride to the real war, not this sissy shit job you've had here."

What a jerk, barking like that in front of the kids. I have developed such a rapport with the kids that they can sense when something is wrong. They ask the nurses what that "bad man" said to me. The mood turns solemn. I suspect the nurses told them my time with them is up and that I have to go back to my unit in the field, the boonies.

Although I try to cheer them up, a few are visibly upset, turning away from my attempts to console them. Four Legs scoots to his corner, curling up with his head buried. I feel terrible, but I know I can't do a damn thing about it. Somehow I have to turn off my affections and concerns for them. Others need me too. My comrades in arms come first, but man, what a price.

As my shift ends at 1300 hours on November 6 1966, I sense an estrangement has taken place between the nurses, the children, and me. Up until this moment, there were always a couple of kids constantly at my side, content just to be near me as I went about my work. The nurses made small talk to learn more about America and me. Toward the latter half of my shift, the atmosphere is unusually quiet. The kids keep their distance, speaking and playing quietly among themselves; the nurses do the same.

The next day at the hospital, around 1000 hours, as is the norm, we open the doors, allowing parents to see their children. Normally, one of the nurses unlocks the solid wood door and chats with the early bird arrivals. But Sandy asks me to open the door because she is busy. Not giving it a second thought, I open the door and see about twenty mothers smiling and cheering, loaded with arms full of food. I am taken aback. "What? What is this all about?" I sheepishly smile when it dawns on me that they are here to throw me their version of a going-away party. Boy, am I ever surprised.

The kids come to life with the festive mood, coming over to see and smell what the women have brought. Some jump up and down when they realize their mothers have brought some of their favorite foods. Normal chow for them is American cuisine from the mess hall. They tolerate it but obviously favor their own as they fervently seek out their mothers, eagerly trying to peek at what they have brought.

During all this excitement, I want to know how Four Legs is reacting. I scan the growing crowd and spot him still curled up in his corner, staring blankly. I make my way to him, eager to cheer him up. While the other kids are too young to understand why we are having a party, he understands and is nearly in tears as I approach him. "Come on, Four Legs!" I smile. "What's the matter, little guy." Rubbing his hair, trying to elicit a positive response, I continue. "Look Four Legs, it's going to be all right. Everything will be just fine. You'll be just fine." He turns his head aside when I see tears falling from his eyes. I pick him up despite his protest and give him a big hug, kissing the side of his neck. "I love you, Four Legs. I love you very much! I will never forget you!" I fight very hard not to cry myself. With tears and his nose running, he pushes away from me, his hands on my chest, and says in the clearest English I have heard from him, "I wove you, Haarwie." And then he hugs me, not wanting to let go.

Muscle spasms begin deep within me. I try to hold them back. I don't want to ruin the otherwise festive mood. Nyguen, sensing what is happening, lovingly pries us apart. Instantly the mothers begin to push their food in front of my face, gauging which food I favor most based on its presentation and smell. I have been to enough family outings with my aunts and uncles to know what to do. I deliberately act as if each food holds a special place in my heart, and smell it as if it is my favorite. They all giggle, pleasantly surprised at my theatrics while nodding their heads and chatting to each other.

I am afraid to ask Nyguen, Sandy, or Kim what each dish is. I am also afraid I won't able to eat their food without gagging. I might be able to fool them into thinking I like their food, but based on experience, if I can't tolerate something, I'll gag. Fortunately none of my fears come to fruition. I sample food from each plate each mother brought as they look on. Fortunately my taste buds allow me to chew their food without incident as I savor each bite of unknown meat, chicken, fish, and vegetable dishes presented to me. I am humbled that they thought enough of me to honor me in such a fashion.

Although I said my goodbyes yesterday, with one hour before my rendezvous with destiny and fully laden down with my combat gear, I want to see the kids one last time. Happily anticipating seeing them and watching their smiling faces light up, I enter the hospital, laboring to walk straight due to the weight of my rucksack. The kids don't recognize me. Many run off in different directions, some cry out in fear. "Hey! Hey, it's me, Harry!" I tell them, trying to calm their fears. I whip off my helmet. "Hey! Four Legs, it's me, Harry; come here, give me a hug." I hold out my arms towards him.

The younger ones are more inquisitive, not having any fear at all. They come toward me, some crawling on all fours, some walking, all smiling. Four Legs admits a small smile, albeit lacking conviction, and struggles to his feet, using his crutches. The first to get to me is Mouse, Four Legs' brother. He is called Mouse because he can't walk. He was born paralyzed from the waist down but can pull himself in the direction he wants to go with fluid speed. His mother brought him here, thinking we could somehow work a miracle and give him the use of his legs. He is also kept here because he is malnourished and to keep Four Legs company.

"Hi, Mouse!" I say as he hugs my ankle. I reach down and pick him up, holding him above my head to give him a view of the world he rarely sees. "How ya doing, Mousey, my boy?" He giggles, staring around the room. A few of the early visiting mothers have already arrived. Each greets me, some from a distance while holding their children; some are comfortable enough to touch me and examine my equipment. They have never really been this close to a combat-laden soldier before. Fortunately, I don't have any grenades with me. The rules don't allow us to have them when we're not flying out to a hot zone.

Some of the youngsters want to examine my M-16. Because it is empty I permit it, cautioning them it isn't a toy. Suddenly one mother thrusts her child at me, bursting into tears as she does so. It is "Frankenstein," an eighteen-month old little boy whom I personally examined and bandaged when he came to us two weeks ago. The little guy has multiple scabies that are badly infected, but have since begun to heal. He is still, however, heavily bandaged on over fifty percent of his body. "What, mamason?" I ask as I put down Mouse to take Frankenstein. I turn to one of the nurses to explain what she is gibbering and crying about. Nyguen sympathetically smiles while speaking to the woman. Then she softly says to me, "She wants you to take her son to America with you. She says he has no future here in Vietnam."

We both try to calm her fear in our different ways: Nyguen talks with her; I gently touch her cheek, wiping away her tears saying, "I understand, mamason. I'm sorry, but I can't. I wish I could, but I can't. I'm terribly sorry." She gathers herself and apologizes for her outburst, backing up slowly as she does.

Four Legs suddenly punches my thigh to get my attention. I look down at him; he's wearing my helmet and says, "Haarwie, You number ten thousand!" He hands me my helmet and walks away with the aid of four legs—two legs and two crutches. "Goo-bye Haarwie."

I catch myself. Nyguen catches me too and grabs my arm, leading me toward the door. I am grateful for her intervention. Her arm is intertwined with mine as if we are on a date. Once outside, I tell her how much I appreciated working with her, Sandy, and Kim. I will remember them always and wish her well. Nyguen, a college-educated woman in her late twenties, puts her index finger to my lips to stop me from talking. Her face tightens as she attempts to control her emotions and she speaks. "Haarwie, you very good man. I please to know you." She drops her finger from my lips and grabs my hand, casting her head downward "We have saying," she tries to enunciate clearly, deliberately, and concisely. "To live is to feel pain. Vietnamese people know this. Maybe you feel pain for a very long time, Haarwie."

She turns, not bothering to look me in the eye and states, "Goodbye, my friend," as she lets loose of my hand, then, putting her hand to her face, she bursts into tears. She moves quickly to the hospital, allowing one more "Goodbye." Christ, if ever I had an empty feeling, that goodbye was it. I drop my head, take off my steel pot and walk away. I vow though that one day, when I write my book, I will write about them. "Goodbye, Nyguen."

Slowly, I make my way to the pick-up point to meet the chopper. The war with Charlie and the NVA won't wait. It is again my turn on the line, the boonies. The itching in my crotch gets my attention. Damn. I've been out of the bush for a month. That jungle rot should have healed by now.

My spirit is so low that while sitting on my equipment waiting on the chopper, I write a message to my parents and my siblings in my diary . . . just in case.

> *My dearest mother, father, brothers and sisters:*
> *As of this writing, I have been in Vietnam for nearly six months. During this time I have seen many sights and sounds, all of which have scared and fascinated me. I have witnessed death and it's not something I can talk about right now. But I do want you to know I love and miss you all very much. I am writing this because there is a chance I may not come back as I hope to.*
> *Mom and Dad, I'm sorry. I know I have caused you much pain and grief while growing up, and for that I apologize. Please forgive me. Joey, my older brother, thank you for buying me that '54 Chevy. Even though it cost less than your first bicycle (a mere $ 25.00) it is the thought and the expres-*

sion of love I appreciated, but never expressed. So now, I want you to know I appreciated it very much.

To my younger brother Glennie, I wish you well and hope you don't ever have to experience what I have here in Vietnam. Maybe you'll be more lucky than I. I hope so.

To my younger brother Allen, I hope for your sake you'll wise up and fly right because the path you're currently on leads to a world you may not be able to handle.

To my sister Martha, thank you for the troll doll. I'm carrying it strapped to my helmet. It has seen everything I have and as of this writing has brought me the luck you wished me when you gave it to me at the airport, as that was the last time we saw each other.

And my youngest brother and sister, Bobby and Connie. Let's see, Bobby, you're about six now and Connie, you're just four years old. We haven't had very much time to get to know one another since you were only four and two when I left home. But I wish the very best for you two in all that you do. And everywhere you go, for the rest of your lives, please know I think about you two often.

These are the thoughts and the words I want you to remember me by because if you ever read this, I am no longer in the flesh. But I trust, forever in your memory. Goodbye.

Your Son

and

Your Brother, Harry 11/8/66

Chapter 12

HILL 358

SERGEANT FLOCK APPROACHES me as I finish writing in my diary. "Still writing, huh, Spencer?" I look up and tuck the diary away. Shit. He is the last person I want to see right now. Sensing I am down, he toys with me, saying, "What's the matter, trooper? You sad 'cause you didn't get any pussy from the nurses?" It is his way of cheering me up, I guess. But he angers me enough that I respond, "Look, Sarge, haven't you got anything better to do than to come here and bother me?" Half pleading, because I sense he doesn't like what I said, I continue. "I'm just sitting here, minding my own business. Give me a break, will ya?"

He stops just a few feet from me and puts his hands on his hips while a sneer crawls over his face. In his own defense, he barks, "Look, Spencer, I'm here to make certain you get on that chopper. That's my job. Do you have a problem with me doing my job, trooper? In case you forgot, while in the rear, (meaning base camp), I'm your boss. You got that, mister?"

I drop my head in submission stating, "Yeah, Sarge, how could I ever forget that? You be the bossman. No problem. How could I forget? Every time I look at my sleeve and see my PFC stripes, I remember, Sergeant."

He becomes agitated. "Look here, you smart ass. You've been a pain in my ass since I've known you. You had the makings to go a long way in this man's army, but you had to go and screw it up, you dumb shit. And you're nowhere near where I want you to be. Remember my promise, Spencer?" His tone is steady and deadly, eyes level, voice filled with determination and anger. I dare not push him any further.

"Yes, Sarge. I remember." And then, out of nowhere and without premeditation, I rise to his threatening remark. "Yeah, I remember. But do you remember my promise in return, Sergeant?" I am shocked at what I just said, but it's too late now. I might as well finish and do it right. "Fight fire with fire, Spence," comes that inner voice. Before he can interrupt, as I know he will, I beat him to the punch. In that momentary pause between words his eyes narrow to meet my challenge. I continue, not giving him the courtesy of addressing him as sergeant, "Flock, if I ever catch your black ass humping out on the line in a squad patrol, I'll see to it personally that you don't come out of it." Holy shit! There I go again! I snap my head around, thinking for a second someone may have heard me. Whew. Nobody is close enough to have heard. I look away from his penetrating stare. What the hell is wrong with you, Harry! Have you lost your fucking mind? Things had been cooling down a bit between us the last couple of months, and, although he continues to take swipes at me, I haven't bit the bait. Now, you stupid shit, I think, now you've really got to him.

Flock screams his response. "You want a piece of me motherfucker? Is that what you want?" As he steps closer, still screaming, I involuntarily tighten up. I'm not too sure if I should go into a fight or flight mode. He reaches for the .45 he always carries, jumps back, and dares me to make a move for my ammo. I go onto automatic. Others going out on the line have gathered some twenty feet from us. They sure as hell heard Flock challenge me. So I want to be sure they hear me back down.

Still sitting on my rucksack, I do not dare make a move. I put my hands up in surrender. "Sergeant," I yell for everyone to hear. "Knock off the theatrics, you're scaring those guys. They'll think you're serious." I force a smile for them to see. Flock knows what I have done. He relaxes his posture, putting his hands out to his side. I won—this round anyway. My smile broadens. Check, asshole!

But he leans a little closer, trying to conceal his teeming anger. He is heaving for air, trying to conceal that too, when he states, "OK, you son of a bitch," while nodding, as in recognition of my ability to outmaneuver him mentally, and whispers. "What would you like your headstone to read, motherfucker?" I have to give it him; he always had a come back.

Two guys are slowly moving our way, I'm sure, out of morbid fascination. I feel the comfort zone returning just as surely as I felt the danger zone building and put my head down. I shake it from side to side slowly and say with one raised hand, "Sergeant Flock, you win. You always win. What can I say? You are the man."

He grunts as if he won the exchange and turns and walks away. Two of the guys going out on the line with me approach and one of them asks, "What the hell was that all about, Doc? I've never seen that man so mad. What did you say to him?"

Making light of what happened, but with an eye to potential witnesses, I reply, "Oh, nothing more than he wants to see me get killed."

"Whoa! That's pretty heavy shit, man! What did you say back to him?"

One of the two standing before me is a crazy; I know he'll understand. I reply, "Just that I'd *off him* if I ever caught him out on squad patrol."

They jump back when hearing that, slap each other five and laugh. "Doc, you be one tough dude to tangle with!" then one asks, "You sure you said that?" His tone is serious. He is probing me to determine if I am one of them.

"Naw, I'm just bullshitting you. I just told him to get the hell out of my face with his REMF mentality," (slang, which stands for Rear Echelon Motherfucker).

They break out laughing, seemingly relieved I'm not really one of them. After all, I'm a medic, a person who tries to preserve life, not take it. All infantrymen admire and respect medics. It's their way of making sure they are tight with those who might possibly save their life if they take a hit.

I let my mind drift, counting how many more days before I'm discharged. I stop counting at around 200 when I hear the unmistakable sound of a Huey helicopter approaching. Here I go. Here I go . . .

My chariot to war has come for me. Once airborne, within fifteen minutes, I'm helping unload hot meals the chopper carries as cargo.

The hot meals will come to us every other day. The days in between, we'll eat c-rations. God bless the cooks who labor under the intense heat and humidity to cook for us. Guys on line would never speak negatively about the cooks. As far as we're concerned, cooks are cool—cool, indeed.

The view from atop Hill 358 is breathtaking. From here we can see the whole of Da Nang Harbor with its sandy beaches. From this vantage point, it looks like a resort. I strain to see if I can spot the Hoa Kahn Children's Hospital. Although I can't see it, I know I am close, if only in my mind's eye. Scanning 360 degrees, I admire the entire landscape. Its beauty belies the tortuous conditions encountered on patrol.

Later, I am shown a sandbagged bunker I'll be sharing with one of the infantrymen, Oliver Lamont, a soft-spoken black guy from Arkansas. Oliver is an ammo bearer in the weapons squad. The bunker has a steel corrugated roof, standing about four and half feet high. The walls, seven feet wide by ten feet long, are made of sand-bags. Bunks are nothing more than rectangular boxes filled with sand, which serve as our mattresses.

We lay out our ponchos to cover the sand, sort of like a bed sheet, to keep the sand away from our bodies as we sleep. Invariably, however, during the night the sand finds its way up and onto the topside of the ponchos. We simply shake it out in the morning. This bunker will be my home for the next twenty-three days. Other bunkers are strategically erected and scattered throughout the craggy, jagged hillside/mountain top.

Although it is called a hill, to me it is a mountaintop. I guess its elevation from sea level to be nearly 1,700 feet. Hills to our south are smaller, affording us an unobstructed view of the ocean with its waves slowly lapping the shoreline. To our north lies a valley, which gradually gives way to a higher mountain by some 1,000 feet teeming with the heavy foliage of trees and underbrush. To our east and west are smaller rolling hills rising in the distance to various mountain ridges resplendent with green trees indigenous to the Southeast Asian forests. The thermals provide a constant twenty-mph wind. Because of the elevation, it is much colder up here than down below in the marine garrison, perhaps by as much as ten degrees. Couple that with the wind chill factor—I feel cold.

The jungle rot I have is healing well, looking the best it has since I got to Vietnam. Affected areas of my feet, ankles, and shins show definite signs of healing. Dark purple and black skin is giving way to pale white dried scaly skin—which is a good sign. But that itching in my crotch has really kicked in since I arrived. At night while sleeping is the worst time. I've got to do something about this pretty damn soon.

Unlike the hospital, which had real lights and switches, the only form of illumination up here are candles. Outside, at night, we make our way around by memory and feel, sometimes stumbling, sometimes falling flat on our face, until we learn the areas to avoid.

The next morning, around 0800 hours, just after our morning pickings of C rations, we hear automatic weapons fire coming from somewhere just southeast of our position. A two-lane highway, which runs east and west, is just over two small hills south of us. We all stand still, wondering what is taking place somewhere off in the distance. This is our assigned sector to protect, and we know we will very shortly mobilize to ascertain what is happening down there. The men instinctively start moving towards their bunkers to get to their equipment.

Within a minute we identify two distinctly different weapons engaged in a firefight. The loud authoritative booming of an automatic weapon followed by a single shot semi-automatic rifle plays out a deadly beat.

Within five minutes Lieutenant Pilgrim bursts out of his bunker along with my true buddy, Sergeant James Lims. "First Squad, with the M-60, load up. Light load only." This means weapons, ammo, and a minimum amount of water. Pilgrim shouts to the platoon's radio operator, "Hoornstra!"

"Yo," he replies.

"Move out."

Then Pilgrim adds, "Medic?"

I call out, "Got it, Sir!"

Shit. There is no such thing as a light load for me. I've got to take everything with me. Got to be prepared for anything. I scramble to put on my gear when I hear a jeep start and men yelling "Go, go!" I am still in my bunker tucking things and double-checking to make sure

I have everything when I yell, "I'm coming! Slow down a minute will you!" I emerge to see them pulling away.

Realizing they are, in fact, going to leave without me, I scream to Lims to stop the jeep as I run after them. In my haste, I don't take the time to slip into my rucksack. Instead, I carry it on one arm, slung over my shoulder. My M-16 is in the other hand. Lims lets out a loud whistle, getting the attention of men in the jeep as it pulls away and heads down a winding, rapidly descending dirt road. Fortunately, they hear Lims and stop and wait for me.

The men are really impatient. "Come on, goddamn it, Doc. Let's go, move, move, man!" screams the squad leader, Homer Oscar Pop (Hop, as we refer to him).

Just when I realize I haven't even got around to lacing my boots, I trip and fall face first while descending the hill on a dead run. A couple of the guys jerk me back onto my feet. They grab my gear and hustle me toward the jeep, saying, "Come on, Doc, we've got ya, let's go." When we get to the jeep I am amazed to see how laden down it is. The men are piled on top of one another. Some are standing on the back bumper straps, some lie on the hood, and some are barely sitting on the front fenders, clutching the windshield to keep from falling off.

The driver maneuvers like a mad man hell bent on killing us prior to giving Charlie his chance. The severely overloaded jeep is slow to respond to the driver's input, so much so that I scream at him to slow down. Within a couple of minutes (because of the rate of speed the idiot driver chose), we come across another jeep in the middle of the road. One man lies face up on the side of the jeep. The other man is crouched on his knees along side of the jeep, firing intermittently into the mountainside.

He is shooting at about a sixty-degree angle, oblivious to our arrival. I notice they are marines. Sergeant Hop is the first to call out to the guy while we scramble to take cover. "Hey, fella," he yells. "How many are there? Are you hit? Is your partner hit?" But before the guy can respond, the enemy's powerful automatic comes alive with at least ten to twenty rounds spewing forth with just one pull of the trigger. We all press into the mountainside. Large boulders overhead provide cover. With that twenty-round burst of fire, Charlie lets us know he knows we're here.

The bullets dance our way, hitting and penetrating the asphalt surface of the road, "Do you see that, Hop?" I ask. With his head pushing into the boulder, he glances my way, simply nodding his head, eyes wide with fear. The marine lets out a few more rounds as I careen my head and neck to see him. Charlie opens fire again while I still have my fix on the marine behind the jeep. The body on the ground rises and falls slightly as the bullets hit it. I jerk back in horror in seeing a body hit like that. While Charlie keeps his finger on the trigger, I scream at Hop, *"Jesus Christ, Hop! They're killing him—they're really killing him!"*

Hop chances a glance as the firing continues and responds, "Goddamn it! You're right!" "Hop, I've got to do something!" And before he can say anything, I bolt forward, not even thinking about the danger. I am mad, mad as hell mad. I want to defy Charlie.

Bullets are hitting the ground. Jesus! Then my training takes charge of my movements. I start zigzagging. Almost instantly the men in the squad open fire. In the time it takes me to run to the jeep, I feel as if I am in the middle of a ubiquitous thunderclap. The thunder vibrates my eardrums, tickling my inner ear.

When I get to the jeep the marine is shocked to see me. I think for a second that he'll shit his pants from his surprise. "United States Paratroopers at your service," I say. "Are you hit?" He responds by showing me a through-and-through bullet hole on his forearm. But before I can say anything he states, "I'm all right. Just check the colonel. They ambushed us, man. Came out of nowhere." I reach for the colonel, pulling him by the legs to get him and keep him out of the line of fire.

The squad is not letting up. They have settled into an alternate-firing pattern, conserving their ammo, keeping Charlie at bay . . . I hope. I rip open the colonel's fatigue shirt and then his T-shirt. Christ. There are four quarter-sized holes running from his left shoulder down his mid-chest maybe two inches apart. No blood present. I feel for a pulse on his carotid artery. Nothing. I put my ear to his chest over his heart, but I can't hear a damn thing over the weapons fire. He has the look though. I roll him over and the backside of his shirt is covered with blood. I lift it, trying to see anything that—Aw, shit.

When the bullets passed through him, they ripped his back apart—

exposing tissue, muscle and vertebrae. I look away from the sight of this atrocity but take another glance to look for blood flow indicative of the beating of a heart. Nothing. He is gone. I lean back, my head up against the back tire of the jeep, feet to the side, keeping myself out of the line of fire. "He's dead, Marine," I say. "I'm sorry." The firing suddenly stops.

A marine Ontos, a tracked vehicle, rumbles toward us. I cautiously look up and down the road. About a quarter mile in the opposite direction from where the Ontos is approaching, I spot a Vietnamese bus. Its passengers are outside, mingling and waiting, I assume, for the situation to end so they can resume their journey. In the silence, I dress the marine's wounds. The bullet appears to have cauterized his veins and capillaries as it passed through his forearm— not much bleeding.

As I apply a four-by-four gauze pad to the wound's entrance and exit points and wrap his arm, the marine begins to relax, stating, "I was driving the colonel to say goodbye to his troops. He was scheduled to go home tomorrow. He wanted to say his goodbyes. That's all he wanted to do." He puts his other hand to his forehead, shaking it, and continues, "He'd been here thirteen months without any problems." His voice decreases in volume, lowering in tone. "And now this shit has to happen."

I strongly suggest he get this incident out of his head. "If you don't put it aside, man, it'll get to you. Just be thankful you're OK," I say as our eyes meet.

"Yeah, right," he says in a satirical tone as he looks away, "Easy for you to say."

I don't want to bother him any further. I know he is beyond talking to; he can't rationalize away the incident at this point.

Hop calls for a Medevac, informing them to bring a spare body bag. We put the colonel in the one that I carry. I'll take theirs once it gets here.

As the marine Ontos pulls up, a guy calls to the wounded marine. "Woodchoppers again, Bill?" The wounded marine obviously knew those guys.

"Yeah," he responds.

I interject, "What do you mean, woodchoppers?"

The marine looks at me, annoyed, like I am supposed to know. "Look man, everyone around here knows they blend in with the local population, disguised as simple woodchoppers. But in the woodpile they carry, they hide their weapons or they bury them along the trails up there," he says, pointing up the mountain. "Right now you can bet your ass they've already ditched that weapon and are going on their way playing woodchopper. If you caught them right now, there is no way you could prove they are Vietcong or the NVA. It's like they're invisible. We don't know who, where, or when. Since I've been here, they've been picking us off a little at a time. It's bullshit, man, pure bullshit."

A line of cars has formed behind the bus. A few of them are bold enough to honk their horns. They are growing impatient, wanting to go about their business. Irritated, I think, this is their war. We are here to help them and here they are telling us to get this shit over with? So they can do what? Join the army and help us? Or perhaps is it because they could care less who runs their country!

If you ask the average Vietnamese who started the war, the response would be equally divided. Fifty percent would say the communists, fifty percent would say we did. Go figure. I learned a lot working with the nurses. They told me things many Americans don't want to know or hear.

Off in the distance we hear the thunder of the approaching Medevac chopper. The marines' power with their Ontos and its six mounted recoiless rifles is held in check. If they fire into the mountainside, it might start an avalanche. They spin their tracked vehicle 180 degrees and head back, grumbling that they want to kill every "gook" in this country.

Hop, on the other hand, is yelling at a couple of his men. "What the hell do you mean you can't get the damn cartridge out of the bore? Here, give me that rifle." The guy hands Hop his rifle, who tries to get the weapon un-jammed. "Mine's stuck too, Sarge," says another.

My mind wanders, reflecting on the events. Charlie's won another one. This is definitely Charlie's war. He won't allow himself to meet us on our terms; he is too smart for that. In direct battle, *might* proves who's *right*. He knows that all too well. He's fighting us with the same strategy our forefathers used fighting for independence: stick 'em and run. And quite often, they didn't wear uniforms either. We were successful using that strategy back then against a world power, and Charlie might prove to be just as successful. That thought scares me. All that we are going through, all the sacrifices and hardships, might, in the end, be all for naught.

After five days of humping the mountains, I know I need help. While the previous medic went on squad patrols one out of three days, I am going out every single day. When I make radio contact, Flock just happens to be at battalion headquarters. When I explain the circumstances, he responds, "Permission denied Alpha Connecticut Sierra Papa Mike. Permission denied."

Sergeant Lims, who shares our command bunker with Lieutenant Pilgrim, is standing next to me during the exchange. After hearing Flock turn me down without substantial reason, he shrugs his shoulders and says, "Sorry, Doc. I know we're wearing you down, but I've got to send out patrols daily." I can tell he genuinely feels bad for me but won't go up against another career soldier.

Tomorrow will be the sixth straight day of humping the mountains—another tortuous ten-hour day, if we don't make contact, and if we're lucky. While out on patrol, the men carry a light load while mine barely decreases in weight. I guess I could have decreased the number of rounds of ammo to maybe 300, but I have that boy scout mentality—"always be prepared." I am also still carrying that spare bullet in my breast pocket, the one not meant for Charlie. Six hours on patrol, following a path used by the woodchoppers, the terrain changes from trees to tall elephant grass. The edges of the grass are sharp enough to cut you if you rub up against them the wrong way.

A different squad leader is in charge of this patrol. Sergeant Bob Pepper orders me to take the point position. Although I can object for a number of reasons, one of which is that I'm a medic, I accept his command because I want to show the guys that I have no reservations about leading them into battle. As I take the lead and move out, I think, if you guys respected me before for my capabilities, respect this. I may be the first among us to take a hit from a booby trap. Inside though, I am sweating bullets.

Two hours later I turn ninety degrees to follow the path and damn near run into a woodchopper! He jumps—as much surprised as I am. Holy shit! I speak first, smiling at him, scared shitless though trying not to show it. "What the hell are you doing here?" He tries to recover from the shock of running into me as well. The guys behind me freeze and hit the ground, sending word back to Pepper that I made physical contact with someone. They can't see the woodchopper from their vantage point, just me.

On his back there's a load of wood stacked so high that he has to bend forward at the waist. If he stood up straight, the weight of the wood would surely cause him to fall backwards. He tries very hard to convince me that he is friendly and means no harm, chattering incessantly in his native tongue. We don't have a translator with us to interrogate him. As I wait for Pepper, I study him while he continues to beg me to let him go, or so I assume. But for all I know, he could be telling me that he is going to blow my fucking head off.

He is too young looking and physically fit to be a woodchopper. Most of those we encountered on previous patrols were either young teenagers or older men from their late twenties to early forties. This guy standing before me appears to be too physically fit. His hair is even cut shorter than most, and he is between eighteen and twenty-two years of age. I just turned twenty myself.

"What have we got here, Harry?" Pepper asks as he rounds the corner in the elephant grass.

I reply in a low cautious tone, not taking my eyes off of him. "I think we've got ourselves a real live NVA soldier, Sergeant."

The woodchopper picks up on my saying NVA and responds as if he was just given a death sentence. In a barely discernible voice, he interrupts before Pepper can say a word, "No, no, no, no! No NVA! NVA number ten thousand!" He shakes his head so hard that he almost falls backward.

Pepper then speaks up, "Spencer, what are you, some kind of psychic? He's a simple woodchopper. Let's go." He nods his head at the woodchopper, waving at him to go by us.

I reluctantly step aside and gave him the room to walk between us. But I have to speak up, just one more time and say, "Look Sergeant, he's the exact age of a soldier. Look at his build. Ever see a woodchopper that physically fit? Come on, Sarge, let's at least search him."

Pepper doesn't like being challenged and snaps, "Shut the fuck up, Spencer. You're a fucking medic. You stick to your job and I'll do mine." His tone is threatening. It is dangerous to get into a heated debate on a squad patrol. For that matter, it is dangerous to raise your voice on a squad patrol. Squad patrols operate most effectively by stealth and secrecy. I search Pepper's face, looking for an opening in his words but find none. "Now just move out, goddamn it. That's an order. Understand, Private?" I give in, not wanting to push the issue any further. But I am convinced the son of a bitch is an NVA soldier.

Ten minutes later an AK 47 assault rifle opens fire from the direction the woodchopper walked. He knows where the path has taken us. His aim is pretty damn close, but he didn't count on my setting the pace of our forced march up the mountainside. After making contact with him, I purposely led the men at a much faster pace than I normally would have. We aren't out of range by any means, just further along than he thinks when he fires in our direction.

The side of the mountain seems to explode as we try to bury ourselves, diving in different directions. Some of the guys dive into the elephant grass, some drop where they are. I take refuge behind a large rock alongside the path. Once secure in my hiding place, I let out a bloodcurdling scream of frustration at Pepper's stupidity in not searching him. I am also angry with that fucking NVA scout for acting with such melodrama, convincing Pepper to let him go. I envision him laughing down there as he has us pinned down, firing on full automatic. That son of a bitch. I yell at Pepper who is somewhere behind me. "Now what do you think, Pepper? Is he NVA or what, you stupid . . ." I stop myself before I go any further.

Just as suddenly as the firing began, it stops. After about thirty seconds, Pepper shouts, "Anybody hit? Everybody OK?" Each man responds sequentially. I listen carefully, thinking I may have to respond, but to the man we are OK. No one was hit. All's well that ends well. Let it go Harry, let it go. I am still boiling mad at Pepper. That could have been a very costly mistake, but through some fluke of luck, we escaped unscathed. The remainder of the day, I can't shake the thought that I want to get wounded in action just to get the hell out of Vietnam. Just a small million dollar wound, nothing serious enough to cripple me for life or anything. I try to fight off that thought, but I can't get it out of my head.

After this patrol, my legs begin to show signs of serious muscle strain. My quadriceps are sending out incipient signs of break down;

even my butt is sore. Trudging up and down the mountains is taking its toll on me. I know it, and I pray I won't let the guys down because of my inability to keep up. I can also tell that I am losing more weight. I have to tighten my belt again. Since I've been in Vietnam, I've lost three inches from my svelte physique. I estimate my waist to be just twenty-seven inches. I had a thirty-inch waistline at Fort Campbell. I know because I had most of my stateside issue fatigues tailored.

No one ever thought of having his jungle fatigues tailored. It just isn't in the cards. Who are we going to impress with tailored fatigues? The comfort of loose fatigues comes well before vanity. Besides, if our fatigues were tailored, they'd cut into us while humping the boonies. That is the last thing we want out here.

As night falls upon us, my bunker partner produces a portable radio he received from his girlfriend. We're listening to music by light of candle, sort of cozy, but I wish I had better company than him. Given the reality of the situation, however, Oliver will do just fine, for the time being.

Hanoi Hanna plays Mick Jagger's "Can't Get No Satisfaction." In a seductive voice she says, "Does this song bring anything to mind, boys? Can't win at love and you certainly can't win at war with us, The People's Party. Think about that on your date tonight with Mary Palm." She closes her satirical commentary by climbing onto her soapbox. "We also want you to know we have been at war for thousands of years. We have defeated every conqueror starting with China, which ruled over us for 1000 years. Their reign of terror ended in 938 A.D. France, and its allies ruled over us for 150 years. We defeated them at Dien Bien Phu, in the fall of 1954, taking thousands as prisoners. Did you know that G.I.? Do you know that thousands of Frenchmen died while in captivity! And like you G.I., they never felt they could possibly lose in battle to us, a frail little yellow-skinned people. Like you, they too, couldn't adapt to our way of life. Like you G.I., they didn't really want to be here in Vietnam. How you doing out there, G.I.? Are you lonely? Are you tired? Do you want to go home? We, The People's Republic are at home, and *you*, G.I., *you* are the invader to our homeland. Go home, G.I., go home. You won't win this war, G.I., and no matter how long you stay here, you will not win. And now for your listening pleasure, I play for you 'Can't Get No Satisfaction,' by Englishman Mick Jagger."

Oliver and I laugh at Hanoi Hanna, while we get into the groove, twitching to the music's beat as we sit on our sand-filled bunks. There is no room to dance in the bunker. So, without commenting on Hanoi Hanna's words, for deep down within us we know she is right, we devise a little game of who has the better moves to the beat of the music. When it is Oliver's turn to watch, he asks if I had any black blood, "For a white boy, you can move, brother. You got soul!" I stop to watch him and reply in kind, "Olive Oil (his nickname), you sure you're black? You ain't got no sense of timing, man." Then we slap each other five, enjoying the camaraderie.

Our lives are on the line and if necessary, we'll all go down together. Ergo, *we are brothers bound in a fraternity of fear and fatigue facing the possibility of death on every step of every patrol.* Oliver makes me laugh when he says, "Brother, when I get back to the block, I'm gonna find those dude's Fear and Fatigue and I'm gonna whip them to death. No lie, Spence. When I look them up, I'm gonna wax 'em."

The next song Hanoi Hanna plays chills us out. This is one we can relate to and makes me think of Beatrice. I trust she is fine. I wish her well. The music plays as the words allow our minds to drift. *"Over the mountain, across the sea, there's a girl just waiting for me."* We both become rather melancholy during the song.

After three more long days out on patrol, I'm more exhausted than ever. I have no energy. My nerves are on the edge, and I have a growing anger about myself, the men in the platoon, the weather— you name it. I can't go on without some relief. I feel like I could sleep for a month. Instinctively I sense I am experiencing a meltdown of mind and body.

I go to Sergeant Lims and tell him I'm at my mental and physical limits of endurance and need to call battalion headquarters and request relief. I am so tired and edgy that when I get on the radio, I violate all established protocol. Instead of coming up on the frequency saying "Hotel Hotel," symbolizing headquarters, I simply state, "Hey, battalion headquarters, you out there man?"

Lims eyes nearly pop out of his head. He grabs for the mike and says, "Harry, have you lost your mind? Give me that mike." As he wrestles the mike from my grasp, a slightly confused voice comes back over the radio. Lims barks for me to get the hell out of his bunker, saying, "You don't know what you're doing, trooper. I'll take it from here." As he begins to talk on the radio, he raises his arm and points the way out. I don't argue.

Walking back to my bunker as dusk approaches, I think, no problem, Sergeant Lims. I'm simply not going out on patrol tomorrow. Sorry 'bout that. I'm just too pooped to participate. That little voice within me tries speaking to me, but I am in no mood for rational thoughts. I simply don't care anymore.

After twelve hours of solid sleep I step out of my bunker at the first sound of the chopper delivering breakfast. Once it lands, I am surprised to see Steve Best, my ole buddy. He looks as fine as a hair on a frog's head. It is great to see him. He has been recuperating for the last three weeks from malaria. He looks refreshed and clean. I don't realize how dirty we all are until I see how clean he is. What a sight! I run up to him anxious to find out what the hell he is doing here. When I see him carrying his equipment, it dawns on me. Oh, my God! He's here to relieve me! But the chopper has already begun to rev its engine to take off. Still advancing toward him, my mood tempers. The chopper lurches forward with its nose pointing down and goes airborne. Nope, he's not relieving me.

We shake hands vigorously and he says with a broad smile, "Ass Kick Two to Ass Kick One, I hereby officially inform you that I'm here to go out on patrol every other day, thereby affording you some rest." He puts his left hand on my right shoulder and says, "You look terrible. What's the matter, kid? Can't take it any longer?"

My muscles relax some and I answer, "You're damn right, Best. I was minutes from refusing an order to go out on another patrol. You're a godsend. How'd you hear about that?"

"Our platoon leader, Lieutenant Edmore," he responds. "Someone got a hold of him directly and said you were in tough shape, needed a break. That's it. No big thing man. I was sick of just laying around that hospital with all those fine . . ."

"Stop," I say, "I've got the picture."

Steve looks great compared to the last time I saw him. I felt much better then, but my crotch rot is itching nonstop. As I go to my bunker with Steve in tow, I introduce him to Oliver Lamont. I then ask Oliver if he wouldn't mind finding another place to sleep, explaining that medics should be together to discuss medical stuff.

Oliver is cool with that and pokes fun at me, saying, " I knew it all along, dude; you just don't like black folk." I respond jokingly. "Is it that obvious?" We all laugh while Steve and I help Oliver find and set up new diggs. All is right by the world. I feel a huge sense of relief having Steve with me. As it turned out we all had the day off—no patrol would take place this day.

During the night, it starts to rain without let up. The noise of the rain hitting the steel roof of our bunker wakes us both.

"Hey, Spence, you awake?" he asks.

"Yeah, Steve, what's up?"

"I was just thinking, how do you take a shower out here?"

I smile to myself and respond, "Oh, we have a lot of bathtubs up here," and wait for his response.

"OK, I'll bite. What the hell are you talking about? Bathtubs. Shit." He is a little agitated. He knows that I am toying with him

"It's called your steel pot, Steve. You pour water in it, stick your ass down near it and wash your asshole and balls, man. That's it, buddy."

"Are you shitting me, Harry?'

"That's all we've got to clean up with, Steve. Each man is allocated three steel pots full of water per day to bath in."

"Tell me you're shitting me, man. Don't bullshit me, Spencer, I'm in no mood for bullshit."

I begin to laugh with such intensity I can't answer him. The more I laugh, the angrier he gets. The angrier he gets, the more I laugh. I'm so hysterical laughing that it's difficult to breathe. Somehow, I manage to tell him that I'm not bullshitting him.

When it sinks in, he mutters, "Well I'll be a son of a bitch."

I can't resist a shot at that comment. "Always have been as long as I've known you, Steve."

He barks, "Shut the fuck up, will ya? I've got to get some shuteye. I'm the one going out tomorrow, remember?"

"Sure do, Steve. Good night."

After about thirty minutes and just before I nod off, Steve speaks up again. "Knock it off will you?" His voice indicates he is serious.

"Knock what off? Steve, I was nearly asleep."

"Stop fucking with me, Spencer. Keep your goddamn hands to yourself. Don't be playing any of that funny shit on me, man. I know you're a goddamn queer, you asshole. This ain't some frat house with some Mickey Mouse initiation rituals to pull on me. Now I'm telling you, if you touch me one more time, I'll knock your fucking block off. Got that?"

I want to string him along as far as I can, but I guess I should tell him before he jumps on me. I am smiling in the dark on the verge of laughing uncontrollably again. But I manage to say, in a sincere tone so he doesn't think I am pulling his leg again, "Oh, oh that! What you felt was not me, Best." I mock his agitated demeanor. "It's the rats." I pause for a reaction. Not hearing one I continue. "They come in here every time it rains. No big thing, man, chill."

Steve goes ballistic. He reacts with such force that he hits his head on the steel roof at least three times while he desperately scrambles to get out of the bunker despite the pouring rain. Steve has gone mental. He is screaming like a madman. "Rats! Are you crazy? Jesus! Get me out of here! Holy shit!"

Steve pushes the bunker door so hard it rips off its hinges. He crawls right out into the fucking rain. I lose it. I laugh so hard that, not only do I cry, but I also damn near lose control of my faculties. I have to beat myself in the stomach to stop from laughing so hard. It is hilarious. I have never laughed so hard in my life. Rats are no big deal to me. I grew up with them, the four-legged variety as well as the two-legged ones.

After he comes to his senses, he cautiously crawls back into the bunker. I lit a candle while he was outside. His eyes dart about, genuine fear written all over his face. He says to me, as he inches his way back in. "Do you know there are rats in here? Or are you just bullshitting me again?" He looks like he'll kick the shit out of me if I say the wrong thing.

While reaching for my M-16 to remove the cleaning rod taped to the front stock, I try to calm him down. "Look," I tell him as I put the rod between the end of the bunk where it meets the sandbag wall, "they're harmless."

I poke down where I know the rats are. One of them lets out a screech of objection. Steve, still on his knees, halfway in the bunker, reacts again. He fights hard to control himself as he watches three of them scurry out in the open, running to their next hiding place.

"Jesus Christ, you're crazy. You know that, Spencer. You're absolutely crazy." He backs out the doorway again with rain bouncing off his back. He is soaking wet.

I coax him back in saying, "It'll be all right. Now, just get your wet ass back in here or you'll catch your death."

"Yeah," he allows, "I'll catch your death if they bite me, you son of a bitch."

The next morning, the rain has stopped, and it is warmer than usual. Steve is already out with the first squad, so I decide to take a steel pot bath. Lims is near by. As I finish cleaning myself and towel off, he walks toward me. I always keep my boots and pants on when I bathe—simply dropping them down around my ankles. Lims goes into what looks like an Irish jig. "Jumping Jahosaphat! Those are the biggest damn crabs I've ever seen!" He jumps back as if horrified by the sight.

Of course I think he is just pulling my leg. Innocently I respond, "What are you talking about?" trying to cover my modesty.

"What am I talking about? Jesus, Spencer! Those are the biggest crabs I've ever seen! How long have you had them? You look to have ten generations of them on you."

I begin to believe him. "You sure, Sarge?" I ask, eyeing him to see if he is pulling my leg. "Are they really crabs? Maybe I just got them." I am looking for a way to hide my stupidity.

Lims is genuinely concerned. "Not a chance, Harry. Those guys have been on you for months." And with an inquisitive tone he asks. "Haven't you been itching, son? Go ahead, use your fingernail. You can scrape them off. Try it."

I look down at the black mass huddled around my crotch and hairline and pick at one. Holy shit! It moved! This is the most embarrassing moment of my life! A medic with the crabs who doesn't even know it. "Jesus, Harry, you stupid shit." I hurriedly pull my pants up.

"Sergeant Lims, I need to use the radio. I've got to call for some crab powder and ointment. I don't normally carry that stuff. Having the crabs is not a qualified emergency that warrants the need to carry it while out in the field."

He retorts, "In your case, it sure as hell is an emergency. Get enough for everybody. We all might have them now." He turns to walk away, saying, "Just keep your distance, will ya?"

Within a couple of hours, I convince Sergeant Lims not to divulge the fact I have the crabs. If he tells anyone, I argue, it may start a psychosomatic epidemic. "Look, Sarge, if you tell them, it may distract them while humping the boonies. They have enough on their minds as it is."

Lims shakes his head smiling and responds, "Harry, I cannot fault your sense of reasoning. OK, I'll keep your condition confidential." As I thank him and he turns to walk away, he reiterates his admonition for me to keep my distance. "Boy, Harry, if I catch just one of those little sucking biting crabs, I won't be a happy camper. Now, just stay the hell away from me." He lets out a grin and goes about his business.

"Thanks, Sarge. Thanks a lot," I say and go about my business.

Later, a chopper drops off some items that Lieutenant Pilgrim requested along with two cases of crab ointment and powder. After unloading the crates, Pilgrim calls me to his bunker and asks in an alarmed tone, "What the hell are we doing up here with two cases of crab medicine, Harry?"

My face turns bright red with a wave of embarrassment. I stammer, not wanting to tell him the truth, and state, "Every now and then, Lieutenant, we are asked to pass out various medicines as preventative measure—similar to giving the men salt tablets." I say it as if I believed it.

He searches my face trying to determine if the statement is plausible. "OK," he responds in a cautionary tone. "Go ahead then, do some of that medical shit you're trained to do." He is somewhat perturbed, as if my rationale for having the medicines irritates him. He closes with, "But leave me a tube of that shit. Now out. I've got work to do."

As I carry the medicines to my bunker, I feel proud of the spontaneous and believable explanation I improvised. Way to go, Spence. You pulled the wool over his eyes with that one. Back in my bunker, alone, I tear open the boxes as if my life depended on getting the ointment onto my body. I feel like a junkie in critical need of his next fix. Ever since Lims informed me of the truth, the itching is very acute. I put an entire tube of the ointment on my crotch and asshole. God, it *itches*! I apply the ointment as if in a movie playing fast forward.

Tonight, as Best returns from patrol, I go to meet and study the men, to gauge their mood and energy levels as they carefully remove the protective barbed wire surrounding our mountaintop encampment. I nod at a few men, and speak to some, when I spot Steve near the end of the column laboring to walk. I smile, knowing he has tasted the strain of humping the boonies of the mountain chain.

When he sees me, he theatrically pretends to not be able to make it up the slope to Hill 358. I chuckle when he yells, "Ass Kick Two to Ass Kick One, Hhheeelllppp!" I then walk briskly toward him, anxious to hear his reaction to the struggles of climbing and descending the mountains. I knew before they approached they had not made any contact with Charlie. It was just another ass-kicking routine patrol. His eyes light up as I approach him, and he says, "Man, I must have lost a lot of strength when I got malaria. That shit damn near killed me. Forget Charlie. He doesn't have to kill me. Just going out there did the job." We laugh hard. It is a good laugh.

We stay at the barbed-wire fence, letting the remainder of the squad pass into the compound. After the last man in the patrol passes, we secure the gate and walk back to our bunker. Once inside, it begins to rain.

"Boy, Steve," I say, "you got lucky with that one."

Steve flings himself onto his bunk after dropping his rucksack just inside of the doorway. "Lucky? Shit. Take a look at me, will ya? I'm soaking wet—saturated with stinking sweat. I would've welcomed the rain. It would have cooled me off." He then digs around for a bar of soap in his toilet article kit, strips naked, save his boots, and steps out into the pouring rain to shower.

Later we settle down for the night, taking comfort from the elements when he asks, "What's that smell, Harry?" He sniffs the air, then his armpits and says, "It's not me, man. It's got to be you. What the hell do you have on that smells so bad, Harry?"

I hadn't realized what the stuff really smells like. It has been on me for nearly eight hours. I act surprised, stating, "Oh, that. It's just some ointment I put on to help out with the jungle rot I have on my legs and groin area."

He sniffs the air, satisfied that it isn't a dead rat and states, "Well, get better quick, will ya? That stuff stinks!"

Just before we drift off to sleep in the dark of night, Steve makes one final comment, "By the way, Spence, I'm calling Flock in the morning to tell him I quit. I hate this job." We both chuckle a little. Quitting is simply not in the cards.

We finally awake around noon, sleeping right through the chopper's earlier landing that brought us breakfast and fresh water. It is a beautiful sunny and warm day. We learned last night we have the day off. No patrol—great!

The men are in an unusually good mood with spirits running high. It is a pleasant change to see them smiling. While taking in the view, I notice a group of guys sitting in a circle. A Mexican guy has a small guitar and is singing, "They Call Me Mellow Yellow." He sounds pretty good too. A couple of brothers play the chorus role, responding with appropriate timing, "That's right." They are entertaining.

A group of guys not participating gather on their periphery, appreciating the spontaneous show, when Lieutenant Pilgrim pops his head out of his bunker and shouts for them to disperse, saying, "You guys are making a great target for Charlie. Now spread out, or so help me I'll send you all out on patrol." A patrol is the last thing we want on this beautiful day. The guys scatter like rats in different directions.

Sometime later, around 1400 hours, just killing time, and taking in the beautiful scenery, I can actually feel the crabs moving. I rationalize the medicine must be working. Suddenly, I feel one actually trying to escape by making a mad dash for my armpit. I swat instinctively, and look down to see it—yikes! It is a fucking crab and it's about the size of my baby fingernail. I pick at it and it falls off. Jesus! I've got to do something pretty damn quick—they're attempting a jailbreak, trying to get to my armpits and head hair.

Based upon the rapport I have with Sergeant Hop, I seek him out to share with him my dilemma, of course in total confidence. After I explain my problem, he states, "That's no big deal. I've had the crabs at least a dozen times in my life." His voice is truly convincing, resounding with confidence. "You got any alcohol, Harry?"

"Yeah."

"Well, you're in luck. It's a good sunny day, hot too. Take some alcohol with you and find a nice quiet spot. Drop your drawers, lay down and pour it on to them. Then take some sand and immediately sprinkle it on them. Then just kick back, and let the sun, alcohol, and sand do their thing."

I smile in relief, knowing that within a couple of hours my troubles and my embarrassment will be over. He then says, "I know this sounds crazy, but you've got to expose your asshole, too. They'll try to take refuge there and you *do not* want that to happen."

I nod in agreement, anxious to go do it, but ask, "What bearing do these items have on them? How does it actually work?"

In a sincere tone he responds, "The sun, which they don't like, will disorient them. The alcohol will sting them and sand will confuse them. They'll think they're out in the open and scramble for cover, leaping off you. That's it, brother, that's all you have to do."

I am grateful to have this homegrown recipe and anxious to go try it. Hell, what do I have to lose? I straighten up from the familiar Vietnamese crouched position I am in, turn slightly and thank him for the advice, and then tell him I'll keep him posted on the results within the next two hours. He casually waves me off stating, "You're welcome. Good luck." I make a beeline to my bunker to get some alcohol. Within a few minutes, I find a somewhat secluded spot on the hillside, position myself facing west and just do it.

With my pants pulled down around my ankles, I pour a half a bottle of alcohol on my crotch, grab a handful of sand, being careful to spread it evenly, and kick back. As I lie there, I think I feel movement. Good. It must be working. I raise my legs as a woman would in a sexual position, sunning my asshole. The tropical sun's rays begin to heat my unaccustomed-to-exposure parts with a vengeance. But it feels like it is working. As I lie there, I raise and lower my legs to keep from getting a cramp. I have never thought about it before, but holding ones legs up while lying prone is work.

After twenty minutes I pour more alcohol and apply more sand, thinking I'll give it a double dose for good measure. My ass is sweating profusely. It is an unusually hot and windless day. I have to wipe the sweat repeatedly as it runs into my eyes, burning and blurring my vision. I glance at my watch. One hour to go, hang in there, I think. It'll be worth it.

Off in the distance I hear a faint giggle. I careen my neck around to find where it is coming from. There it is again. Then I spot a head ducking behind the knoll I descended from to get to this remote spot and I yell, "OK you pervert! Haven't you ever seen a pair of balls before? Get the fuck out of here, you asshole!"

Suddenly the entire platoon stands up, laughing uncontrollably at the sight of me naked with my feet in the air. I jump to my feet, pulling my pants up in one move. Embarrassed and humiliated, I yell at them, scolding them, trying to shame them for "getting off" watching me. I begin to walk in their direction. Christ, I think, if one of them took a picture, I'll just die.

Hop, trying to control his laughter, is on his hands and knees, but manages a response in between fits of laughter. "Harry, my boy. you've just been had!" More laughter erupts.

I stop moving toward him and just stand there, in a state of shock, watching them bust a gut. When it dawns on me that Hop set me up, I scream with growing anger, "You mean to tell me this is all bullshit?" Their laughter increases.

After about thirty seconds, Hop manages to contain himself. I can tell he has something more to say, so I just wait, looking around in a state of bewilderment and embarrassment. I feel like a hooked fish with the fisherman holding me just above the water, letting me dangle, wither, and twist in the wind. "OK," I say in a resolute tone. "What the hell is so funny? Come on, Hop, fill me in." Then it dawns on me he might have even concocted the recipe.

In horror I scream, "You mean to tell me it doesn't work! You just made that shit up?" The guys were falling on the ground, laughing with abandon as if they just heard the funniest joke in the world. Even my "ole buddy," Steve, is on all fours, pounding on the ground, laughing right alongside them.

At the sight of them laughing so hard, I begin to laugh myself. Still smiling, I step closer toward them, saying in earnest, "Come on, guys, let me in on it will ya? Hop," I say with a smile, "It doesn't work, does it?"

He wipes the tears from his eyes and responds, "If they get drunk enough, it will! They'll then stone themselves to death and you'd be rid of them!"

In a valiant effort to ward off my humiliation I manage to laugh with them. It feels good to laugh and to see all of them laughing in return. "Get them drunk and they'll stone themselves to death." Not bad, I think, not bad at all. Suffice it to say, Hop's homegrown recipe didn't work!

December 3 1966

I have been struggling to maintain mind, body, and soul, going out on patrol every other day without contact with Charlie. But with each step of each patrol I wonder if this will be the day, or, as the terrain changes, if this will this be the spot. That little voice inside me keeps me on guard. "Be careful, Harry. He's out there. You don't know where or when, but he's coming." I try hard to make that voice shut up. I don't need distractions while on patrol. Anything less than full concentration will give Charlie the edge. If he's out there, I want to spot him before he spots me. I don't want to consciously contribute to my own demise by arguing with myself and walking into a trap.

Somehow I have to be more diligent in my note taking, in documenting this madness. Hell, if I weren't here, I'd think it was a nightmare myself. I miss being home. I miss a flushing toilet, a light switch, and I miss not being able to go see Beatrice anytime I want. She doesn't know it, but I carry a picture of her in my diary. I have to put in for R&R. In our last two letters we've nailed down the time we'll meet in Hawaii. I'm looking forward to not just seeing her, but to getting out of this country and onto American soil, even if it's not the mainland.

We're slated to go back to Bien Hoa tomorrow. Operation Winchester is over. This operation claimed one more medic killed in action, while four were wounded. I never really knew Bill Williams. He came to our platoon a couple of days prior to shipping out. I do, however, remember his theme song, *"Don't Mess With Bill."* Williams repeatedly played that song, dancing to it, reinforcing the image he wanted us to believe. While dancing he'd say, "You really don't want to mess with me," and would continue to dance and sing along in harmony, *"Leave my Billy alone."*

Of those medics wounded, three were minor, not requiring a major hospital stay. The fourth medic sustained a serious injury. Gary Bartmore was involved in an accident with a utility vehicle called a "mule." It flipped on him, crushing his face. No word whether he'll return. I was not that close to him, but Steve Best was. They are from the same hometown and the same neighborhood—NYC, Queens.

In what is fast becoming a custom, a battalion formation is held within two days after the termination of each operation. The ceremonies honor our fallen comrades. A total of eight guys lost their lives in Operation Winchester, while sixteen were wounded. Eight rifles with bayonets are stuck in the ground draped with steel pots. Boots lay in front of each. In tribute to them, we salute their memory as taps plays in the background. Others among us are awarded various ribbons.

After being in country nearly six months, approximately two-thirds of the medics have been issued their Combat Medical Badges (CMB). You earn a combat medical badge for coming under fire while tending to the wounded. Despite the number of times I have made contact with Charlie and tended to the wounded, I haven't received mine. I have my suspicions as to why, but deep down, I don't think I have come under fire as much or as often as those who were awarded their CMB's—least I thought so listening to their stories.

Chapter 13

SURROUNDED BY CHARLIE

OUR NEXT OPERATION begins December 7 and will run through December 23; this one is entitled Canary Duck. We snicker amongst ourselves, saying "Canary shmary, how about Sitting Duck!" Twelve choppers will be in the first assault wave. They'll drop us off—God knows where—and return for more men. As a rule, we are never told where we were going. It could be China for all we know. Once on the ground, we'll scramble to set up a perimeter of defense. Because the LZ is initially unsecured, the first wave is inherently more dangerous than the second wave. The first wave on the LZ will provide the second wave security if Charlie decides to welcome us.

Flock sees fit to not only put me on the first wave, but in the lead chopper. As we fly low and fast to the LZ, I think about that and just shake my head in silence, smirking. He's really trying. I had to give him credit; the son of a bitch is consistent.

Our landing, much to the chagrin of Flock, is uneventful, as was the second wave. We are in a large clearing surrounded by dense foliage. The jungle. The almighty omnipotent jungle. We respect its beauty and its power to humble us both physically and mentally. A small red ant can bring a man down, withering in pain, if it bites him in the wrong place; leeches, if left clinging in numbers, can sap not only your strength but your life's blood, as can the infamous Vietnamese mosquito. If bitten by a Bamboo Viper, the size of a benign American field snake, you'll be dead within minutes. Yes, the jungle, the boonies of Vietnam, reigns unparalleled in power and mystery. Charlie, however, is a close second.

Pilgrim is unusually tense, overseeing and positioning each man as we established a perimeter securing the area. Within fifteen minutes, squad patrols are sent to sweep the area about 100 yards into the jungle directly in front of the perimeter. Something's definitely up here. There are 250 of us on the ground, two infantry companies— Alpha and Charlie Company—set up in a semi-circle defense. Word has it that Bravo Company is holding back as ready relief in case we need them.

Two uneventful hours later, word spreads that we are going to be visited by General Abraham, whoever the hell he is. Therefore, this must be some kind of a show set up for him. I suspect it is a way for him to say he's been out on the line, in the jungle, with his men. Oh, well, Harry, I think, can't do a damn thing about it, so just go along with it.

To help pass the time I count the days before I can go to Hawaii to meet Beatrice. There are just eighty-one to go. Then I wonder how many more before I'm a free man. As I begin to calculate, the thunder of approaching choppers is heard off in the distance. The sound dictates that there are definitely more than one—I guess three. Sergeant Lims hurriedly walks up and down the line of us at jungle's edge, encouraging us by saying, "Look sharp, men, stay awake. The general's coming. Let's not make any mistakes. Look sharp, stay awake." Jesus, that pisses me off. The implication is that we're not normally on our toes. Give me a break. I'm always on my fucking toes. My life depends on it, you asshole.

But of course, I keep that part to myself, responding instead with, "No problem, Sarge." He winks at me, "Good man, Doc, good man!" The powerful choppers rise above the tree line. The pilots slow their aircraft, three of them, with a nose-up attitude, blades chopping at the air. Two of the choppers are gunships. The third looks like it just came out of the factory—all shiny and polished compared to the other war raptors that bear the scars of contact with Charlie. No doubt, that is the general's chopper.

As his chopper descends, the order is given to fire into the tree line in sequence of squads. Each man is required to empty two magazines.

Pilgrim raises one hand in the air while listening to the telephone-type handset with the other. As if someone gave him the order, he yells, "First squad, fire." And the jungle's power falls to the barrage of bullets penetrating it, knocking down small trees, while the underbrush sways back and forth.

The noise is deafening, our collective power frightening. If anyone is out there, they are in a world of big hurt. The firing lasts as long as it is designed to. It takes about ten minutes to complete the exercise. This little get together is nothing more than an exercise to show off our military might for the general. We are convinced Charlie is nowhere near us. Besides, when was the last time a general came out to view a firefight? Not a chance, Mack!

A few minutes after firing in to the jungle, I glance in the direction of those who have gathered, instinctively knowing they are the general's welcome party. Our battalion commander, Iron Mike, is on sight and is flanked by members of his staff—along with the two company commanders of Alpha and Charlie companies, as well as their XOs. The general is escorted by members of his entourage and a couple of reporters. Man, do they ever look clean! All I want in life right now is to be clean and not feel tired.

It takes about another ten minutes for them to shake hands and greet one another. Iron Mike then proceeds to walk the general up and down the line of us lying on the ground. Lieutenant Pilgrim notices me staring at them rather than looking into the jungle and snaps, "Turn your goddamn head around, Spencer. We're here to protect the man, not ogle him." Like a good soldier, I obey his command.

Seconds later, out the corner of my eye, I see Pilgrim snap the general a salute as they approach our position. Well, I'll be a son of a bitch! The last time I saluted an officer in the jungle, I got my ass reamed. And here this West Point officer is saluting another West Point officer in the fucking jungle! Now I am convinced this is just a charade—a fucking show for the general! I feel totally disgusted. "Lieutenant Pilgrim, Class of '64, it's a pleasure to meet you, Sir." Shit, give me a break!

The general stops to make small talk with Pilgrim and then moves on, returning his attention to our battalion commander. He points as he walks, asking, "Is that where we suspect they are, Mike?" Iron

Mike responds with military staccato; his words are sharp, fast, and clear. "Yes, Sir," he glances at his watch and continues uninterrupted, "Smart Darts due in two minutes sharp, Sir. We'll do a sweep of the area once you depart, for a body count."

Smart Darts, as we called them, are F-5 Freedom Fighter bombers—sleek, air force jet aircraft that fly exceptionally fast. They are probably based in Thailand or the air base at Bien Hoa. They are tried and true, highly maneuverable, and fast moving aircraft. And they look like darts. One of the greatest aircraft the United States has to offer.

Within two minutes, just as Iron Mike said, two Freedom Fighters shoot over the LZ at a remarkable rate of speed. They are so fast, if I hadn't been looking in the direction they came from, I would not have seen them. The guys just ten feet to my left and right are staring into the jungle when the aircraft shoot over us. One, James Johnson, reacts as if they scared the hell out of him. With eyes wild in bewilderment he looks at me and asks, "What the hell was that man? I hope to God they're on our side!" I smile and respond, "You bet your sweet ass, James! They be ours!" He likes the way I said that and lets out a cry of "Airborne!" His prompt is followed up by someone else who responds, "All the way."

The sounds of the jets' engines continue to rumble because their afterburners are engaged and because they're going vertical right over the LZ. The guys are excited, not only from firing into the jungle, but by the sounds of raw power coming from the jet aircraft. Within a minute we can no longer hear the jets.

All falls quiet. We're just waiting for the hammer to fall. Then I hear a low deep whine and look up to where it might be coming from. One of the jets is streaking toward earth in an attack angle. Wow! What an amazing sight. Then he releases two bombs, heading for the jungle somewhere in front of us. But, wait a second! He's not pulling up. Oh, my God, he's not going to make it!

He ejects from the aircraft, looking like a rag doll attached to a string. But his parachute fails to fully deploy, and he is falling at an incredible rate of speed. He's too far away for me to make out if he is conscious or not. But he isn't kicking or struggling to untangle his risers above each shoulder, which appear tightly wound together. I watch in fascination as the jet continues straight and true to the pilot's last commands, right toward the ground.

It doesn't look like it was hit or lost control. It simply continues on its earthbound path until I lose sight of it as it passes over the tree line. Seconds later I heard the distant sound of an explosion and then the shock wave ripples through us. Holy shit, I hope the guy's OK. But then I can't help myself from thinking, "OK, Mr. Pilot, now you're going to taste my world. How do you like that shit?"

Iron Mike orders Charlie Company to hightail it to the crash sight. My company, Alpha Company, goes in a different direction, sweeping the area for a "body count." Within two minutes of the jet crashing, the general is airborne, accompanied by the two gunships.

Later, I'll read in a *Detroit News* article about the incident.

December 7
PARACHUTE FAILS
SAIGON (AP)—An American pilot was killed today over South Vietnam after bailing out of his crippled F-5 Freedom jet. His parachute failed to open. The pilot was on a tactical air strike 10 miles from Bien Hoa. Troops of the 173rd Airborne were in the vicinity in a firefight with Viet Cong. It is not known whether communist ground fire struck the craft . . .

On Operation Canary Duck, the crabs who have made themselves at home for some five months really let me know they don't appreciate my attempts to eradicate them with chemical warfare. I itch so bad that I am left with one alternative—shave them off, along with all my hair, from pubic to asshole. Settling down after a company-size patrol near dusk, I feel confident enough to venture some twenty-five yards out from our perimeter and find a small creek. It is perfect for what I have in mind. I strip down to my birthday suit, but keep my boots on, just in case. With a can of shaving cream and a fresh shaving blade, I lather up, committed to win the war with these suckers. I wash what I don't shave. Afterwards, while walking back to our defensive perimeter, a growing warmth emanates from my groin and asshole, which triggers an alarm. Oh, shit. I glance at the can to see what type of shaving cream I used. And sure enough, the cream was spiked with menthol! Damn, it burns like hell. Well, here's another fine mess you've gotten yourself into, Spencer, you conflagrating fornicating sphincter canal. Way to go, Harry, you stupid shit!

DECEMBER 12 1966

Tonight, while I am writing in my diary, Lims walks by and asks that I put his name in it. I laugh and tell him I will. It's amazing how many guys want to have their names recorded in my diary. Word is getting around that I'm keeping a diary, recording events as they occur. But I've got to be careful—they can confiscate it. Keeping a diary while out on line is strictly forbidden.

The next day we move from the rubber plantation to Bear Cat. We are 16,000 meters north of the LZ that we were dropped off at a few days ago. No contact with Charlie—yet.

The next day as we hump the boonies, I feel pretty secure with 120 guys cutting through the jungle's underbrush. We're supposed to get to our destination, a former NVA base camp, around noon. They tell us our objective after we're in the bush, but never while in base camp. Once we come upon their base camp, it's apparent they left in a hurry, leaving many personal artifacts behind. I scavenge a large water pan and some rope to build a makeshift portable shower. The only problem is that I don't have any spare water. But it looks like it'll work. Oh, well!

Mail call this evening produces two letters. One is from my mother informing me that my dad had a serious heart attack and is not working. She is going to attempt to get me reassigned under the terms of what the army calls a "Compassionate Reassignment." The other letter is from Beatrice confirming that she's booked for our rendezvous in Hawaii. She talked a couple of her friends from college into going with her. While I don't particularly like that idea and its implications, I have no control over it. It is her choice. And I will be more than pleased just to see her.

As darkness falls, Charlie pays us an unusual visit. Truth sometimes is stranger than fiction. He has actually surrounded an entire company of 120 men with bullhorns, and now he's calling out to us. It is absolutely fascinating to listen to him. Although he is a good distance from us, occasionally we understand what he is saying. "Hey, hey, G.I.," and then laughter followed by, "Hey, Joe, go home—you die." It gives us the creeps. For whatever reason, our company commander doesn't call for an air strike or artillery support.

Then the words come from a different direction. A couple of times, Charlie calls to us simultaneously from different directions. It turns out to be a sleepless night for all of us. Because I am not assigned to be on perimeter watch, I stretch a test market hammock sent to me by a company stateside between two trees and drift off to sleep.

At 0100 hours, I am thrown from my hammock by several explosions dancing around our perimeter. Crawling on all fours, I make my way toward Lieutenant Pilgrim and the radio operator's position. If anyone knows what is going on, they will. The explosions come so close I feel the barometric pressure drop in that nanosecond before the shells' thunder hits. The impacts hurt my chest, sucking the air from my lungs, and vibrating my inner ear. Trying hard not to panic and feeling disoriented, I crawl on my hands and knees in the dark, not quite sure if I am headed in the right direction. Another explosion forces me to cry out, "Someone tell me that's friendly fire!"

Lims responds, "Yeah, Harry, just be cool, keep your head down and shut the fuck up."

I am immediately relieved to hear that and kiss the earth, responding, "It would have been nice if you had given us some kind of warning, Sarge."

Lims retorts, "You don't need to know everything, Harry, just shut up."

The shelling lasts about ten minutes. The 175-millimeter howitzers about twenty miles from us provided the honors tonight, keeping Charlie or the NVA at bay. Part of me is content to fight this way, any way that doesn't call for direct contact with the enemy. The other part of me wants the direct and deciding battle we've been trained to fight. Sometime later I learned we are the advanced "securing" party for the 9th Infantry Division that will soon arrive. Perhaps another way to look at it is that we are the advance target to divert Charlie's attention while the 9th Infantry comes in on our heels as we vacate the area.

While humping the boonies the next day, I try to take my mind off the misery I have been subjected to since arriving in this godforsaken land. I feel as if I've been betrayed, both at home and here in the army. It's not what they led me to believe it would be. And I know I'm here because of the judge who gave me no choice. "It's either jail or the service." As an infantry soldier, I've had two years of preparation and experience. I'm trained to kill, fire, maneuver, contact, outflank, and squeeze the enemy into submission or death. But, as a medic, I'm trained to protect and save my fellow paratroopers, if necessary, at the expense of my own life. That feeling is growing and I cannot fight it— I'm not going to make it out of here in one piece.

According to the *Stars and Stripes*, U.S. casualties are averaging a thousand a week. Broken down, this figure equates to 200 a week killed or missing in action, 800 wounded. Those are American— not Charlie or his cousin the NVA—casualties. It's a phenomenal number that I find hard to believe. Those figures swirl in my head as I hump the bush.

Still humping the jungle, looking for "the most dangerous game," my right arm brushes up against a large tropical leaf. Casually, I look down and am shocked to see my arm is covered with hundreds of red ants. I stop dead in my tracks. They haven't bitten me yet, thank God.

Without fanfare I lower my M-16 to the ground and reach for the mosquito repellent I have strapped to my helmet. Very slowly, careful not to agitate them into a biting frenzy, I pour the liquid over them. Ninety percent of them fall off of me in seconds. I smack the remainder, getting bit just a few times. Man, am I lucky. If I hadn't spotted them when I did, they could have done a lot of damage in mere seconds.

December 24 1966

Christmas Eve finds us back at base camp. It is quiet—our platoon tent is nearly empty—it's just me and Arthur Gamesmore, a white guy from Mississippi who is a devout racist. Most of the guys are attending one of many religious ceremonies taking place or getting smashed at the Friendly Fire Club. Because it is unusually quiet, I hear angry voices not far away, heading toward us. As they get closer, I hear one of them say, "Fuck 'em. I'm going to get me a fucking white boy. Them white motherfucker's gonna die."

Racial tensions run high in base camp, but not in the bush. In base camp fights between whites and blacks are common. Suddenly, one of four black men rips open the wooden screen door of our platoon tent. The first one through the door has a .45 pistol in his hand. I jump up from my bunk, simultaneously reaching for my M-16 hanging right above my head and a magazine of twenty rounds in my pilllow case. I secretly stashed some ammo after each operation until I had enough for a full magazine.

"Freeze motherfucker! Don't come out of there," he shouts, looking at my hand in the pillow case. "Don't be pulling nothing out of there you don't want shot off. Understand, motherfucker?" We make eye contact. "Don't do it man," he commands.

I have the magazine firmly in hand, but decide not to take it out. If he sees it, he'll blow my fucking brains out. I look up at him and state, "All right, guy, just be cool." I slowly pull my hand out of the pillowcase. "I'm cool. You just be cool, too," I chance a look at Gamesmore. His eyes are wide with fear.

I can feel my heart beating, pushing against my chest, and I'm short of breath. Gamesmore meets my gaze and makes a gesture that says, "All things equal, better you than me, brother." I respond to his look of indifference and say to the would-be shooter, "Look, man, all things being equal, I'm from Detroit," and with false bravado add, "you've got the wrong guy."

The brother screams, "Shut the fuck up, motherfucker." His coal black eyes burn right through me when he continues, "get the fuck over here," pointing with his free hand at the ground just a few feet from him. "Now!"

With my hands outstretched at my sides, I reluctantly obey, eyes cast down. As I slowly walk toward him, my mind races—he's not really going to do this, is he? No, he can't. Then it hits me. Oh my God, this is the place! This is the time! I try summoning that little voice within me, but he isn't speaking. He's probably in as much shock as I am.

He screams, "On your fucking knees *white boy*."

Surprisingly, a relaxed feeling comes over me. A calm I have never experienced, free of anything I felt just seconds earlier—no apprehension, just a peace. So, this is how it ends, my Father. OK. It's OK. While kneeling, my eyes are cast down. Out of nowhere I think about Sergeant Ugly, my platoon sergeant who said to me in basic training, "Look at me, boy. Look a man in the eye before he's about to eat you alive."

As I raise my head to look at him, the black hole of the barrel aimed at my forehead is the first thing I see. I let my gaze travel upward, where our eyes meet. At that very instant the guy leans forward to make sure he won't miss his target. I close my eyes, accepting what is about to happen. I then hear an M-16's bolt slam into the rifle's bore, pushing a bullet into the chamber. It is followed immediately by the booming voice of Leon Dallas, a.k.a. Brutus, "Give me a righteous reason, nigga. Go ahead. You kill my brother, you're dead, nigga."

He then pulls so hard on the screen door that it comes off its hinges, and walks into the tent, weapon on hip, aiming at the shooter. The shooter turns toward Brutus as if annoyed, not threatened. He and the other three guys turn their backs to me. The sight of Brutus just standing there—feet spread, slightly bent at the knee—all 210 beautiful pounds of him, makes me feel as if everything will turn out alright. Without a shirt, his muscular physic alone is intimidating, but add an M-16 firmly in hand and he looks like the Grim Reaper. The guy with the .45 walks toward Leon saying in a high-pitched tone, "What be wrong with you, brotha? I be playing, man. Shoot, I ain't about to do noffin. I jus fithen to fuck him up a little, brotha? That's all."

Leon cuts him off with a mocking smile, "Put that weapon down, brotha." The would-be shooter slowly, ever-so-cautiously obeys. The guy may have been playing, but it is quite apparent that Leon, the Brutus, isn't. Brutus scares the hell out of them as he continues, "And there won't be any of you left alive to dispute our story of how you came busting in here, the medical platoon tent, wanting to take one of us out. Now, nigga, bend down again and pick up your weapon. I want you to die with it in your fucking hands. Go on. Pick it up."

Before anything can happen, I jump from the kneeling position, grab the gun, and with a roundhouse right, I slam the weapon right into the side of his head. The sound of cold metal contacting bone startles even me. It sounds like the snapping of a two-foot chicken wishbone. The guy never knew what hit him. His upper body follows his legs as they bend at an awkward angle. When he hits the ground, air is forced out of him by the impact.

For a second, I think I killed him. I bend down to check his pulse as blood flows from the side of his head too quickly. The shooter's friends immediately begin begging for their lives when I scream, "We're goddamn medics, for Christ's sake!"

"Sorry, man, we didn't know you's be medics."

Leon barks, "Get him up and get your black asses outta here, right now. And, if somebody wants to know where his weapon is, tell him to look me up. My name is Brutus, you got that, nigga? Now, get the fuck outta here!"

As they scramble to pick up the shooter, I give them a pressure dressing to put over the gaping indentation I put into his head and tell them, "Here, put this over his head and take him to your aid station, wherever you guys are from. And if you want, tell them the medics from the 4th battalion did that to him, and make sure you tell them why." They seem grateful to get out of the situation they created just a minute earlier. "No problem, man. We're sorry. We didn't know you guys was medics."

As soon as the guys are out of the tent, and with my heart racing, I look at Leon with hands outstretched, as if to give him a hug, but he cuts me off with a shrug of his shoulders and a wave of his hand, saying, "No big deal, man. Chill, Spence."

"No big deal? No big deal? Leon, you saved my fucking life!" I embrace him, kissing him on the neck and say, "Thank you, my brother. I'll never ever forget this . . . never!"

For reasons unknown, Operation Canary Duck is extended from its original December 23 termination date to January 6 1967.

Chapter 14

CEASE FIRE TRUCE

DECEMBER 26 1966

I AM BACK ABOARD an assault wave of twelve choppers with Alpha company's second platoon. As we board the choppers, we ask each other if anyone knows where we are going or what we might be encountering. As usual, no one knows a damn thing. There's supposed to be a cease fire truce during the holiday period, allegedly agreed to by both sides. I wonder what gives.

As the choppers fly in tight formation, I think of Karl Lessnau, the kid from Kentucky, whose chopper crashed. I close my eyes to block out that memory. Just another bullshit mission, I think. Thirty-some minutes later, the choppers begin to slow and descend, I look out, straining to see our landing zone. Immediately I jerk back, pressing up against the back of the pilot's seat in disbelief. One of the door gunners raises his microphone from his lips and screams, *"Hot LZ, hot LZ!"*

Both machine guns on each side of the chopper open up, firing nonstop. *This is not good.* Each of us instinctively arms our M-16's; bullets slam into fire-ready position. What I saw scares me like I've never been scared before. We are landing in Charlie's base camp! Small tents are pitched with a number of fires still smoldering. As our chopper slows, the door gunners are still firing when a gunship shoots past us, spewing forth rockets, jettisoned from its pods.

On the other side of the chopper, two guys from the platoon open fire with their M-16s. The door gunner screams at them to stop, but they pay no attention to him. As we near the ground, the gunners wave us off. Jesus Christ, we're still five feet in the air! With all this weight I have strapped to me, the fall could kill me if Charlie doesn't. Screw it, I'm airborne, I tell myself as I step onto the skids of the chopper and leap away. I hit the ground and roll just as I was taught in jump school.

As I momentarily lie there, I am pleasantly surprised that I did not hurt myself, which is only a minor relief! I roll onto my belly and spot a tent just twenty-five feet from me and let out a burst from my M-16, just in case Charlie is hiding in there. Sorry, Charlie, I say to myself. I just want to live.

Others among us are not as fortunate in jumping off the chopper. Some were carrying upwards of 2,000 rounds of ammo, and the weight caused them to hit the ground too hard, too fast. As we fan out, crawling on our bellies, firing into various tents, the choppers take off at a sixty-degree angle of attack. With the nose of the aircraft pointed skyward, I think they might go into a stall and fall back onto us. And to add to the confusion, because of the aircrafts' noise, we can't tell if we are being shot at. Gunships continue making passes over us, releasing their payload on the hidden enemy. God, Louie, help me, big fella, wherever you are.

Lims jumps up as the noise dissipates, yelling, "Second platoon— follow me!" We all rise to our feet and start running and firing at the invisible enemy. The thunder of the choppers begins to grow again. Bravo Company, all 120 of them, is coming on the second wave. Lims realizes he has little time to shout out his plan of action before the second wave of choppers arrives. He screams between bursts of fire. "We've got to get off this LZ now."

He then goes into action. "OK, men," he yells. "By the numbers we're going to fire and maneuver just as we've trained. Stay in your present positions. By squads, first squad is first, take ten paces men, firing into the tree line as you go, and drop. All other squads follow on my command. Sergeant Pepper, you ready?"

"Yo!" Pepper shouts in return.

"Hop, you with me?'

"Let's do it, Jimmy," Hop responds.

After Lims hears from the other squad leaders, he adds an addendum, "Medic and radio operator, move only when I say so. Got that?"

Hoornstra and I respond, shouting over the growing thunder of the approaching choppers. Lims turns his attention back to the others nearby. "OK, first squad only, go! Go!"

Eventually we all make it to a mound of earth, which affords us a small degree of protection. At best, the rise of the mound is only two feet high. Hunkered down behind the mound, I hear the buzz and pop of bullets as they pass overhead. Then, above the noise of dozens of men shooting, I think I hear Chuck Holt screaming. "I can't take it. *I can't take it anymore!*" I look around and see him running in my direction, side-shuffling, still screaming while trying to shoot at the enemy. Unfortunately, his bullets are hitting the ground five feet in front of him. It's apparent he's lost it.

Chuck is screaming at the enemy, but I can't make out what he is saying. As he gets closer, I can tell he is crying. In an effort to get his attention, I scream, "Chuck, get the fuck down! Get down, Chuck!" I frantically wave my arms at him. Suddenly his helmet flips forward, falling to the ground. His face jerks slightly upward, then it snaps backward, violently forcing his chin toward the sky. He drops where he stood, never knowing or feeling what hit him. Brain fluid spews forth from his forehead with the pressure of a small water faucet. I close my eyes to block it out. I know he is dead, and I scream in agony, "You stupid goddamn son of a bitch, Chuck!" as if he can hear me. "What the fuck is wrong . . . with . . ." And then that inner voice takes control. "Forget it, Harry. It's a done deal."

I bury my face in the earth to block out the madness. Chuck Holt, the guy who told me on board the ship coming here that he wouldn't make it. And I chastised him for thinking that way.

Lims crawls over to me, "Harry, are you OK?" Sensing that I might crack myself, he doesn't wait for an answer. "Look, Harry, he got what was coming to him. He brought it on himself. Just stay cool —stay with me, and everything will be all right."

He searches my face to determine my state of mind, and a smile spreads across his face. The bullets fly over our heads, some closer than others. In a light-hearted tone, he continues, "Remember West

Point, son?" He winks at me, and barks, as if to elicit a positive response, "Airborne, son. This is what it is all about!"

I acknowledge his prompt with a weak but determined, "All the way, Sarge." Then I gather myself, feeling a growing sense of anger and state, "Let's get this shit over with, Lims." And then with increasing anger I scream, "Air fucking borne! Let's do it!"

He winks again, just as he did back at West Point. "You'll be just fine, Harry. Stick close to me and you'll be just fine." In a situation of near chaos, this man makes me feel better and more secure in this otherwise horribly uncertain environment. I love him for that, and, as our eyes make contact one more time, I nod, saying, "Thanks, Sarge. I think I'll be OK." In an upbeat manner, he responds, "Then let's get this show on the road, trooper," returning his attention to the ensuing battle.

Meanwhile, Lieutenant Pilgrim has taken control of moving the squads forward, having reached the safety of an abandoned VC bunker about seventy-five feet in front of us. He gives Lims a number of different hand signals as Lims chances a peek over the mound of earth protecting us. "OK, men, it's our turn." There are just three of us left to leave the security blanket of the mound of earth—Lims, Hoornstra, and me. Lims states, "On the count of three—one, two, three." And we bolt over the mound, firing into the tree line while those to our front also lay down cover fire for us. As I run, I feel strange sensations of wind brushing by my cheeks while firing my rifle at the distant treeline. And then it dawns on me while I'm still running toward the safety of the bunker—*those are goddamned bullets!*

Recognizing that, I drop like I've been hit, right on top of my M-16. The rifle pushes into my chest with such force that I think for a second that I broke my sternum. The barrel brushes up against my face, burning my cheek from the heat of firing it. I recoil in the shock, not only from the heat of the barrel, but the fact that I could have shot my own face off. Jesus Christ, Harry. Think, man, think. Don't panic.

Deep inside me, I begin to hear the clapping of hands with boots, hitting the pavement in unison. The beat has been drummed into me. It jumps to the fore of my thoughts. I begin to laugh, openly laugh at the incredible stupidity of this situation and of the war itself. How incredibly stupid it all seems.

As Lims, Hornstra, and I crawl the remaining distance to reach the safety of the bunker, I think I hear the faint thud a mortar makes somewhere off in the distance followed by someone yelling, "Incoming! Incoming!"

Five to ten seconds later the earth shakes near the bunker that the platoon used for shelter. "Medic! Medic! We need a medic over here!" The thought of Chuck's body still lying behind the mound of earth fifty feet to my rear makes me wonder who'll take care of it . . . him. "I'm coming!" I scream as my toes and knees dig into the soft earth, propelling me forward. "Medic! Medic!" the pleas for help continue. In anger I shout back. "Shut the fuck up! How many times have I told you not to yell *medic*, goddamn it? I'm coming."

Another thud is heard along with another scream of, "Incoming!" The earth shakes. That one was so close that the tall grass I have been crawling through ripples from the shock wave. The nanosecond implosion hurts my ears and the upper part of my lungs as it attempts to suck the air out of me. When we reach the relative safety of the bunker, I ask, "Where is he?" Three guys point down the span of stacked rocks that Charlie constructed as a fortification for the bunker.

Upon first glance, I am relieved that he appears to be in good shape. The men used their personal pressure bandages and wrapped his thigh prior to my arrival. However, blood has already saturated most of the dressings. The guy grimaces in pain. To get a better picture of the extent of his injury, I carefully remove the dressings, checking the wound for any arterial bleeding. He convulses with pain and is going into shock. He looks chalky—ashen—as he screams through clenched teeth, "It burns, goddamn it. It feels like it's on fire, Doc!" I acknowledge his pain, saying, "I know, man. You'll be OK though, no major bleeding. You'll be fine."

He has a gaping, jagged tear in his outer thigh with internal fibrous tissue oozing from its opening. His blood is dark red, indicative of venial bleeding, not arterial, which in comparison flows fast and is bright red. I struggle with the question: Should I or shouldn't I get an I.V. into him? I've never had to administer one before while in the field. When in doubt, there is no doubt.

While the men continue to take cover from the mortar attack and occasionally fire back at Charlie, I struggle to get a vein. Despite the on-going firefight, I keep poking and prodding, looking for a back flow of blood in the intravenous line, which will indicate I am in his vein successfully. His two arms are full of tiny holes when I finally hit pay dirt. Up until then, I was beginning to doubt my own abilities. I inject some morphine and fill out his evacuation tag, giving the date, time, and the treatment I performed on him. My hands shake so badly that I can barely decipher my own writing. But the doctors and nurses need to know what has or hasn't been done to the patient along with the timeline involved.

Despite gunships strafing the tree line, the firefight lasts about four hours. Ten guys in the platoon are wounded during this firefight. First aid supplies are nearly depleted. Fortunately, none of their injuries are critical. Most injuries are from the shelling. A couple of others are from bullets, minor wounds. Luck lends its hand on this operation, this day.

Due to the large number of men injured, their evacuation proves to be a major undertaking. Some simply twisted their knees or ankles when jumping from the choppers as we landed. Others need medical attention STAT. Tom Brown, the senior medic on this operation, sets up a triage point where the wounded are to be taken. The firefight has all but ended, save a few snipers left behind to keep us guessing. Per Runner's direction, we take the injured to the helicopter's designated pick-up point. Each medic is called by radio in order of company and platoon. We have to report the conditions and number of our wounded.

Once this information is collected, Runner prioritizes movement based upon the severity of injury. We form a line that leads to his position, where each medic reports who in his platoon needs more attention than others. In a macabre way, it reminds me of the meat truck driver delivering his goods to the corner grocery stores in my neighborhood—the medic states which cuts are better than others.

Because of the constant peppering we are getting from the elusive snipers, we dare not use the LZ where we initially landed. A new LZ and triage area is hastily hacked from the jungle, but the choppers can't land. The surrounding trees are too close for them to attempt a landing and too big for us to chop down. Therefore, the injured have to be hoisted out on either a stretcher or the penetrator, thereby dangerously exposing both the chopper and patient to Charlie's wrath.

Meanwhile the guys are fanned out in all directions in various platoons doing their best to suppress Charlie. But every now and then Charlie gets through, shooting at the Medevac choppers and wounded being pulled to safety. No Geneva Convention Codes honored in this war. "Time out" to evacuate the wounded is not honored. The Red Cross painted on the nose of a Medevac chopper simply serves as a bull's eye.

Choppers line up in the sky, constantly moving, waiting for their turn to pick up the wounded. The evacuation process takes a couple of hours to complete. When it is my turn to get my guys on to the chopper, I stand in awe, looking up as each man is hoisted up by a thin metal wire rope.

I happen to be looking at the pilot, taking in his footwork as he pushes on his rudder pedals, holding the chopper steady, when I see the Plexiglas window near his feet shatter. Incredibly, he doesn't even flinch.

Jesus. Either that guy has nerves of steel or he doesn't realize he was shot at. Whichever it is, it doesn't matter. Looking up at his aircraft, I respect his intelligence in mastering the art of flying and his nerve to come here and let himself be shot at or killed. At that point I develop a new-found respect for chopper pilots, all pilots really, but especially for Medevac pilots. Thank you, I say to myself silently. Thank you for being here.

While walking back to my platoon's location, I pay very close attention to the snipers' bullets, as they seem to be flying in all directions. Feeling somewhat satisfied that I have done the best I could for the wounded, my mind drifts to the Medevac chopper pilots. What greater love does a man have than he who would lay his life down for a stranger? All on the ground respect them for coming to us in our time of greatest need. Thank you, my brothers. God speed.

As I continue to walk, sometimes crawl, I reflect on what is happening. Every time someone is wounded and/or killed, part of me is also injured and/or dies along with him. Feelings of loneliness and despair continue to grow within me. I am beginning to feel a void of emotion. Thinking of my mother's last letter to me, a "Compassionate

Reassignment" is fine by me. But I will not return home. I had too
many beatings growing up. I can't forget all the times my dad belittled
and ridiculed me. No way, Jose.

In fact, I remember a time when I got into a fight with my older
brother. As he walked away, I went to kick him in the ass, but my foot
missed its mark, hitting him in the groin, striking his testicles. When
I saw the pain I inflicted, I was immediately horrified and terribly
sorry. Later, however, when I went home, my father decided to inflict
the same pain upon me. He wouldn't stop hitting me with his belt
until he found the exact spot where I had kicked my brother! Even as
a kid I thought that was cruel and unusual punishment. Once you
leave home, you can never really go back. Tough shit, old man, life is
not fair. Those are your words, not mine.

After three more hours, Charlie vanishes. It always ends as
abruptly as it begins—no warning, just silence. Even though the firing
has stopped, we believe it is a trap. After any engagement, we sweep
the area and look for bodies. This time proved to be no exception, and
we uncovered only two enemy dead. Seven hours of intense exchanges
produces two fucking enemy dead. In my mind, Charlie won this
round . . . again.

Later, I'll read this article published by the *Detroit News*:

NO MAJOR VIOLATIONS MAR TRUCE
SAIGON (AP)—The lunar New Year truce eased
through its second day today with neither side in the
Vietnam War claiming a major victory. But U.S. and
Vietnamese military authorities reported 114 incidents and
said 28 are considered significant. Among the significant
actions was a seven-hour firefight between a company of the
173rd Airborne Brigade and an estimated 30 Viet Cong
yesterday in War Zone D north of Saigon.

A U.S. spokesman said the American company of about
120 infantrymen suffered moderate casualties. Two Viet
Cong are reported killed. He said the Americans were
moving to a new position and the guerillas opened up from
bunkers and the trees. The Viet Cong used more than 100
hand grenades, rifle fire and Claymore mines in the engagement, the spokesman said, while the Americans called in
artillery and air strikes. The air attacks continued for four

hours while the Americans removed their wounded. The U.S. company was making a positioning movement and was not conducting an offensive operation, the spokesman said. He gave no further details.

With at least two more days to go in the cease-fire and all reports for the second day not yet in, the number of incidents is running slightly behind the total of 122 reported during the two-day truce at Christmas. But it is considerably below the 178 for the same period over the New Year's weekend.

Meanwhile, the U.S. Command announced that 118 Americans were killed in South Vietnam last week, 290 are wounded and 11 are missing or captured. The report for the previous week had been 131 killed, 822 wounded and 6 missing. A Vietnamese spokesman reported 170 government troops killed last week and 26 missing, up from 157 and 17 missing the previous week. The enemy casualties are reported at 1,309, a rise from 1,256 the week before and a Vietnamese spokesman said 276 enemy soldiers were captured last week.

Other allied forces—South Korea, Australians and New Zealanders—reported one of their heaviest weekly casualty tolls of the war: 38 men killed and 53 wounded.

The U.S. Command also announced that 6,000 more men are added to the American military force in Vietnam last week, bringing it to a total of 410,000. Apparently, most of the new arrivals are to fill out the 9th Infantry Division, the last major organization to arrive in the country.

Chapter 15

ENOUGH IS ENOUGH

B ACK AT BASE camp, we have a couple of days to relax and get cleaned up. My orders for a Combat Medical Badge (a CMB) still haven't been approved. I don't understand why ninety percent of the medics have received their CMB and I haven't received mine. Christ, even Flock has a CMB! Now there's a scam if I ever saw one. The only time Flock ever came close to combat was when he flew out in resupply choppers, never stepping foot in the jungle or going out on a patrol. What a pathetic joke. The man has no conscience.

Medics have died in combat, and here this son of a bitch has the nerve to wear a CMB. Bullshit, pure, unadulterated bullshit! Because I know in my heart I have earned a CMB, I had Lum's laundry sew CMBs on my fatigue shirts. I am so proud when I put on a fresh pair of fatigues and look down on my left breast where the CMB is sewn just above my wings. It looks great.

While walking into the aid station where we all congregate and hang out when in base camp, I bump into Flock in the doorway. He immediately sees that I have a CMB sewn on and states, "Who the hell gave you permission to wear a CMB?" Not waiting for my explanation, he shouts right in my face, "Take that CMB off, Spencer. You do not have *orders* to wear one and as far as I'm concerned, you *haven't* earned one!"

He must be pulling my leg! He couldn't possibly be serious. Before I open my mouth, I search his face for any clues that he just might be busting my chops, but I don't see one, and respond, "Look, Sarge, you and I both know I've earned the right to wear a CMB. The orders are just late coming down the pike. I'm sure they're in the system somewhere. Come on—give me a break, will ya? What's the big deal?"

He draws back his lips, exposing his teeth in what looks like the snarl before the bite. "What's the big deal? Well, I'll tell you, Private," he says as he reaches to rip the CMB off my chest, "you haven't earned it!" I recoil from him touching me.

"Are you serious, Sergeant?" I ask, dismayed and bewildered.

"You're goddamned right I'm serious. Now take it off, or I'll write up an Article 15 on you for being out of uniform. Is that what you want, Spencer?"

My mind flashes back to all the injured to whom I have attended. I remember the bullets, the mortars exploding, the artillery sucking the wind out of me, and the choppers reigning hell fire as the rockets pass overhead. I then look at the CMB sewn on Flock's fatigue shirt and ask, "Why? Why are you putting me through all this bullshit?" In a pleading tone, trying to hide my growing anger, I continue, "You've busted me by two paygrades, put me on hard labor until I bled, stuck me out on the line presumably to get me killed and now this? Why, Sergeant Flock? Why?" Fighting to control my emotions, I am shaking inside as my eyes began to fill with tears—tears of rage, and tears of sorrow. "What have I done to you to make you to treat me like this?"

He senses his victory. Throwing his head back, he breaks out in a smile then leans closer so no one can hear, "Because you were born, boy!"

I step back, nod my head in acknowledgment, thinking, I just poured my heart out in capitulation, pleading for mercy, and this son of a bitch says that? I'll kill him. My thoughts pass through my lips before I can stop them. While trying to control my rage, I step forward to get closer to him and whisper, "I swear to God, Flock, if it's the last thing I do, I'm going to kill you."

I storm back to my platoon tent hell-bent on a mission. I know what I have to do. Nothing can stop me. My thoughts turn to God.

God, why have you forsaken me? What have I done so wrong as to deserve this? If you cannot or will not tell me, I will kill him. I have to. I'm sorry, I just have to.

Sitting on my footlocker at the end of my bunk, I bury my face in my hands and cry. Spasms of sorrow convulse my body. Somehow, up until now I have managed to contain the feelings that have been festering deep inside of me for the past six months, but now it is impossible to hold them back. The floodgates of sorrow open up. One of the medics in the tent, Ted Dziengelewski, tries to console me, saying. "Harry, it ain't about nothing, man. Relax. You've got less than six months to go and you walk out a free man. I know how you feel. Don't even think about it. He's not worth throwing your life away for."

I take my hands from my face to look at Ted. I feel as if I already killed Flock and state, "I'm sorry, Ted, I have to do this. I just have to. I can't take it anymore." At that statement the tent slowly begins to empty out. One by one the guys file out, no one saying a word. I am left alone to think about how and when I will do it. I play and replay the actions over and over in my head. I then decide now is as good a time as any. I grab my M-16 and that fully-loaded magazine I keep hidden.

A calm comes over me as I let the bolt slam the bullet into the chamber. Upon leaving the tent I flip the switch to full automatic. I want to make it quick. I'll empty the twenty rounds in him within five seconds and then kick him in his goddamned face for good measure.

As I walk briskly past other tents on my way to the aid station, various guys along the way look at me, my weapon with the magazine in it, and give me room. Some just stare, and some state in hushed tones, "He's going to do it. Hey, psst . . . Spencer is actually going to do it." My only concern at that point is that word might get to Flock before I do.

Some of the guys however, plead weakly, cautiously, trying not to provoke me, saying, "Don't, Harry, don't do it. Put that weapon back. You'll get yourself in deep shit man." Undeterred, I think about my father and wish he were here. I'd take him out, too, for good measure. That son of a bitch would never hit me, my mother, or any of my brothers or sisters again. Then I think about Captain Martin. Yeah, if he were here, he'd have to go as well.

At this point nothing in the world matters to me. I am committed to do the unthinkable. Others among us have shot their sergeants, but failed to kill them. I won't fail. It's a done deal. In the doorway of the aid station I pause, weapon-at-ready, expecting Flock to be there. Everyone present, including the infantrymen who were there on sick call, stare at me. Some stare out of fear, some out of curiosity. A couple of the Crazies smile—they know the look.

"Where is he?" I demand. "Where's Flock?" Dan Reynolds is the only one of ten medics present to speak up. "He's in his tent, Spence." As I turn to go to Flock's tent, which he shares with other senior NCO's, he adds, "You sure you really want to do this, Spence?" But I don't acknowledge him. I continue, hell-bent on what I have committed myself to do.

On the way to my "rendezvous with destiny," my mind plays back all the wrongs Flock has committed: how he laughed when Chuck Holt tried to confide in him his fears, how he berated Steve Best for not keeping up with us as we ran around Johnson field at Fort Campbell, how he favored blacks over whites, and how he gloated aboard ship as Lieutenant Wronges put his .45 to my head.

Just as I am about fifty feet from Flock's tent, I am blindsided and tackled from my left rear. The force is so overpowering. I go down, my weapon accidentally firing. The bullets penetrate the sandy soil right in front of me, and, as I fall face forward, the M-16 slips from my grasp. I am sure it is Flock, and immediately fight back—kicking and punching until I realize it is Leon Dallas and Ted Dziengelewski, both very big men. They pin me in seconds.

A foot pushes on my chest. I look up to see the barrel of an M-16 just inches from my face. It is Flock! Jesus Christ! I'm going to jail for sure, and I failed to kill him! Son of a bitch! As our eyes meet, he states in a very non-threatening tone, "OK, Spencer, we're even. I've got your point, but have you gotten mine?"

I don't know what the hell he is talking about, but respond, "Yeah, yeah, I've got your point, Sarge."

"Then get your punk-ass self up and out of my sight."

He takes his foot off my chest while Leon and Ted let loose of me. I don't understand anything at this point. I'm numb. Have I gotten off attempting to kill him? Scott free? Are Ted and Leon on his side? I stand and brush off the dust and sand from my fatigues, still trying to comprehend what has just taken place, but nothing registers.

With his rifle still pointed at me, he bends down and pushes the magazine release on my weapon, which is on the ground, ejecting it, and tells Leon to clear my weapon of the lone cartridge still in the bore. Having accomplished that, he lowers his weapon and states, "If I have to tell you one more time to get out of my sight, I'll reconsider my options, Spencer."

Ted and Leon pick up on the cue before I do, each grabbing me by an arm with such force that my feet leave the ground as they hustle me off towards the aid station. Once we are out of Flock's hearing range, Leon is the first to speak, "You are one crazy son of a bitch. Do you know that, Spencer?" Ted joins in, "I might add a lucky one too. Do you realize he just let you go after what you pulled?"

It begins to sink in. "Oh, my, God. I'm not going to jail. Holy shit! I can't believe it." I then state to them in a tone of disbelief, "Do you guys think he'll take me down on charges?"

Innocently they both respond, "We don't think so," with a smug look about them. I dare not ask anything further. Instead, I count my blessings. Holy shit! I just tried to kill my Sergeant and got away with it. The guys escort me all the way back to our tent and tell me to take the day off, saying, "Flock won't be bothering you anymore, Harry. We think he got your message—loud and clear." They both smile as if they know something I don't. Since I am afraid to ask, I just let a sleeping dog lie.

On yet another note, Gary Bartmore came back today after that accident he had while driving the "mule." His face is still swollen; he looks different. After I realize I got away with attempted murder, my spirits are up; I feel good. Had a long conversation with Doctor Pierce this eve. He heard about the incident with Flock and seems very concerned. I try playing it off as a joke, but I don't think he buys it. Tomorrow we're off to the boonies again.

Chapter 16

ATROCITIES

O UR NEXT OPERATION is entitled Operation Cedar Falls. It runs from January 8 through the 25 and we are told it is the largest operation of the Vietnam War for U.S. Armed Forces. It is another hot, muggy day, and our pace is agonizingly laborious and slow. After six hours of humping the boonies, we come upon a small campsite vacated by Charlie. It provides me an excuse to sit back and relax, while the others wade through the personal belongings of our enemy and the spoils of war.

Finding a shady cool spot away from the intense rays of the tropical sun, I slip out of my rucksack and drop to the cool earth. Nearby a couple of guys are reading the markings on a stack of large burlap bags. One of them calls out to me, "Get this, Doc. These bags read: *Donated by the Lone Star State of Texas, U.S.A., to the People's Republic of North Vietnam.* What do you make of that, Doc?" He closes with, "Make sure you record that one in your diary, man. Nobody would believe it otherwise."

My curiosity is aroused so I get up to go to see for myself. At first I thought the guys were making it up just because I found a nice, quiet, shady spot and want to screw with me. Well, I'll be a son of a gun! I look at the wording and sure enough, it reads exactly as he said: *Donated by the Lone Star State of Texas, U.S.A., to the People's Republic of North Vietnam.* I shake my head in disbelief, thinking, whose side are we really on in this war?

Seconds after reading the writing, I hear in a tone of bewilderment and surprise, "Hey, come see what I found. It's a tunnel, a fucking tunnel." My curiosity gets the better of me, and I walk over to where a group of guys have gathered. One of them is on his knees pushing aside the camouflage. With the enthusiasm of a child, he describes how he accidentally stepped on it and how one leg sank into the earth as if to swallow him. The tunnel's opening is no more than an eighteen-inch hole. Too small for any one of us to slip down into, I think.

Within a couple of minutes Sergeant Lims walks up to us, looks down at the tunnel opening and asks with a smile, "OK, who's going in, guys?" We look and feel like kids in elementary school, afraid to take the dare. I speak up before someone volunteers me. "I don't know about you guys, but I'm no hero. I ain't going down there!" I have heard stories of booby traps and of coming face to face with the barrel of a gun in total darkness. Still, I have a morbid fascination to learn firsthand what it would be like in a tunnel, but I tell them again, "No not me, fellas, besides I'm a medic, not a tunnel rat."

Lims studies the other's faces, trying to glean if any of them could be goaded into going down the tunnel.

"Hey, will you look here," someone else calls out. "I found a Honda motorbike." He emerges from the foliage into the clearing where we are congregated. The red motorbike looks brand new. Since I always wanted a motorcycle, I eye it with fascination, especially since it was found here in the thick of the jungle.

Meanwhile, Lieutenant Pilgrim, serious as ever, is at the tunnel's opening, picking at the ground, smelling it, studying it. I can tell he is concerned about what might be down there. He confides in Lims, saying, "What do you think, Sergeant Lims? Here, smell this, will you?" He offers his hand to Lims, who bends down to meet his outstretched hand, palm up. Lims studies it cautiously, studiously trying to recall the smell's origin. He gently rubs it between his fingers with deliberation one might give a fine wine before tasting it. "I'm not sure, Lieutenant. I've smelled that before. I just can't place it."

The lieutenant grows agitated as the men continue to find more personal items Charlie left behind. He has a look that says something is wrong with this picture. He then snaps at the men who are carrying on like they're in some bizarre Easter egg hunt. "Knock it off, men. We are not on a picnic out here. Put all that shit down. Squad leaders, set up a perimeter of defense 180 degrees to the front." He adds, "All of the other platoons are to our rear and our flanks."

Because the men don't jump like Pavlov's dogs to his command as they would in base camp, he adds sarcastically, "Now, gentleman. Right fucking now!" He stands up to emphasize his authority. "That's an order, if you hadn't noticed." The men reluctantly obey, but it is obvious they don't like it. A couple of the crazies are even bold enough to toss out a negative response, saying, "Yeah, whatever, Lou. You be the bossman." However, Pilgrim wisely decides not to follow up on the guy who made that insubordinate remark. He is smart enough to know just how far he can push those guys while in the bush.

As the squads fan out in a defensive semicircle, they find more spoils of war. I stay with Sergeant Lims and Lieutenant Pilgrim for the time being, figuring if there are booby traps, I'll let those guys trip them before I venture to see what they uncovered. Pilgrim points to a man who was a little too slow to move out with his squad and just happens to be small enough to squeeze into the tunnel's opening. "You, trooper. Yes, I'm talking to you. You think you're that well camouflaged? Come here."

The guy turns and casually responds while rolling his eyes, "Yes, Lieutenant Pilgrim, what can I do for you?" Pilgrim, not wanting to waste any more time, doesn't beat around the bush. "Take off your equipment and go down into this tunnel. I want to know what's down there. The white powdery stuff just might be an explosive. We might be sitting on a powder keg."

The guy's eyes widen when he responds, "Oh, I see. We're sitting on a powder keg, and you want me to go down there and do what, light a match to see?" The atmosphere is tense. The guy looks at me, then at Hoornstra, I presume to see where we stand on the issue. Although I think it's a debatable order, I'm not sure about taking sides. Hoornstra, at six foot four inches tall, is comfortable that he won't be ordered down the tunnel.

Hoornstra surprises me though, saying to the guy, "An order is an order, trooper. Get your ass down there, you fucking pussy." Even though I personally think that Hoornstra overstepped his jurisdiction, I offer no counter. I am just glad it isn't me going down there. I'm down to about 145 pounds, thin enough to slip past the opening to the tunnel. I cringe at the thought.

The guy gazes at both the Lieutenant and Sergeant Lims and slips out of his rucksack. Pilgrim is relieved, saying, "Here, take my .45 and flashlight. Be careful. If you see any trip-wires, back out immediately, but we've got to learn what is down there. Do you understand, trooper?" The guy nods his head, but his eye contact with the lieutenant tells his true feelings. Like a snake slithering its way through the jungle, the guy squeezes past the small opening, head first. Instinctively, I back up, thinking any second its going to blow. But nothing happens.

After about five minutes, we all become concerned for his safety. Pilgrim is on pins and needles. Ten minutes pass, and he erupts. "Jesus Christ, where the fuck is he?" He is visibly shaken, perhaps at the prospect of ordering a man to his death. Pilgrim screams down the tunnel, "Brown, where are you? Can you hear me? Are you all right?" He listens intently for a response, but doesn't hear anything. Meanwhile the men who have fanned out find another campsite and are hooping and hollering at what they have found. It's like a carnival atmosphere. Not good, I think. Not good at all. It is all too easy. Too relaxing, too convenient.

Pilgrim suddenly snaps at Sergeant Lims to have the men shut up, saying, "Jesus Christ, Lims, can't you control your men?" Pilgrim leaves no doubt that he blames Lims for what the men are doing fifty-five feet away, even though the squad leaders are with their men. Lims sprints in the direction of the wayward men, tearing through the dense foliage. Within a few minutes, he returns. All we can hear now are the distant sounds of the men hacking at the jungle with occasional grunts.

Again, Lieutenant Pilgrim shouts down into the tunnel. Just as he does, Brown pops out of the tunnel headfirst. That not only startles the Lieutenant, who had his head at the opening, but all of us as well. Brown is ecstatic. "You won't believe what I found!" Pilgrim and Lims pull Brown up by reaching under his armpits. "Lieutenant," Brown says, "about twenty feet down the tunnel turns ninety degrees for a couple feet, then back up another ninety degrees, then sideways again and that leads into a large room—maybe six feet high and twenty-by-twenty-feet square. Another tunnel leads to a room that looks like a morgue—medical shit all over the tables and stuff and it stinks bad."

I interrupt, "Maybe a hospital, Brown?"

"Yeah, a hospital. It's a hospital. But in that first room, Lieutenant, it looks like some kind of factory setup. White powder, fuses, wire, that kind of shit, all over the floor and even tables are down there. Know what I mean, Sir?"

Before I am enlisted to go down into the tunnel, I turn and walk in the direction of the other squads, taking all my gear with me. Out of sight, out of mind, I hope. They're not getting me to go down there. No way, man, no way.

I leave the four of them and make my way to the others, curious to learn what the men discovered on their "Easter egg hunt." I had sent a cherry medic, Doug Fields, along with the other squads while I stayed with Pilgrim and Lims. I was interested in what he thinks of all this. It is his first time in the boonies. Replacements filter in as my fellow medics are either killed or injured. Fields is one of about eight FNG's (fucking new guys) to join us during the "cease fire truce." Therefore, my concern is not that my services might have been needed. Fields can handle that. I am simply curious about what was found and what Fields' impressions are.

I come upon Sergeant Hop's squad just as Hop is beginning to leave, heading deeper into the jungle for parts unknown. I have a great relationship with Hop. I like him and call out, "Wait up, Hop; I'll go with you." When we are a few feet into the jungle, clear of the others, he stops, turning slightly and whispers, "Be quiet, I think I smell Charlie." He is a prankster. I never know when he is pulling my leg, but I sniff the air. Sure enough, I smell something fowl.

We inch forward, weapons ready, stopping every few feet to listen. As we get closer, I recognize the odor as marijuana. We were told Charlie likes to smoke it as much as some of our guys. We begin to make out voices—they are Americans. Somehow, despite the fact there aren't supposed to be any of our guys beyond our platoon's position, a group of six guys are laying about in a small clearing. When we come upon them, they attempt to hide the reefer. The jungle is so thick that the air is stagnant. Hop, always the gentleman, engages them, "Hi, guys. What's going on? We're told no one was supposed to be out this far. Where's the rest of your squad?"

Despite their buzz, the men are scared that Hop will do something stupid and one of them responds, "This is my squad." The guy responding is a Spec 4. Strange, I think. In rifle companies, squad leaders are generally buck sergeants. "This," he points to those who sit near him, "is all we have left from Canary Duck. Charlie took out five guys from our squad. Got the squad leader too, that motherfucking son of a bitch."

Hop sniffs the air suspiciously. "What's that smell, guys? Smells like shit." As he takes a step toward the men, I step closer, following him. The dumb shit. Doesn't even know what reefer smells like. The men tense, thinking that Hop will do something stupid if he finds out that they're smoking pot. I recognize four of the six. They are from Bravo Company, but I don't know which platoon.

What really bothers me, though, is that four of the six are a part of the crazies. I'm not sure what they'll do if Hop does the right thing in the wrong place at the wrong time.

"Psst, Hop," I whisper. "Leave them alone. What you smell is marijuana. Let's get out of here." Hop looks me in the eye, thinking that I am playing a prank on him. I stare him dead in the eye, and say, "I ain't bullshitting, man. Now, let's go."

Fortunately, he believes me and we walk away. But I can tell he is mad at himself for not standing up to them. "Look," I say in an effort to calm him down, "they outnumber us three to one. Four of them are crazies. You chose well, Hop, stop thinking about it." As we continue back toward the men in our platoon, he mutters something about wanting to kick their asses, when the earth shakes from an explosion, damn near causing us to lose our footing.

It was an unusual explosion—muffled, but powerful. Then I hear the cry of medic shouted repeatedly. It seems that all the men are screaming for me. Immediately my breath leaves me. I begin sucking air in to compensate, pushing my way right up to and over Hop. As I trample over him, he yells for me to "be cool." In panic, I forge my way through the bush, ripping foliage and being ripped in return.

My M-16 snags a wait-a-minute vine, and, rather than struggle, I drop it, thinking, I'm a medic, I don't need a weapon to do my job. Suddenly, I hear screams that rattle me to the marrow of my soul. At first I think they are animal screams, but they turn out to be humans crying out in agony—a low-base tone at first, then building to a wail as if they recognize the severity of their wounds. I have never heard sounds like that from a human being before.

It scares me. There is more than one screaming. I try increasing my speed, but the jungle claws at my every move. The harder I try to bust through the foliage, the more I become entangled in it. Fuck! My goddamned rucksack is stripped from me as if some mythical entity has pulled it off. Fuck that, too. I still have my small aid kit with me when I come upon the first clearing, the one where Pilgrim sent the squads to form a perimeter of defense. The men are just standing there listening to the howls from further ahead. Fifty-five more feet to go through the foliage.

I catch a glimpse of Fields out of the corner of my eye just standing there too, as dumbfounded as the others. I scream at him to follow and to bring my rucksack. My heart increases its tempo like a race car suddenly shifting into low gear. Knowing I am headed toward Pilgrim and Lims causes the heart's rpms to jump two-fold. No! Not Jim Lims, please. Lieutenant Pilgrim OK, but not Sergeant First Class James Lims. My God, help me help them. The wails of unabated agony send jolts of adrenaline through my body.

As I break through the jungle into the clearing, the smell of burnt human flesh violates my senses with the power of a skunk's odor. Simultaneously, I see two men I don't recognize at first glance and then I gasp in horror. My God! It is Sergeant Lims and Lieutenant Pilgrim! I recognize them only because Skip Hoornstra has already removed Pilgrim's gas mask and is delicately taking off Lims' mask. Their burned jungle fatigues hang on them in shreds. Their hair is gone. And their skin has ballooned, some of it discolored white, some of it hanging from their arms and the sides of their faces. The bulk of their faces are unscathed, saved by the gas masks they wore when they went down into the tunnel. What a queer, morbid sight.

The contrast from face to body defies perception. Lims is on one knee with head down, trying, I'm sure, to understand what has happened and what is happening. The skin of his massive forearms, once covered with Irish red hair, now hangs as if he were wearing some Indian costume with strips of leather shredded for decorative purposes. Only this is no costume and this ain't no show! I gag in reaction to the sight and the smell. Fields, behind me, vomits, falling to his knees. I turn and grab his aid kit as fluid escapes, gushing forth from my mouth uncontrollably, spewing on top and down my arm. Fuck it. I don't care. My only thought is to get to Sergeant Lims. God will bless him, but I have to help him.

Through a closed jaw, so I don't vomit on Lims, I ask if he is all right, even though I know better. I want to know if he knows who he is and where he is—a way to gauge his conscious state of mind. Lims raises his head from its resting position on his forearm, and before he can speak, my question is answered in a heartbeat. He is dying from shock and the loss of his protective armor, his skin.

Instinctively, I grab his wrist, checking his pulse rate. But upon contact, his skin slithers under my fingers. I recoil in shock, looking him in the eye for his reaction to my involuntary response. Lims simply nods at me without saying a word, and, with teeth chattering uncontrollably, he lowers his head as he whispers something to me. I get closer to hear him, fighting back the internal spasms to vomit again, mucus dripping from my nose. "What, what is it Sarge?" I plead. "Talk to me, goddamn it! Tell me! What are you trying to say?'

Lims slowly raises his head again, making eye contact with me, fighting a battle deep within himself to speak, "Don't touch me. Take care of the lieutenant." I fall backwards in shock, wiping my nose and mouth, not believing what he said, and I try to get him to lie down on the ground. He tightens up, looks at me and manages to say it again. "Don't you dare touch me until you look at the lieutenant. That's an order, trooper!" I look in the direction of the lieutenant. Fields has done nothing other than to try to restrain Pilgrim from thrashing about in pain. "Oh, Jesus!" Pilgrim screams. "Oh, God, help me. What the fuck happened?"

By my observation, Sergeant Lims is far worse off than the lieutenant. And yet the lieutenant is kicking the ground rolling from side to side, writhing in pain. Not bothering to stand up, I crawl the distance, some ten feet to get to him and Fields. Fields looks at me soberly and apologizes for not doing anything to help him. His eyes are filled with tears, his nose dripping with vomit and mucus. "I'm sorry, man," he says in a defeated tone of pain and remorse. I grab him, but the stench of his vomit causes me to vomit again. It splatters on him as I scream, "You're a fucking paratrooper! We'll make it . . . together! Now get me an I.V. line set up now, goddamn it!" I push him away from me, partly out of disgust, partly to wake him up to this reality. We can't just click our heels and wake up in Kansas; Dorothy doesn't live here.

As Fields prepares the I.V., I grab the morphine from his aid kit and inject it into the lieutenant. An audience has gathered, some twenty guys stand around and take in this gruesome sight and smell. I manage to think proactively, screaming to no one in particular, "*Get me a One Alpha Dust-Off now!*" The second in command's face goes blank—Sergeant Pepper. When our eyes meet I yell, "Don't tell me you don't know where we are, goddamn it!"

Pepper's eyes go into the 1,000-yard stare as if he and we weren't here, when somehow Pilgrim has the sense to scream out our last known position. "We're 1,000 meters south by southwest of our LZ!" He then continues to convulse and writhe in pain while vomiting.

Within twenty minutes, the chopper is hovering over us. Pilgrim will be the first to go up, but before that can happen, the stretcher has to be lowered. The chopper can't land because of the dense foliage. I have been taught never to touch the stretcher or the penetrator prior to it hitting the ground because of the possibility of receiving an electrical shock. Tom, our machine gunner, doesn't know this. Despite my screaming at him not to touch it, Tom can't hear me over the noise of the chopper, and sure enough, he gets such a jolt that it knocks him unconscious. Fields is with Pilgrim. I'm huddled next to Lims. Seeing what happened to Tom, I yell for Fields to go check on him. Great, a third casualty. That's just what I need.

I leave Lims' side and signal for a couple of men to help me carry Lieutenant Pilgrim to the stretcher. It is safe to touch now. I let the guys strap him in while I step back and give the pilot the go-ahead to activate the winch, hoisting Pilgrim up to him. Once the stretcher begins the one-hundred-foot journey to the chopper, I run back to get

Sergeant Lims who is sitting on the ground, legs crossed and band-aged with everything I had in the two aid kits. Fields helps the machine gunner to his feet. He looks to be OK, but I can see he is in a state of shock.

As the pilot lowers the stretcher for the second time, Lims catches sight of it, shaking his head to get my attention. The noise of the chopper is nearly deafening. "What, Sarge, what is it? Why are you shaking your head?" I want to put my arms around him but can't. His skin is burned and oozing fluid. I put my ear to his lips, trying to hear him, but he can't speak beyond a whisper, his teeth chattering. He says it twice, but I only catch it the second time, "I'm not going out on my back. Lower the penetrator, I'm not going out on my back." I recoil, looking him in the eye to make sure he is cognizant. He makes eye contact and nods in the affirmative. Holy shit! I don't believe it, but I'll honor his wishes. I run out so the pilot can see me, and wave off the lowering of the stretcher. I signal him to lower the penetrator instead of the stretcher.

The only problem is that I have to strap Lims in to secure him in case he passes out while ascending, which requires a strap to run across his back 180 degrees, locking him in like a seatbelt. I hesitate momentarily before I pull the strap across his back and yell, "Sorry, Jimmy, it's going to hurt." He winces in pain as I lock the strap in place. I want to kiss him but that won't happen. I love this man that much. I served with him on and off for eighteen months, first meeting him at West Point. Sergeant James Lims, a man's man, a soldier's soldier . . . Goodbye, my friend. God speed.

As he is being hoisted, the seat spins 180 degrees, affording us the opportunity to make eye contact one last time. And the son of a bitch actually winks at me. Holy shit. I throw him a kiss screaming, "I love you, Jimmy!" I then turn and think, "I'll always remember you, and I will always miss you." I can't watch anymore. Tears of sorrow obscure my vision. I feel that my hero is going to die.

Once the chopper leaves and things settle down, Sergeant Pepper, a squad leader until now, takes command. Men are milling around wondering and speculating how in the world the explosion occurred. I walk up to Hoornstra and ask if he has any idea. Hoornstra and Brown stayed with Lieutenant Pilgrim and Sergeant Lims when I left to go exploring to check out the other campsite Hop's squad found.

Hoornstra's face looks as if he has the weight of the world on his shoulders. "Yeah," he nods, not looking at me, just staring into the jungle. He lowers his voice to a whisper and says, "It was Brown. He threw a cigarette down the tunnel, discarding it, and said jokingly, '*Here you go, Lieutenant Pilgrim, this one's for you.*' And then laughed about it. Nothing happened for about five minutes. Pilgrim, after listening to Brown and what he encountered, went down into the tunnel with Lims, to check out what Brown saw down there. They put on their gas masks and went in. Five to ten minutes later, you know what I know. But, I tell ya, that fucking flame shot out twenty feet straight up. It was like a giant blowtorch. Scared the living shit out of me. Did you feel the earth shake, Spence?" I nod I had. He continues, "It knocked me off my feet. I thought it might have been a fucking earthquake."

Sergeant Pepper finishes speaking over the radio and tells us to form-up, single file. We will meet and assemble with the other platoons, pushing our way north by northwest. As we begin to form a column to penetrate the boonies, all fall silent. I think about Lims and Pilgrim. Did I do enough? Could I have done more? Hell, yes! I couldn't find a vein on either one of them. I hope the salt water does the trick. Will they live? The *what ifs* haunt me every time I attend to the wounded. Then I think about Brown—the guy Hoornstra feels caused the explosion—flipping his cigarette butt into the tunnel.

I debate turning Brown in, but then decide it would be a suicidal move. Brown is one of the crazies. All I want, all I expect, is to get grazed by a bullet or take a small piece of shrapnel, get a Purple Heart, and go home—forgetting I ever came to this place. Deep down I know neither Hoornstra or I will turn Brown in. I chose to file into the forming column at the tail end to be near Hop and his squad.

As we pass the second campsite, the one Hop's squad found earlier, through thick bush we hear men cursing and grunting. Then I hear someone say, "Pull it, man. It'll come off. Just give it a fucking tug." Hop turns to me to verify that I heard it, too. I nod. Without a word, he signals his men to keep going, while he and I peel off to investigate the source of the sounds.

I am not prepared for what I am about to see. Nothing in the world could have prepared me, nor should it have. As we break into the campsite of those six guys we came upon earlier, smoking marijuana, they are in the process of dismembering a human being! One of the men is pulling on the corpse's leg, one is standing on his torso, while the third is hacking at the groin area. "Jesus, mother of God!" Hop screams. I recoil at the gruesome sight, standing behind Hop. "Stop it! For the love of God! Stop it!"

There's more blood than I have ever seen in my life. The brown and green floor of the jungle is saturated with it. And then I see the head of a Vietnamese man severed from its body. Hop runs up to the guy with the machete, wrestling it from his grip. Two others move slowly toward their weapons, which are on the ground. The guy who had the machete speaks first. "Look, Sergeant, we didn't kill this guy. When that explosion occurred he came crawling out of that tunnel. And dropped dead." He points to the tunnel long enough for Hop and I to spot it.

"Let's go look at it, Hop. Come here," I say. I want to get him out of the men's hearing range, I coax him to follow me. He reluctantly responds, eyes darting between the crazies and me.

When I get to the tunnel, I bend down, examining the opening. Hop bends down with me and I whisper, "If you persist, if you push these guys, they'll kill us both, man. Don't push them. Let's just get out of here . . . alive. You can do anything you like once we get back to base camp, but not now, not here."

I pretend to examine the soil and actually point out blood on the ground at the tunnel's opening. "Look here, Hop, that's blood. Maybe what they said is true. Maybe they didn't kill him. Maybe he just managed to make it out and then died."

Hop looks at me with disgust.

I continue quietly, "It could have happened that way. You're not a goddamn pathologist. The best you'll be able to pin on them is disrespecting the body of a dead man, and that ain't gonna stick either. Now be cool. Take a look at them—no, don't turn now. They've all picked up their weapons. Why do you think they did that? Now let's just stand up and get the fuck outta here."

With a deep breath, he shakes his head as if to wake himself up from a nightmare then looks at me and states, "OK, you win. Maybe we'll get lucky and they'll let us go."

I smile at him encouragingly and raise my voice for the six guys to hear, "Well, then, there's nothing more to say—it looks like you guys caught yourself a Mr. Victor Charlie. And with an encouraging tone, I add, "You guys just might get a Bronze Star."

"Yeah," Hop allows, "maybe with a 'V' designation as well."

As we pass the men to go on our way, the six guys give us looks that scare the hell out of me. I just know any second they'd open up on us. I feel like whistling Dixie, but because five of them are black, I think twice about doing that!

When we're out of their hearing range, Hop, who is ahead of me, turns abruptly and vents his horror and rage while trying to be quiet. He is shaking with emotion as he spills his guts. "Do you believe what we just saw, Harry? Those motherfuckers are crazier than hell, hacking a human being like that. They ought to be court marshaled, those sick-ass bastards!"

"Yeah, I know, Hop. Just let it go."

"Let it go, shit! I want you to be my witness when we get back. I want you to testify."

I know I don't want to testify. Not a snowball's chance in hell will I testify. But I didn't want to upset Hop anymore than he already is, so I respond, "We'll talk about this later, OK? Now let's just hurry and catch up to our platoon."

As we hurriedly push our way through the jungle, we soon spot trampled underbrush, indicating we are on the path our guys took. We press on in silence.

Just as we make contact with our platoon, I tap Hop on the shoulder and say, "Hop, if you think I'm going to testify, you're wrong—dead wrong. I never saw a thing and will deny anything you say to anyone." He shoots me a dirty look of disgust. Tough shit, I think. I want to live. I've got enough enemies. I don't need anymore. Enemies like Flock and my father. I don't need the crazies after me, too, thank you.

Chapter 17

MINEFIELD

A S THE OLD saying goes, "another day, another dollar." And, I might add, I'm another day closer to going on R&R in Hawaii with Beatrice, as well as another day closer to my discharge. Most of the guys in the medical platoon have already taken their R&R. Some stayed in-country at Vung Tau. The military has set up a sort of resort area there with nice, comfortable sleeping accommodations and entertainment, and they look the other way if one brings a prostitute back to his hooch. Others went to Thailand or Australia. Because of the cost and time constraints, few go to Hawaii.

I also give brief thought to my mother's efforts to get me out of the army early, but little does she know I have no intentions of ever going home. Compassionate Reassignment, my ass! As far as I am concerned, my father can rot in hell. Though I have to admit that the bullshit he put me through as a kid has paid dividends. Those who have come from stable families are having a hard time dealing with all the uncertainties of life here and the insanity of the military.

A few of the men have wondered why, outside of Flock, nothing seems to get to me. I just smile at their comments, responding, "I've been more schooled on the subject of survival."

Some buy my explanation, some don't, saying in a accusatory tone, "You know something we don't, Spencer, and one of these days we're going to pin you down with a case of beer to find out what it is."

I always laugh at them and say in response, "When you've been screwed by the best, the rest are just practicing their acts. I don't let amateurs get to me, save the lovable Sergeant Flock. Thank you."

A couple of days later, as we gracefully smash our way through the jungle in stealth mode on a company-sized patrol, someone yells, "Freeze! Don't move! Don't any one of you move!" The others around me respond, "What's going on?" The word is passed at the speed of a raging fire—*minefield*! We're in the middle of a minefield!

Holy fucking mackerel, Andy! A minefield. We have been trained on what to do. We freeze in position. Not moving a foot and not grabbing a tree, we pull a 180. In an attempt to retrace our steps exactly as we entered the minefield, each man silently communicates to the man directly behind him the exact position of his feet. I glance around my immediate vicinity trying to spot a mine. A "push-pull-release" mine is the most deadly mine we could possibly encounter. It is damn near impossible to deactivate it; unless you have the training and experience, you're history.

As minutes seem to turn into hours and meters covered into miles, we slowly, cautiously back out of the minefield. The minefield lies within a cluster of heavily-laden jungle, thick underbrush, and small trees approximately one hundred meters wide. Open fields of deep swamp are on either side of it. On the positive side, at least we know just how far we have to backtrack to safety. Charlie is good, very good at his craft. Hanoi Hanna's words come to mind. "No one has ever been successful in defeating us . . . no one." I'm learning firsthand why. Damn, he's good.

Sweat drips profusely from my brow and streams into my eyes, burning and blurring my vision. In response, I shake my head a little too hard, knocking off my helmet. Big mistake. It rolls slowly down the incline we're on. I watch it roll toward the guy in front of me. He sees it too and crouches down, waiting for the explosion. When it stops at his feet, and he realizes nothing is going to happen, he looks up at me with a smile coming across his face.

Then we hear the unmistakable sound of incoming mortar fire. Seconds later he disappears, vaporized by the explosion, while I am knocked off my feet and showered by some wet substance. "Oh damn, God Almighty, it's his blood." The last thing I saw was his helmet shoot off him as if it had been shot out of a cannon. How in the fucking world wasn't I hit? I touch my arms, a reality check, and notice more blood. I want to run, but I can't. This must be *it*. *This must be how it ends*. Without prompt, the cadence comes to the fore of my thinking. "Discipline. Don't panic. Don't fucking panic in the middle of a minefield. Hold on, Spence, hold fucking on."

Then the sounds of explosions seem to surround us. The explosions are occurring overhead, decimating the trees. What the fuck is going on? Where is that shit coming from? The cries of medic are coming from all directions. It must be incoming, a mortar attack lobbing shells on us and the minefield. *Shit!*

All I can hear are screams for medic between the explosions. Have I started all this? God, Is it my fault the guy in front of me was killed? You stupid goddamn son of a bitch, Spencer. If I could, I would kill myself right here and now, if I had the nerve. The officers are screaming "Retreat! Back! Backtrack exactly as you came in, goddamn it! Move, men, move. Now!"

"Air fucking borne," someone screams. Another voice booms, *"All the fucking way, let's go, let's go!"* More cries for medic are heard, but are overridden by various officers yelling. "The medics cannot help you. If you can crawl, do it. Just get the fuck out of here." Explosions are coming from both the booby traps and incoming mortar fire. Thirty seconds later, just as suddenly as it began, the attack stops.

The first sounds I hear after the horrific thunder of explosions stop are the officers yelling out to the medics, "Medics, do not attempt to get to the injured. They're on their own. That's a direct fucking order." From my rear, a guy comes stumbling up to me, his face and neck boiling with "Willie Peter," a benign name for white phosphorus, a chemical that burns until it completely consumes itself or your skin, unless it is cut off from oxygen. "Doc, Doc, help me, I'm burning alive. Please, man, do something, I'm dying." He falls at my feet, thrashing in unstoppable pain.

In his condition he didn't care if he sets off any more booby traps. In fact he probably wants to, to put himself out of his misery. I slip out of my rucksack, careful not to hit any of the small trees where more traps may be hidden. Someone shouts, "They're in the trees! The trees are booby-trapped." I freeze, rucksack still in hand, and look right above me. A foreign-looking hand grenade, its pin removed, is jammed between two skinny branches of a small thin tree. I almost grabbed the tree when the guy came up to me. The wounded guy is kicking at the ground at my feet, convulsing in pain, but at least he's not too near the tree.

I open my aid kit and grab three tubes of ointments—any kind will do. His screaming intensifies as he writhes on the ground like a mortally-wounded snake. I find a pair of surgical gloves and put them on, then smear the creams over the gloves. Jumping on him, I force the cream on him, spreading it, attempting to cut off the oxygen from feeding the chemical that is slowly and painfully killing him. Together, we roll further down the incline, totally out of control. This guy is going to get me killed! But, then again, death has got to be the absence of pain. So I keep applying ointment as we tumble together, locked in a dance of death.

It seems to be working, he is coming back to his senses. Good, because the white phosphorus is beginning to burn me. I rip off the gloves and rub my hands feverishly into the soil to get the remnants of white phosphorous off. The guy jumps up and bolts, screaming and crying that he is burning. He's lost his weapon, his helmet, and his rucksack. I guess if I were in his condition I might do the same. He isn't playing soldier anymore. He is pleading for his life as he runs into men who are carefully making their way to safety.

When we reach the clearing again, I immediately yell for Sergeant Pepper to call for three Medevacs. I surmise many more men are injured, and it's better to have too many evacuation choppers than too few. As I chase after the injured guy, who keeps running even after reaching the clearing, Pepper yells to me, "Choppers en route, ETA thirty minutes." I chase down my crazed patient, coming upon him as he lies face down. He is holding his face in his hands and kicking, but with less intensity and strength. His energy is being sapped. He is either succumbing to death by shock or from the toxins of the white phosphorus finding their lethal way into his blood stream.

As I turn him over, I want to run out of fear and shock at seeing a man's face so desecrated. He looks like something out of a horror movie. His eyes are fixed in the open position due to the loss of eyelids. His nose is partially eaten away. A gaping hole has taken the spot where the nose once was. His windpipe is also partially exposed. I watch it expand and contract as he takes in air.

His breathing is rapid and shallow, not a good sign. And then as I watch in terror and morbid fascination, he stops breathing. I let out the air I unknowingly held, and close my eyes. This is the first transition from life to death I have actually witnessed, with the exception of those three V.C. Sappers at the maternity hospital six months ago. The body jerks with post mortem spasms as trapped air in his torso escapes, sounding like snores and belches. The last movement his body makes is the passing of gas accompanied by stool oozing from his bowels.

I gulp back what tries to escape from me, turning away from him on all fours, as the gag reflex kicks in. I let my mind and body go through their natural reactions to what I witnessed as I remain on all fours. I tried, I really tried to help him by taking the chance to smear ointment on him and rolling around with him in a minefield. In an attempt to cope, I rationalize he is now back to the blessed calm from whence he came. I want to look at his nametag, but I can't. I know who he once was. His name doesn't really matter anymore. Goodbye, my friend. God be with you.

Because it is impractical to circumnavigate the one-hundred-meter patch of jungle, our company commander calls for an air strike. We back away from the minefield, distancing ourselves the length of half a football field and prepare for the show. This, however, has to wait until the Medevacs evacuate our wounded and, our dead. To the best of my knowledge, there are two KIA and seven WIA, maybe more, maybe less. Numbers at this point don't mean a whole hell of a lot.

The wounded are assigned to other platoon medics. As I oversee the bodies of the two dead men being put into body bags, I caution the men. "Be careful not to get any of that white phosphorous on you, or you might end up just like him." After that comment, the guys handle the body as if it carries the plague. The remains of the guy who was vaporized, which aren't much, are also put in a body bag.

The jets this time are F-4 Phantom bombers, two of them. As they make a couple of passes, they fly right over us, maybe just 200 feet high, sounding more powerful than anything I have heard to date. After their second pass, word spreads that that the next one will have live fire. "Keep your heads down, men. The next pass is not practice," shout the sergeants spread out among us. But I can't help myself. I have to watch.

The jet aircraft come from left to right. Each drops two 650-pound bombs into the patch of jungle. The first wave of four bombs disappears beneath the canopy of trees. The resulting shock wave is so intense it lifts us off the ground, sucking the air from each of us. I feel as if someone kicked me in the stomach and knocked the wind out of me. The pain is more than any of us bargained for. I roll from side to side while opening my jaw to ward off the pressure in my ears.

Once my ears pop, I hear buzzing sounds like hummingbirds all around us. Some of the buzzing, however, has the pitch of a bumblebee, some a mosquito, all traveling at nearly supersonic speed. I continue to roll, writhing and recoiling after having the air sucked out of me. I look up at the sky and see a wave of earth descending. I am horrified as I think, my God, that was just four bombs!

I struggle to prepare for the next percussion wave, rolling back on my stomach as small debris still rains upon us. When I see them coming, again I watch. Only this time, as the bombs fall below the tree line, I let out a scream of defiance. Without knowing it, my scream counters the effect of the percussion wave. Shouting causes my stomach muscles to tighten so this second shock wave doesn't hurt as much as the first. I also put my fingers in my ears. Having satisfactorily escaped the second bombing's effects, I muse, huh, there's another one they never told me about.

A chunk of shrapnel lands within arm's reach of me, burying itself into the ground. My curiosity is piqued and I decide it will make a neat souvenir. So I reach out and grab it. By the sound it made coming toward me, I figure it will be about the size of a golfball. When I put my hand over it to scoop it out of the ground, it burns my hand like a piece of charcoal would right off a barbecue grill. Jesus! That's hot! I pull back, staring at my hand, inspecting the damage it created in that split-second contact. Holy shit. Now I really know what those guys mean when they are hit with a bullet or shrapnel. That shit is hot. Before leaving, the jets strafe the jungle on either side of the swamps from where we must have been shelled at the start of this encounter.

Thirty minutes after the jets drop their payload, we carefully hump through the former minefield. The jungle looks like something you'd see on the moon. Most everything that was green earlier is now burned and charred, still smoldering, a surreal setting. The sun is obscured by smoke hanging from the surface like a fog. The fog doesn't move though. The air is dead calm and hot.

LATE JANUARY 1967

The next day, while in base camp, mail call produces a letter from a high school buddy. I wonder how in the world he got my address. In his letter, he informs me he is in the navy, at boot camp, at the Great Lakes Naval Center. He writes:

> *"How ya doing ol' buddy? Long time no see and no hear. Surprise! I'm in the Navy. Couldn't get a college deferment, I was drafted and fortunately they gave me a choice of branch of service. I've been following the war on television and have thought about you often being in the thick of it and all. You unknowingly helped me make the choice of going into the Navy. No way was I going to follow your footsteps (nothing personal). But I tell ya, this boot camp shit is crazy. They got me doing all kinds of bullshit work— cleaning heads, pulling KP, it's hell buddy, they won't even let us smoke. Can you believe that? I hate it! I'll close for now ol' pal. Take care and keep your head down will ya?*
> *Jerry Miracle*

I ball up the letter and throw it toward the trash can in disgust. "Boot camp is hell," he says. He has no fucking idea what hell is, not a fucking clue! And, "they won't even let us smoke"—give me a break!

Chapter 18

THE ULTIMATE EDUCATION

TONIGHT IN THE mess hall, the Vietnamese movies we captured during Operation Cedar Falls will be shown for our amusement. Rumors circulate throughout the day that the contents will shock us, but the brass thinks we ought to know what we're up against. Based on that endorsement, I decide to see what all the brouhaha is about. Viewing the films is not mandatory, but my curiosity gets the better of me. Previously all movies, for either training or entertainment, were played outdoors. This one is being played indoors, a red flag. But I don't heed the significance of the movie being shown indoors, so I take a seat in the mess hall.

The movie begins with credits and an introduction, of course, in Vietnamese. I am immediately impressed. Our training has taught us we are up against a primitive people, implying that they lack any sophistication or state of art technology. The first thirty seconds of the film dispels that myth.

After the opening credits, the camera pans skyward, taking in an American aircraft with actual sounds accompanied by music and narration. Because we don't understand Vietnamese, we focus on the images and the sounds. The scene then changes to the obvious aftermath of the aircraft's attack and the destruction it caused. Bodies of men, women, and children are graphically filmed. I watch in awe and determine very quickly that the people in the film are not actors—they are real people, and they're really dead.

The camera rises to the sky once again, and we see another American jet flying very low over them while it drops its payload. My mind flashes to the bombing I witnessed that destroyed the minefield. But these bombs are dropped on a city. From the speed of the aircraft as it releases its bombs, I reason they'll hit a good distance from the men and women being filmed, who are running in all directions, panic plainly visible on their faces. While the camera films the panicking population, the percussion from the bombs is plainly evident. The camera shakes momentarily as people stagger in response to the shelling. Film fades to black.

The next scene is of the jungle: A slow pan from left to right with the faint whisper of Vietnamese. The picture widens and pulls back revealing a small stream in front of the cameraman. The camera zooms across the stream and focuses on movement within the jungle—the face of an American appears. He is a Green Beret, a staff sergeant.

Up until this point, most of the guys were making small wisecracks about the film and its intended purposes. However, everyone falls silent at seeing a real live American on patrol being filmed. I smirk to myself, thinking this is one elaborate movie depicting Americans, who are probably being played by Russians.

The Green Beret approaches the creek cautiously as we would while on patrol. Slowly, cautiously, the sergeant puts his hand in the air for the others to stop behind him. He bends down at the creek's edge, looking left, looking right, while the camera zooms in on his face. Another faint whisper in Vietnamese, and the camera pans slowly to its left, showing well-camouflaged North Vietnamese uniformed soldiers, rifles poised to strike. Jesus Christ, I think, this can't be for real! Come on, give me a fucking break.

Others in the audience can't contain themselves. It's as if we are there with them, and they yell, "It's a fucking ambush! Get back, man, get back!"

Others state in an angry tone, "This shit can't be real!"

"Fuck this shit," someone else yells, then he stands up and leaves before he can see any more of the film. "I ain't watching a goddamned snuff film, I'm outta here!"

A voice calls from the back of the room, "Sit down, goddamn it. This shit can happen to anyone of you, watch and learn from it."

A heated argument erupts as men take sides. Some argue that it's sensationalism at its worst, when one of them states, "It's goddamned violating my very sense of morality, man. I don't want any part of this." Someone else interjects, "Then why in the fuck are you a paratrooper, man? You goddamn pussy. Get outta my sight, you wimp." The two guys square off, swinging wildly at one other, but are ignored. Most are glued to what is unfolding on the screen.

The camera pans back slowly, showing the Green Beret still at the creek's edge. He appears as if he thinks something is terribly wrong. His eyes shift to the side of the bank that lies before him, the side where the North Vietnamese are filming. Inside of my own head I'm screaming, get back man. It's an ambush.

The staff sergeant is joined at the creek's edge by a local Montagnard tribesman who has taken our side in the war over joining the ranks of the Viet Cong. The Montagnards know the terrain and act as interpreters. It appears the two know each other as they speak and smile, but their voices are muffled. The film crew's microphone cannot pick up their conversation. The pair decide to cross the creek, which looks to be one hundred feet wide with a fast-moving current. The body language of the Green Beret says that he does not want to cross the creek, but the Montagnard encourages him, waving him on with a smile and a nod of the head.

At this point the camera doesn't move. It just pulls back to get a panoramic view of the squad of men as they wade into the knee-high water. We can hear the men forging through the water. One guy nearly falls due to the strong current.

The fight between the two paratroopers stops. Someone in the audience screams, "Jesus mother of God, *stop, go back.*" Just then the music in the film stops, and the sounds of the swift-moving water grows louder. I can even hear sounds of birds in the jungle. I count the men as they wade into the water: One, two three, four, five, six, seven, eight men out in the water. Oh God, *no.* Please let this be just a film with actors, please. My heart is racing. I want to cry out in agony. I want to want to run away. But I just sit there staring.

One guy couldn't take it any longer. He stands up, waving his arms, yelling, "Fuck this, fuck this war, fuck the North Vietnamese, and fuck all of you for watching this shit." He puts his hands over his ears as the enemy spring their trap. At this point, reality sets in. This is not just a movie.

The men barely have a chance to return fire. Eight men are slaughtered. They fired less than twenty rounds in their defense before they all went down. Not even a scream is heard. All present sit in total silence, stunned. We know it could be any one of us, anytime, anywhere out on the next patrol.

As soon as the men fall, the North Vietnamese jump from their positions, wearing foliage that allows them to blend in to the jungle. They shoot the floating bodies while wading into the water, and catch them before the swift-moving current carries them away. However, one lone Green Beret struggles to get back to his feet. The look on his face I will never forget. It is a look of fear, like that of a small child just before he cries out in pain and disbelief. He is then shot in the head at close range. A spout of brain fluid gushes forth as his head hits the water. I suddenly have a pain in my gut, sweat beads on my forehead and below my eyes. The scene fades to black.

The next scene shows the same men lying next to one another, still soaking wet, but with their equipment off. One can hear a pin drop despite the one hundred men watching. The cameraman walks up and films each man's face. Displayed for all to see are their Army ID cards, along with their dog tags. This is not an act of film fantasy where the cast of characters stands up and brushes themselves off after the director yells cut.

The men are deader than shit. As a medic I know that at first glance. I understood what the army wanted us to learn. The lesson was simple: They should have had only one man cross the creek at a time. I get up to walk out, saying to myself, I wish I hadn't gone to see that film. It will be etched in my mind forever. Once outside another sobering thought jumps to the fore: How could I possibly tell someone not only what I have gone through, but what I have seen? And do I want to?

It is dark as I walk alone back to my tent, feeling that this could one day be just a dream when Flock walks up to me. "Here, you goddamn cry baby. Here's your orders to wear a CMB." He throws the paper at me and walks away. But I don't feel anything and don't really want to. I guess he thought that might make my day. But after what I have just seen it means nothing, absolutely nothing. I don't respond to him and simply continue walking toward my tent.

Just as I reach my tent's doorway, an explosion lights up the night somewhere between the mess hall and battalion headquarters building. A shower of sparks flies over the tents. Fireworks, I think satirically. Then multiple screams for medic echo throughout the compound. Jesus Christ, now what? I grab my rucksack that is considerably lighter than it is in the bush. In base camp I only have the aid kit attached to it—No spare clothing, socks, water, c-rations, or ammo. Then I sprint in the direction of the blast.

More screams for medic come out of the darkness. We always have medics on duty at the aid station just for emergencies. It will be their role to officially respond and take charge of any emergency in the compound. I'll be back-up. My pace is tempered by that thought as I slow my strides.

Approaching the chaos, I pull out a pen flashlight I carry in my breast pocket and illuminate the area immediately in front of me. Others have beaten me to the scene, including the "on duty" medics. Six guys lie on the ground in various stages of injury. Doctor Pierce and the duty medics are already attending to the injured. Some of the injured are screaming like wounded animals, crying out in disbelief, "I didn't pull the pin, man. Who pulled the pin?"

A couple of jeeps arrive, their headlights illuminating the area. I get a good look at the carnage. A man's leg lies near his torso, it was obviously ripped from his body. The boot still has the foot and ankle in it. An arm is totally severed. I don't recognize the guy trying to get an I.V. started; he is shaking so badly that I bend down asking him if he needs assistance. The smell is nauseating, but nothing I can't handle. He snaps back that he is a doctor, saying, "I know what I'm doing, young man." One of the spectators responds, "So fucking what, Doc. I've been watching you repeatedly try and fail to get that fucking needle in him. Let the medic do it!" The doctor shoots me a look and asks if I am a medic. When I respond that I am, he hands me the needle, stating, "Here, see if you can get it. He's lost so much blood. I can't find a vein."

I feel honored, but challenged. The men are watching us in action, judging our competency to work on them should it come to that. When we attend to the wounded under fire, infantrymen have a tendency to turn their backs. Once I think I've hit a vein, I tell the doctor to let the tourniquet loose a second to see if there is back-flow of blood into the I.V. line. As I wait, I glance at the holes in his arm that aren't bleeding. Not a good sign. And there is no back-flow of blood into the I.V. line. Shit, I missed. I turn the wounded man's hand over, palm down, and smack it. In that fleeting second, I catch sight of a vein and tell the doctor to squeeze his arm at the bicep. I get lucky. There was an immediate back-flow of blood into the I.V. line.

The doctor thanks me as I step out of his way. A couple of guys who have been watching grab me by the shoulders and shout, "Good man, Doc. You're all right in my book." There's no time to take a bow though. I scan the area. My fellow medics are working fast. Some of the injured are already being loaded onto the jeeps. Once onto stretchers, the men are simply thrown across the backs and the hoods of the vehicles.

We have to get them to the 3rd Field Evacuation Hospital, about a mile down the road toward the air base. I notice two legs on the ground where men fell and pick them up, throwing them on top of the injured, and run back, remembering the arm. It is a strange sensation to pick up a part of a human being, feeling its heft and its give to my grip. I note the elbow still flexes as I carry it. A shiver runs through me. I am not sure if the parts can be reattached, but decide it's better to have them go with them than not.

As the jeeps are pulling away, I catch a glimpse of Flock. He looks ashen, as if in shock, riding in the back of one of the jeeps. Good, I think. You son of bitch, you're just getting a small taste of what we, the ground-pounding medics, have gone through, you goddamned bastard. He catches my gaze. I'm sure I look far more in control than he is. I damn near laugh—his eyes are as wide as if he had just seen a ghost.

Once the jeeps pull away, I return to where the explosion occurred to learn what the hell happened. The story unfolds: six guys got drunk and decided to play hot potato with a grenade in the dark. Two of the men were Vietnamese interpreters who introduced the Americans to the game. The ole "I dare you" trick. Someone then either accidentally or purposely pulled the pin. Three or four seconds later the grenade irreversibly changed their lives. One, a father of five, lost an eye, a leg, an arm, and his testicles. Three others were more fortunate . . . two weren't.

Walking back to my tent, I block out what has just happened. I let my mind drift, speaking to Beatrice, baby doll, I'm coming. Somehow, someway I'm coming to meet you. And then I smile at the memory of her beauty and the way she dances, better than anyone I have ever seen. Just thirty more days and I'm there. And then I tense at the thought: Can I tell her what I have been through, what I have seen, what I have smelled?

I decide it will be impossible, and besides, it would ruin the festive occasion of our getting together. I begin to believe that no one would ever know. But then that little voice comes forth, stating, "They must know, Harry. How else will they learn the truest lesson of war? Your book, Harry, must be written." "Yeah, right." I speak aloud, as if arguing with someone. "You think I want to write about this shit! You must be out of your mind, Spencer." Maybe I should stop keeping a diary. I don't want to remember. I don't.

As I enter my tent, I notice one of the guys has left his radio on. The words to a song playing catch my attention, *"summer time, summer time, som som summer time."* Oh yeah, the days of my carefree youth, where have they gone? I fall onto my bunk as another song plays in the background, *"Just a dream—just a dream . . ."*

Chapter 19

A REPRIEVE

THE NEXT MORNING, after reporting to the aid station, Dr. Pierce pulls me aside and informs me that I will not be going out into the field for at least thirty days. He has reviewed records of all the medics, their time spent in the boonies, and their respective encounters. As a result, he and our platoon leader, Lieutenant Edmore, overruled Sergeant Flock's plan to put me out again and states, "You're overdue for some rest. We don't want you looking all haggard when you go to Hawaii to meet your family. In your present condition, you'd scare them, and they might think the army is trying to kill you." He looks at me with a smile coming across his face and continues, "Besides, you need to put on a few pounds. Looks like you've lost twenty pounds since we've been here," and gives me a wink.

I feel bad because I told him I was going to meet my aunt and uncle in Hawaii, not Beatrice. I smile sheepishly, thank him and go about my business thinking that I'd welcome the bullshit that Flock will have in store for me at base camp. And I'll take anything he can throw at me by counting the days until I meet Beatrice.

And, wouldn't you know it, sure as shit, later that day Flock assigns me to burn off fifty-five gallon drums of shit from the enlisted men's as well as the senior NCO's latrines. Even latrines are segregated. The third latrine is for the exclusive use of the officers. I get lucky though. I have to work on just two of the three. The stench of hundreds of human excretions sitting in those full drums is incredible. Coupled with the heat and lack of wind to carry off the smell, it is overbearing. To cope we put handkerchiefs over our faces soaked in after-shave.

The last bit of latrine housekeeping is to pour disinfectant on the areas where men sit to do their business. I'm supposed to let it stand full strength for a few minutes, then rinse the area down, throwing buckets of water over the areas where disinfectant was applied. As I brush the disinfectant onto the senior NCO's latrine seating area, a thought runs through my head. I decide not to rinse off the disinfectant, relishing at the thought of the sergeants' burning asses.

Because our platoon tent is right across the road from the latrines I figure I'll hear their screams, a gleeful thought. Three hours later, we are on another detail planting trees in the walkway alongside our tent. I've forgotten all about that little prank when I hear someone scream, "I'll kill that son of a bitch!" I look up at Mark Baldwin, who has been supervising the three of us medics planting trees, and break out in laughter.

"What the hell's so funny, Spencer?" Mark wasn't in on the joke. In total amazement he says, "Someone screams and you laugh! Are you nuts, man?" I stop digging momentarily, still smiling and meet Jim Chiefoot's gaze. Chiefoot helped me on latrine detail and knows what I have done. We both start laughing so hard that we can't stand still. I run a few yards from those gathered to regain my composure.

My laughing, however, comes to an abrupt halt when I see Flock holding his pants up with his hand, running toward the Water Buffalo (community water bladder). Oooooops, the smile slides from my face. He glances at me as he sticks his bare ass under the spigot. If looks could kill, I'd be history. Trying very hard to keep from smiling, I break eye contact and continue digging.

The next morning, I go to sick call. I have been having problems the last couple of months with minor anal bleeding. I've tried controlling the symptoms with creams and ointments to no avail. The bleeding is worse than ever. Flock, of course, sees this move as a ruse to get out from under his fury. Upon examination by Dr. Pierce, I am diagnosed with, of all things, anal warts! I wince in shock when Pierce informs me and explains the treatment—surgery.

A few days later I am admitted to the 93rd Field Evacuation Hospital, which is located a few miles from our base camp in a neighboring Vietnamese province. I am assigned to a ward with others who have sustained combat wounds. Some patients, however, have malaria. At the foot of each man's bed hangs the insignia of his respective unit along with his medical records. No one in the ward is a paratrooper.

Paratroopers are a minority in the army. To see one is rare among the majority of army personnel. Most regular army personnel know the paratrooper's reputation as tough, and to some extent, crazy. To be a paratrooper as well as a combat medic is looked upon as the ultimate among the elite, and here I am among the wounded in action, some torn up pretty badly from combat—with anal warts. Grrreeat!

Those walking down the hospital aisles naturally look at the unit insignia hanging at the foot of each man's bed then at the man in that bed. Most passing by my bed look puzzled. I have no visible injury, and look as fit and healthy as a thoroughbred racehorse. I exchange sheepish smiles with those who make eye contact with me as they pass. This is also my first real prolonged exposure to round-eyed American women since my arrival in Vietnam. God, they look beautiful and, to me, they're better built than any Vietnamese woman. To keep things in perspective I have to remind myself several times why I am here.

I am scheduled for surgery tomorrow morning, and the usual battery of tests is given. Afterwards I begin to talk with those nearest me, asking what happened to them, their units and what they did. They are equally curious about me, but I am a little embarrassed to tell them why I am in the hospital. The guy next to me is a REMF with malaria. He is a signalman and has never been in the boonies. I stop communicating with him when he confides in me that he purposely exposed himself to mosquitoes by not applying repellent. He brags, "Hell, I'd rather be in here than working. Malaria's no big deal."

The guy on my other side is an infantryman from the 1st Infantry Division—a rifleman, a grunt like me. I stop talking to him too when I learn from an orderly that he shot himself to get out of going back to the jungle. Some of our own guys have talked about shooting themselves to get out, but that's all it is—just talk.

Disgusted, I lie in my bed in silence. Those two guys, in my mind, are cowards. I feel like kicking the shit out of both of them, but decide that each of us has to live with himself. They'll have to face their cowardliness sooner or later. That will be punishment enough. What are they going to say twenty years from now when they're asked what they did in Vietnam, or how they were injured?

I am my own best friend and my fiercest enemy. And while the enemy within has been tempted to do something as stupid and cowardly as the guys beside me here, the friend says, "You've got to sleep at night, Harry. Don't even think about it." *Airborne* rises from within . . . the beat and the boots hitting the ground—and the pride. I think of the situations I've encountered—the faces of the dead who exemplified courage and greatness, heroes because they dared to put themselves in harm's way, heroes because they heeded our nation's call, even if in blind obedience. As Shakespeare put it so eloquently, "Some are born great, some achieve greatness, and some have greatness thrust upon them." Yeah, they had greatness thrust upon them, all right.

Later in the afternoon, we are paid an unexpected visit by none other than "Maverick," James Garner and the "Rifleman" Chuck Connors. Garner appears more sophisticated and arrogant, but not in a condescending manner. Both are very big men. Connors looks to be 6'4" and very thin and has the biggest jaw I've ever seen. Garner is built thicker, standing just a couple of inches shorter than Connors. Both have Hollywood written all over their perfect smiles and store-bought teeth.

The nurses go into lala land at the sight of the pair. Of course, Connors and Garner play to their emotions. In a Texas drawl of sorts, Connors says to them, "My, my, what do we have here gentlemen," as if he were talking to those of us lying in our beds. "Aren't you the luckiest soldiers in the world to be taken care of by such gorgeous women?" The nurses, normally very professional, and officers in the United States Army react as if they are typical teenagers, smiling and giggling among themselves.

Connors and Garner work the ward, going from bed to bed, speaking quietly with each man. The two must have been briefed by the military because they seem to stay longer at beds with the insignia of the 1st Infantry, the 25th Infantry, the 196th Lightning Brigade.

When Connors stops at the guy's bed to my left, the one who shot himself, he asks him how he was wounded. I listen, trying not to be too obvious. I'll kick the shit out of the guy if I hear him lie, but he doesn't. The guy simply states, "I fucking shot myself, Sir. I just couldn't take it any longer." He bursts out crying uncontrollably. I understand and admire his honesty. I grieve for him, as does Connors, who tries to console him, stating as he shoots me a look, "I understand, son. Everyone has a breaking point. Just take care of yourself." He pats the guy's shoulder.

Connors leaves the man and walks toward me, then stops at the foot of my bed to look at the insignia of the 173rd Airborne Brigade. His eyebrows rise in recognition. "Well, I'll be," he says, "a real live paratrooper." He extends his hand to shake mine. Geez, I think as we clasp hands, he's got the biggest paw I've ever grabbed. His face beams, looking unearthly big to me. "And what, pray tell, happened to you, son?"

After the guy next to me pulled everyone's emotions to the ground, and because I really don't want to tell him that I'm here to have my asshole reamed, I state, "Nothing much, Sir. I just got caught in some whorehouse and got the shit kicked out of me by her mamason!" His huge smile gets bigger and he and his accompanying entourage break out in laughter. Even I laugh while I think that I have never even been near a whorehouse!

He gently smacks my arm, shaking my hand again, and, while leaning forward in a soft voice, states, "I hope she was worth it, trooper. You are a paratrooper, aren't you?" I smile and pull my hospital gown sleeve up, exposing my tattoo. "I'm the genuine article, Sir. I earned it the hard way." His eyes indicate he doesn't understand. I then say, "I got it before I went to jump school."

He immediately understands, saying, "I'll bet you did, son," and moves on. James Garner works the other half of the ward. I never met him. But I remember his attitude and demeanor as confident mixed with a little bravado.

The next morning I walk to the operating room—they didn't wheel me in. "Up on the table," the doctor says. I look at the table in disbelief. On top of the table is a device, which I'll have to climb upon and then lay face down on with my ass elevated head-high to the surgeon. No, no modesty here. The nurses are everywhere, busy with their assigned tasks preparing for my surgery, and oblivious (I hope) to my embarrassment. Needless to say, I am a little reluctant and humiliated. Geez, at the very least I thought they'd put me under, so I wouldn't have to be conscious of this.

A nurse informs the doctor that I am a medic. "A medic," he responds. "Are you a line medic soldier?"

Before I can respond, another nurse states as if annoyed by the doctor's comment, "He's a combat medic, a paratrooper with the 173rd. Doctor, paratroopers don't like to be referred to as soldiers. It was on his chart. You did read his chart, didn't you?"

"Well then, no need for me to explain much," he says as he applies tape on one cheek, pulling it aside with such force that I become a little alarmed. Then he tapes the other side and I yell, "Easy, Doc. What the hell you going to do? Drive a fucking truck up my ass?" They all chuckle at that comment. But I am serious!

"Now, now, it's not that bad. I don't feel a thing," he responds.

"Well, good for you," I respond.

More laughs fill the air. I surmise they are upbeat because I am not a trauma patient. One of the nurses says, "I'll bet you'll remember this operation for some time to come." And then the surgery begins.

"You'll feel a few little pokes, I'm injecting the ole numbing agent, Paratrooper. Are you with me?'

"Ready and able, Sir," I respond with my eyes closed, trying to block out my humiliation.

Here are all these beautiful women around me, and I've got my ass hole stuck up in the air! The doctor keeps engaging me, wanting me to speak so he can gauge my reactions to the injections. "Why did you shave your groin?" he asks, laughing, "And if you'll pardon my French, your asshole?"

Not wanting a dialogue on either subject, I blurt out a partial truth while grunting in pain. "Crabs, Sir. Got them from the bunkers while on Hill 358, north of Da Nang."

He lets out a snicker stating, "I'll bet it hurt while the hair was growing back, humping those boonies huh?"

Holding my breath, eyes still closed, I respond, "Not as much as the hurt you're putting on me now, Sir."

More laughs. I feel strangely good to know my life's experiences are comical to them. It serves to help me put things in perspective . . . almost. As he cauterizes the areas where he lanced the warts, I wince in pain.

Then I hear the softest, sexiest voice speaking right into my face. "Hi there, you young, handsome Mr. Paratrooper. How you holding up?" My eyes open in less than a heartbeat and there, just six inches from my face, is a nurse looking at me, her face covered by a mask. As I look at her, she winks with the sexiest wink I've ever seen.

I gulp heavily and manage to respond in not a very sexy tone, "Fine, ma'am. But right now, nothing I possess could *get up* to meet that lovely voice of yours."

More laughter. Another nurse pats my raised ass, saying, "He's definitely a live one, all right."

I let my military courtesy drop again and say, "You bet your sweet bibby, I'm alive, and I intend to stay that way." More laughter. I am eventually packed, racked, and told to walk back to my ward. They all cheer as I walk away, slightly bent forward, with my legs spread, taking baby steps. I feel like I have the proverbial broomstick stuck up my ass.

A couple of weeks later, nearing the end of February, I walk into the aid station, and as usual, Flock is there at the front desk. He is fumbling with some papers and glances up at me as I enter, saying, "Maybe now, after your brain surgery, you'll be able to think straight." He snickers to himself as if amused by his own remark. He continues to thumb through the papers and shoves a couple toward me.

"What's this, my discharge, Sarge?"

"No, it's your paperwork to go on R&R to Hawaii, that's all."

I snatch the papers out of his hand before they can disappear, and respond, "Thanks Sarge, it stinks to be back. I was hoping you'd have been blown away by now." It's an obvious dig, but I dug too deep.

"Spencer, the minute you get back count on going on line. I'll stage a firefight with Charlie if I have to just to send your ass out there." And then in his serious tone that I hoped I'd never hear again, he reminds me, "I'm not through with you, Spencer. I'd throw your ass out there right now, if I could. You're either gonna be the greatest hero who ever lived or the deadest. Now, get out of my sight."

Slowly, very deliberately, I walk away, pretending to be in more discomfort than I actually am. He takes a parting shot at me, snickering under his breath, "Fucking pussy." That pisses me off. I stop momentarily, thinking of walking as if nothing is wrong, which I could have, but decide to play out my hand and continue on as if I'm barely ambulatory. He doesn't know it, but I am jumping for joy knowing that I have my ticket to Hawaii in hand. I smile to myself as I walk slowly to my tent.

Finally, February 28th is here! I feel like a kid going to Disneyland with a free pass to ride everything and eat anything. Because of the time and distance to Hawaii, the army gives me one day of travel each way. Seven days of total relief. I am so nervous that I report to Bien Hoa's Air Base at 0900 hours, three hours prior to the scheduled departure. Once there I noticed a silver bullet (a civilian aircraft) securing its doors as its turbines spool up to power.

An air force tech sergeant is busy counting ticket stubs when I ask rather casually, what gate Flight 4234 boards from. He looks up at me with eyes widening and asks, "Are you Harold Spencer?"

I respond with growing alarm, as the jet engines grow louder, "Yes, yes, I'm Harold Spencer, why?" Then I scream in panic, "Don't tell me that's my plane!"

He runs toward the plane frantically waving his arms to get the pilot's attention. I run after him dragging my duffel bag. Oh, my God! This can't be happening to me!

The pilot shakes his head at the sergeant, waving his hands as if to say sorry. Sorry? Like hell you are! I start jumping up and down, screaming in defiance. I damn near pissed in my pants. I guess the pilot has second thoughts after seeing me act like a mad man. He nods his head and waves me aboard, as he throttles back his engines. As I hurriedly ascend the portable staircase to the plane's door, my legs feel weak, and it is difficult to swallow.

The adrenaline shock got to me. I have waited eight painfully long months dreaming, praying, hoping this day would come, and it damn near disappears on me like a mirage. As I continue up the stairs, my legs buckle again. Once at the top, I pause, take in a deep breath and try to compose myself.

The stewardess is friendly and understanding and welcomes me on board. But when I walk down the aisle to find a seat, it appears that the entire plane is full.

Looking for an empty seat, I continue down the aisle, slowly dragging my duffel bag, which should have been put in the cargo bay, when suddenly a voice booms, "Here, Doc, take mine." Another says, "No, take mine. Here, Doc. Sit here." I scan the men sitting in the plane. At least a dozen have stood up offering their seat to me. It's like this is some sort of weird set-up, like Candid Camera. Why are they offering me their seats? And then it dawns on me. Of all the uniforms and accompanying unit insignia worn by those on board, not one is from an infantry division, not one is a paratrooper. Looking closer, none have a Combat Infantrymen's Badge signifying they have been subjected to actual combat. At least half on board are in the air force. I am the lone infantryman, medic, and paratrooper on board. I also have on my Combat Medical Badge right above my parachute wings. I guessed they knew what that meant.

A firm hand touches my shoulder, and I turn to see an air force colonel who states, "Here," pointing to his seat, "sit here please." Without further fanfare I slump into his seat in the first class section. Apparently the colonel is a pilot himself and takes the jump-seat in the plane's cockpit.

I have never known a higher tribute in my life, and feel unworthy when they praise who I am and what I do in the war. Most want to know what combat is really like. I downplay my experiences with most of them, giving limited details. I cannot bring myself to relate the fear, fatigue, and death I have felt and witnessed. Although I attempt to tell some of them, I can't embelish upon details for fear of disgracing those who have died. A combat encounter is nothing to brag about. It's a very humbling experience.

One stop at Wake Island and twelve hours later our plane lands on American soil. Anticipation boils within me at the thought of being with Beatrice, the girl I met in the ninth grade and have loved ever since, the woman I am convinced I will one day marry. All I have to do is convince her. But she is getting her college degree and going on to law school. That thought unnerves me. After all, I am a kid from the inner city of Detroit. She moved to the suburbs in the tenth grade, taking on a new life, new thoughts, and a different direction. Although I feel strongly that she loves me, deep down I suppress what might be the inevitable—the separation of class, separation from the one I love, cherish, and admire. I decide to put that thought off until tomorrow. Why provoke anxiety? I've got enough to handle right now.

As the plane taxis to the terminal's entrance, the men are going absolutely nuts—hooting and hollering like the excited bunch of kids they are. Then, without warning, I feel a growing fear at the thought that maybe she isn't here. Maybe she's decided not to come. Maybe I have been fooling myself into thinking she loves me. I am frozen with fear in my seat as the men file past me. I can't move.

With the plane empty, I sit there, staring at the back of the seat in front of me. A stewardess notices and comes to me, bubbling with excitement. Her excitement is contagious to everyone but me. Realizing something is wrong, she sits down next to me and speaks very softly. "What's wrong, Mr. Paratrooper, no one here to meet you?"

My eyes gloss over. My mind races as if I'm stuck in an emotional tornado that has paralyzed me. I want to speak, but can't. I want to tell her all the pain I feel, and all the apprehensions I have about returning home from Vietnam alive.

I think of Chuck Holt who once tried to express his fears to me, but I cut him off, of Karl Lessnau as his chopper crashed, of Willie Sykes and William "Don't Mess With Me" Williams dancing. I think of Gino Washington crying as he came back from patrol where the sergeant who had seven days until discharge was killed and who was himself later wounded in the minefield along with Tom Brown. I think of my musketeer—Louie Blade. I think of the children at Hoa Khan Children's Hospital—patient number 112, Four Legs, Mouse, and Frankenstein, and my last casualty with his face gone. On and on my mind races.

"Mr. Spencer? Mr. Spencer?" the pilot's voice brings me out of the tornado I am trapped in. "Is there anything I can do for you? Are you all right? Should I summon the military?"

I glance at my watch. I have been sitting here twenty minutes. I jump up startled, in a state of near-panic, thinking that Beatrice may think I didn't make it! That I don't care! Oh God, please be there, Beatrice, I'm coming. I run from the plane.

By this time the terminal is already empty. All who waited and all who arrived have found their way to Disneyland. I let out a scream like a lone wolf might, howling at the loss of his life long mate, "*Beatrice!*" The empty terminal echoes and falls silent. I reach frantically for some change, trying to remember the name of the hotel. Oh, my God, I forgot! I put my hands to my temples, shut my eyes tight, and speak out loud, "What the fuck is the name of the hotel, Spencer? Think! Think!"

A soft voice answers, "It's the Marriott, Harry."

I know her voice instantly, like I know Flock's—yes, a poor comparison, but both have equal but opposite impacts in my life. The one standing before me is filled with love, peace, and security; the other is the essence of evil and ill intent. I embrace her small five-foot, one-hundred pound frame, shaking with excitement and anticipation. As we embrace, she whispers that she thought I had been killed. I push her back slightly to see a stream of tears flowing down her beautiful face.

Her emotions burst as she grabs my shoulders and throws her head onto my chest while managing to say, "I would have died if you hadn't been on that plane, Harry. I agreed to meet here because I could no longer deny my feelings for you," and softly she whispers, "I love you Harry. I always have. I've just been too stubborn and afraid to admit it." She pulls back to look me in the eye and says with a tenderness I have never known, felt or heard, "I love you."

We embrace alone in the terminal, kissing with tenderness and the promise of what will follow. Mellow Hawaiian music plays softly in the background throughout the empty terminal. As far as I am concerned, Hollywood couldn't have set up a better scene. We are the stars, and we don't need or want an audience.

During the ride in the taxi, I take in all of her while asking what happened to the reservations at the other hotel. She is wearing a red mini-dress that has become popular since I left the states. I heard about mini-skirts in Vietnam but never saw one. God, I can't help but notice her legs. Her strongest physical attribute is her legs, which make Betty Grable's look second rate.

As the shock of actually arriving subsides, my hormones begin to kick in. But, as is the norm, whenever we get together, she does most of the talking. This moment proves to be no exception. "I've been here

two days," she says. "I saw the International Market Place, been to
Diamond Head—twice, Waikiki Beach—it's beautiful. You'll like it
there. And I've got you a room that adjoins the one I'm sharing with
my girlfriends. The hotel is very beautiful. You'll like the bar—I told
them you were coming. They said they wouldn't ask you for your ID
once they see you in uniform—as if they didn't believe I was meeting
my hero and that he wasn't really coming here from Vietnam. You've
lost weight. Why? Don't you like Vietnamese food? You look terrible.
How much weight did you—"

"Stop, please, Bea. Hold it a second. Take a breath. What do you
mean you have a room next to mine?"

She bats those big almond eyes as only she can do and starts into
another nonstop monologue, "Harry, we are not married."

I look at the driver, making eye contact via his rear view mirror. He
rolls his eyes, smiling understandingly and interrupts Bea, saying,
"Looks like you're a paratrooper. What outfit? Is that the patch of the
173rd?"

"Yes," I respond. "I'm based out of Bien Hoa, thirty miles northwest of Saigon."

"How long have you been in-country?"

The term he used, "in-country," is a vernacular for those of us who
were or are in Vietnam. He must know it because of the guys who
have taken their R&R here. He looks too old to be a 'Nam vet. He
must be the age of a World War II guy.

"I've been in-country about eight months now, since June of last
year," I state. "What about you? You used the term we use, in-
country. You been there?"

Our eyes meet again in the mirror's reflection. He nods his head,
casting his eyes back on the road. "Yep. Served with the 5th Special
Forces, spending time at Na Trang, Long Binh, and Plekiu." He
sticks out his hand, half turning, "Staff Sergeant Paul
VanDenebeelee, they call me Paulie. Retired, twenty, and out. 1944
to 1964, thirteen months in-country, and I retired." While twisting in
his seat, he looks back at me, saying in a low voice, "Vietnam turned
me off. I would have stayed in another ten years to max out my
pension, but it's bullshit the things they had us doing, just plain bullshit. Know what I mean? What did you say your name was?"

"Harry Spencer," I quip.

"How's it going for you, Harry?"

I think about Bea sitting next to me and decide not to engage him any further. I push back into the seat as he looks at me again in the mirror. "About the same," I respond.

He casts his eyes back on the road, nodding in recognition, realizing I don't want to talk about it and remarks, "I hear ya, man, loud and clear."

In a small way, I take comfort in having come 6,000 miles and meeting someone who knows what I know.

Bea continues as if she had not been interrupted. She puts her hand on the inside of my upper thigh, "Harry, I couldn't tell them we were married. How would it look with two different names on our licenses and two different addresses? Besides, I'm in school, you know. I like it. I'll be going into my third year. Cindy and Valerie are with me. Did you know that? Yes, I think you knew that."

I listen, smiling at how rapidly she speaks and how exuberant, animated, and innocently childlike she is. So full of energy and life. I like that, but it makes me think of how I used to be. There was a time not too far back I was just as outgoing and teeming with life. Looking at her now sitting next to me as we pull up to the hotel, I realize just how much I have changed, how my experiences in Vietnam have affected me. But what hasn't changed is the fact that I still think she is the most beautiful girl I have ever seen, and I feel privileged to be with her.

As I dig in my pocket to pay the fare, the former Green Beret put his hands in the air, saying with conviction, "No charge, trooper, this one's on me. Just have a great time, brother." We shake hands. "Good luck, brother," he states, and turns to get back in his taxi. His tone is kind, empathetic, and somewhat melancholy.

I turn and put my arm around Bea, dragging my duffel bag behind me. She continues to bubble with energy and asks, as we took in the hotel's trappings and art deco, "Well, what do you think?" They even have a doorman who bows slightly as if we were royalty walking up to the king's palace. Bea loves it, but, looking at the posh marble flooring, I feel about as uneasy and unsettled as a goldfish in a coffee mug. Very out of place is an understatement.

When we get to her room no one is there. I expected to meet her schoolmates, Cindy and Valerie. I turn and embrace her, not out of passion or lust, but with the tender love I feel and have always felt for her. Her thinking enough of me to come here, friends along or not, touches me. I am with the one that will be, if only for the next five days, my woman, my soulmate, and my friend. No matter what happens, Bea will forever be etched in my mind. If it is written somewhere in the book of life that I am destined to die in Vietnam, I'll gladly take the next 120 hours and its memories to my grave.

The sound of music is suddenly heard from what Bea said is my room. I hold her away from me at arm's length to determine if she knows what's going on next door. She smiles and says, while taking hold of my hand, "Come on, let me show you."

Even though I don't care for the "mine and her" separation of the sleeping quarters, I follow sheepishly. Opening the door, I am quite surprised to see upwards of twenty people yelling, "Surprise!" as Bea steps aside for me to enter first. I don't know a single person, but that doesn't matter. A sign over the bed reads, "Welcome Harry." Balloons and streamers are taped to the ceiling. As if on cue my favorite songs boom from a stereo that Bea somehow finagled.

Some of the men are servicemen in uniform. Some single, some with their wives. Even members of the hotel came up to help spring this surprise, and what a surprise it is. Bea has set the stage to make me feel special. And that weighted, vexatious feeling I have learned to carry and accept as part of my life vanishes. I am happier than I dared admit, laughing and hugging each and every one of them just for being there. I feel like a kid again, and it feels great. I am on a high without so much as taking a drink and turn to see Beatrice standing there just watching me enjoy the thrill and the excitement of the moment. But the look on her face troubles me. She is forcing herself to smile, trying to hide something. I know her well enough that she can't fool me, though she can fool everyone else.

I walk up to her and touch her face lightly and ask, "What is it? What's wrong, Bea?" She stubbornly won't allow me in.

"Nothing, Harry," she says as tears well up. She then embraces me, clutching my arms, stating, "I'm so glad you're happy. All I ever wanted is for you to be happy, Harry." She snuggles up to me, putting her lips to my ear, standing on her toes, and whispers, "I've worried about you so much—you have no idea." She silently weeps against my neck.

"I've worried about you too," I reply. "Thank you for the gifts— of being here and surprising me so much. I love you, Beasley." I call her Beasley every now and then as a sort of pet name I invented, much to her chagrin. In the background, the lyrics of a song are playing: *"The mountain's so high and the valley's are so deep, don't you give up, don't you cry."* And then the phrase, *"don't you give up till I reach the end of this life,"* causes me to think of my chances of returning to her in less than four months. However, I force myself to concentrate on the here and now. Vietnam can wait. The next song is, "Daddy's Home"—*"You're my love, you're my angel, you're the girl of my dreams, I'd like to thank you for waiting patiently."* We dance slowly to the music.

For four of the five days we refrain from having sex. It is not easy, and just in case we can't fight off the hormones, I purchase a three pack of condoms. Both of us want very badly to have sexual inter- course, but manage to relieve ourselves in other ways. Neither Bea nor I want to face the responsibility of becoming a parent at twenty years of age. Besides, I have nothing going for me other than the service. And I sure as hell am not about to stay in and try to support a family on $300 a month. Beatrice has a bright future and an unwanted preg- nancy at this stage in her life does not compute. She remains steadfast when we neck and pet in intimate moments. I keep the condoms to be prepared if we get carried away, and secretly I am hoping to get lucky.

On the eve of day five, Bea's schoolmates leave us alone in our hotel room. We talk about old times and old friends—who is doing what with their lives, music, her schooling, and where she wants to be in thirty years. Of course she does most of the talking, going on and on with my interjecting an "ah huh" every now and then, letting her know I am following her and that I am interested in what she has to say. As the evening wears on, I find myself tensing. It is as if I am in a dream and about to wake up to find myself back in the jungle out on some ambush patrol. I also feel that emotional tornado getting closer, attempting to overcome me again as it did on the plane. But I manage to suppress its distant calling.

A few drinks later, a song comes on the radio we both like, and we sing it together, thinking we sound like recording artists. We don't care if we are in tune or not. It's the lyrics that matter. The song is entitled, "Dedicated to the One I Love."—*"Each night before you go to bed my baby, tell all the stars above, my baby, this is dedicated to the one I love."*

Afterward the mood is set. I couldn't have a better lead in and feel this might be my last opportunity to consummate and manifest my love in a sexual way. I chance taking the initiative. "Bea," I begin. "Bea, I've got something to say, and it can't wait. Please hear me out. Do not interrupt, please, just listen. It's not easy for me to say what it is I need to say right now . . ." God, I think, I've practiced this over and over. Come on. Then that little voice comes forth stating, "It's no big deal Harry. What have you got to lose? Just say it. You know you love her."

"Bea, I only know what I feel right this very moment. A peace I have never known and a love I have never fully expressed for fear of rejection. But it doesn't matter anymore. Rejection or not, I want to love you tonight as I have dreamed and fantasized about for a very long time. Love me in return for who I am, not for what I may become. For all I know, this may the best I'm capable of being in this life. Love me without the promise of tomorrow."

I cast my gaze down, feeling the tornado pulling me away from her, but I fight back, saying, "Forgive me, you might take this the wrong way, but, Bea, I've seen death. I've been an active participant in it. I'm not proud of that. I simply followed the orders of our Commander-in-Chief, the President. I'm doing what he has asked me to do. That's all, nothing more, nothing less. The fact is I may not make it back to follow up on what we've got going."

She is about to speak, but I stop her, asking her not to interrupt. I put my index finger over her lips tenderly. "Shush now!" And I continue, "Bea, I may not return to you like I am now. That is a reality I live with, a reality I have seen played out too many times. But should I never be able to see you again, please know, I love you as no man has ever loved a woman. I have not pushed the issue of having sex. I respect you. I would never consciously cause you pain, or hurt you, or encumber you. My intentions are honorable."

Her face is taught with emotion, as she searches my eyes, seeing past them, reading my thoughts and emotions, sensing my soul, somehow hearing all I am afraid to say, seeing and feeling all I have seen, all the pain in my life that I have tried to hide. In effect, she sees me for who I am, nothing more, nothing less.

With a tear running down her cheek, she tenderly strokes the side of my face and responds, "Oh Harry, don't you know? I've always loved you too. It nearly killed me when you chose service over college." I try to respond, but she gestures to have me listen while she attempts to compose herself. She then continues. "Harry, you have always held a special part of my heart. I remember the first time I saw you, too. We had a class together, band practice. I was new to the school. I beat you into the classroom and had just opened my flute case when you walked in wearing your letter-sweater you had earned in your first semester in high school. I thought I looked like a fool, puckering my lips to meet the flute's mouthpiece when our eyes met. I knew that very instant that you were the guy I would one day marry. Don't ask me how I knew. I just knew. Call it a girl thing. I knew then as I know now you have greatness within you, a capacity to succeed, the will to win at anything you undertake. You're special. Did you know, that Harry? You're a very special person. I've always loved you and always will. I came here to let you know. I can't let go."

She is beginning to tear again. Music plays softly in the background, intoxicating us. We search each other's eyes, reading each other's thoughts. In those fleeting moments, I think how very much I love and admire her. Growing up together, we could have had sex any number of times, but I could not allow myself to discredit or dishonor her by getting her pregnant. I held her to a higher standard. I loved her that much.

I want her tonight though, to hell with tomorrow. I mean to cash in my chips and go for broke. Tonight I want to taste her love. My heart has chosen her. My "will" will bring me home to her. While in Vietnam, this moment will get me through. "Nothing will keep us apart," I vow, "nothing. This is no ordinary love. We will make it . . . together!" As I pull out the condom, she stops me saying softly, "No, Harry, nothing can come between us."

Back onboard the plane, en route to war, I pull out my diary and date it March 8 1967 and copy what a fellow medic gave me some while back. The author is unknown: "God, I haven't spoken to you as often as I should, but I want to now. How do you do? You see,

God, they told me you didn't exist. And like a fool, I believed all of
this. If I had known then what I know now, I would have spoken to
you more throughout the last decade. If I come to your house tonight,
will you shake my hand, because somehow I think you'll understand.
Look, God, there is going to be a horrible fight—it could be that I
will come to your house tonight. God, it's me. I'm here in Vietnam.
Mary, Joseph, and Jesus of Bethlehem, look out for us in Vietnam.
Oh, God, I'm so sorry. I wish I had known you all these past number
of years."

Although I am not back in the tornado, I sense it's very near. That
heavy, weighted feeling I've learned to accept is bearing down on me.

My last thought after closing my diary was last night with
Beatrice. I smile to myself when a song jumps up in my mind: *Oh
What A Night* by the Dells. Yeah, I think—what a night it was.

Chapter 20

THE LAST CASUALTY

ONCE BACK AT the battalion area, I spot Flock walking out of the mess hall. I run up to him as he walks with his back to me. I want him to know that I'm back, ready to face whatever he has to offer. I feel rejuvenated from R&R and from being with Beatrice. "Sergeant Flock, I'm back. I thought you might like to know that. What's cookin'?" He stops to rinse off his used tray in a heated fifty-five-gallon drum of water. He doesn't bother to make eye contact. But he doesn't ignore me either. His body language indicates he is aware of my presence, although I sense something is bothering him. So I start with the introduction again. "Hey, Sarge, I'm back. How's everything going?"

He rubs his tray with a wet soapy rag and responds, "OK, so you're back, so what?"

My natural high was nose-diving fast. "What's the problem, Sergeant Flock? You look like you lost your best friend."

"I'm fine," he snaps. "But I can't say that about the guy who took your place. While you were partying in Hawaii, he was killed."

"What? Who's dead? Who took my place?" I ask in astonishment. "What happened?'

"Bartmore. Took one in the head trying to get back from saving a guy who was wounded. Almost made it. As he was crawling over a downed tree trunk, Charlie nailed him in the back of the head. I gave him your platoon, Alpha company second platoon."

"No, tell me your shitting me, man; don't fuck with me like this, Flock."

Before I left, Bartmore had just returned from an injury he sustained in Da Nang. I didn't think he was fit for regular duty. I look at Flock, searching for any clue that he's just cruelly pulling my leg, but there isn't any. I knew Bartmore for nearly a year. He was close with Steve Best. Gary, gone. Holy shit. Who's next?

As I walk back to my tent, I keep thinking that it should have been me. I feel like shit. What a contrast to my trip to Hawaii, what a remarkable contrast. I shake my head, feeling partly responsible for his death.

A couple of medics are in the tent. We exchange pleasantries and then I ask if they know the guy Bartmore saved.

"James Johnson," states Dave Trevino, another medic, an FNG.

"I thought he was in Sergeant Garcia's platoon in Bravo Company?" I state.

"He is. Ah, was," exclaims Dan Reynolds. "They transferred him, due to the big hits the second platoon of Alpha Company took while you were gone."

"Alpha Company? Second platoon? How many? When? On second thought, don't tell me, I don't want to know. What are the extent of his injuries?" I ask.

"He's dead," says Chiefoot. "Died while in the evacuation hospital. Took three bullets to the back, the thoracic region."

James Johnson confided in me once that he thought he would take the big hit. I dismissed it as "beer talk" as we were in the EM Club when he said it. Another self-fulfilled prophecy, I think to myself while sitting on the end of my bunk. I turn deeper into my mind, searching for that little voice that seems to speak only when I don't want him to. Where are you, voice? Nothing, zero, zilch, nada! I feel empty, hollow, and horrified as I sit on my footlocker, with elbows on knees, and hands over my face, silently shaking my head.

Sometime later Flock walks into our tent, informing me to get ready. I am going out to join the pool of medics at BSOP in Operation Junction City. I'll be ready-relief for the medics on patrols. I don't bat an eye as he searches my body language for an opening to pounce. The new guys take in the tension between Flock and me.

New medics join us with greater frequency. Most, if not all, keep their distance as if we were senior cadets and they were pleebs at West Point. I don't even want to know their names. The less you knew about them, the less you'll hurt if they take a hit.

Operation Junction City, which saw my brothers from the 2/503rd making a combat jump while I was with Beatrice, will come to a close on March 15th. More of our own have fallen, making the supreme sacrifice, while numerous others were wounded in action. I have grown to accept death as long as it doesn't take someone I know. If I know them, it haunts and frightens me.

During the next three weeks, the majority of medics doing the humping are replacements, FNG's. About a dozen combat-tested medics are back in base camp with the privilege to work under the direction of Flock. Strange as this sounds, most prefer humping the boonies and facing death rather than deal with Flock—that's just how popular the guy is. In the final analysis, Flock is in love with himself and the power he holds over us. A real piece of work.

I think of Fields, my replacement. How he's doing out there without me to guide him? I feel like an upper classman waiting to graduate. The only prerequisite to graduate here in Vietnam is to stay alive and in one piece.

On April 4th, word filters back to us that three FNG medics were wounded in action and some among us will have to replace them. At 1000 hours, Flock barges into our tent, and asks for volunteers to fill their spots in various platoons. Despite our hatred of base camp and Flock's direct control over us, no one in the tent raises his hand. No one wants to replace an FNG. It's bad luck, or so the saying goes.

Not seeing any volunteers, Flock stands in the middle of our tent, hands on hips, scanning us, "Let's see," he toys. "Who shall I pick?" He's not looking my way. Maybe I'll get lucky. "Well then," he muses, barking and pointing, "Dallas, Mike Sand," he spins on his heels, looking dead at me, "and Spencer."

I respond immediately, "Wouldn't you rather have me pull KP or burn shit barrels so you can keep an eye on me, Sarge?"

"Not a chance," he sneers. "As much as I'd love to have you around to do shit details, Spencer, I much prefer to have you out on line facing the real enemy, and you know what else?"

Oh, shit, he has that look again. As I sit on my footlocker staring at him, I think that there are fourteen guys in the tent to pick from, ten of whom have less time out in the bush than me, and I get picked to go. Go figure! He then turns to leave our tent. Before I can stop myself, I rise to his threatening look and state, "Come on, Sarge, leave me here so someone can be around to kiss your ass or polish your fucking boots."

He flips me the bird and keeps walking, saying over his shoulder "Your time's coming, Spencer. Make no mistake about that."

Within an hour I am boarding a chopper with Flock standing alongside its entrance, hands on hips, looking like ever-the-tough guy, snickering at me. Seconds later he gives the pilot the thumbs-up as we get airborne. I briefly entertain the idea of drawing a bead on him, but flip him the bird instead. He sees it and points at me, yelling something, but I can't hear a word over the roar of the chopper's engine and whirling blades. I throw him a kiss, waving bye-bye with much animation.

Thirty minutes later, as our chopper ever so slowly begins its descent, I notice a group of men huddled below. Some are obviously wounded, but others do not show any visual signs of injury. I recognize the medic standing with them, I.V. bag held high with a tube running into a man lying on a stretcher. It is Robert McQueen, a senior medic. I also spot Doug Fields, my replacement. He is lying on a stretcher with his leg heavily wrapped.

That's one of three medics wounded. I wonder where the other two are. I'll find out later. As we touch down they run toward us to board the chopper, even though it isn't a Medevac. I take the initiative to wave them forward, staying by the chopper to help them onboard. Dallas and Sand do the same.

When they are within thirty feet of the chopper, there's an explosion exactly where they were standing just seconds before. Despite the roar of the chopper, I hear and feel the explosion. Holy shit! Seconds later, Robert slumps and falls to the ground. He had covered the distance to me, still helping the injured, while he himself took a hit from the shrapnel. I don't think he knows he is hit. He didn't exhibit any signs that he is injured until he passes out at my feet, dropping the I.V. bag on top of my boots. His back is covered in blood. I hoist him in with help from Leon Dallas, and yell, "Looks like we'll need another medic out here!"

After everyone is on board, I yell to the door gunner that he has an unexpected passenger, a medic, and ask how long to the evac hospital. He holds up one hand, making a fist, and opens with five fingers, telling me fifteen minutes. I motion for him to stay put. I have to check McQueen's wounds, so I cut his fatigue shirt open from the back as he lies unconscious face down on the steel floor of the chopper. The pilot meanwhile has his turbine whirling at the RPM necessary to go airborne. I ignore the obvious sign that he wants out of here. McQueen's wounds are not too bad. Not too much bleeding, several small holes, though none look significant. Then I yell that he'll be all right if they get him to the hospital within fifteen minutes. I tell the crew chief to make sure the pilot knows that he has another injured party aboard who is a medic. In fact, I tell him he's got two medics, one of whom has not been treated and time is critical. He waves me off as if I annoy him.

As I step off the chopper's skids. it leaps into flight just as another explosion rips the earth about one hundred feet from me. I fall to the ground, looking around and see no one. Where in the hell did everybody go? With the noise of the chopper fading, I hear several shouts from the men, "Where in the hell did that shit come from?" And, "Who's supposed to be on the perimeter?'

"Everyone get off the LZ. We have incoming. *Move, move, move!*" I don't need much coaxing. I am simply trying to figure out where to take cover. I don't want to run right up to Charlie and shake his hand, or the barrel of his rifle. But just as suddenly as it began, it ends. Charlie struck when the noise of the chopper covered his movements and drowned out the thud of the mortar when fired. He is smart, alright. I have to give him credit. He knows when and where to strike.

Flock's words come back to mind as I scramble for cover. He stated, "It's only for a couple of days." A couple of days. Hell, it only takes a split second to take a hit. A couple of days might as well be an eternity.

Minutes later a battalion major has come to inform us where our companies will be coming from and when they should enter BSOP for the night. Some patrols went out as company-size units, others went out as single-platoon patrols. I am assigned to Bravo Company's third platoon.

At dusk, the men begin to emerge from the jungle, one by one. As I have already found Bravo Company's entry point, I stand as sentry while they pass by me, nodding at some while speaking to others. Look at that. What a surprise. Willie Lane resigned his cooking job to become a grunt. He appears happy, but certainly looks out of place. I always pictured him in white kitchen attire. Here he looks as dirty and ragged as the rest of us. We shake hands, and I make the comment, "What's up, Willie? Just had to see for yourself how tough it is out here? Couldn't take our word for it, huh?"

He smiles sheepishly. I believe he feels he made a mistake. Disheveled, he not only looks out of place but totally out of character. Even though he says, "Hi, how you doing Harry? Long time no see," he keeps walking. He is in no mood to chat.

Later that night a group of medics get together to chat, not a fireside chat, but guy chat, combat chat. I learn that Fields shot himself. Steve Best is here along with George Shepherd, Mike Sand, and Dallas. Steve Best brings up Doug Fields' injury before I have a chance to ask. "The dumb shit couldn't take it any more. Went to go shoot himself in the foot, but instead he shot his knee cap off." We all flinch on that one. Sand says he'd like to see Fields thrown out of the airborne army. "Banish him, that pussy," he says. Shepherd is a little easier than most, stating, "He's going to pay for that not with just jail time for destroying government property, but living with himself. How's he gonna tell his grandkids?" Dallas jumps on that one, "He's such a fucking pussy. He couldn't have kids."

We sit in darkness, speaking in hushed tones well into the night. The two medics I didn't see when I landed have been killed—Willie Walker and John Savinsky. The count of medics killed now stands at ten, more than thirty percent of my platoon dead. Not good, Spencer, not good. I count the days left to my freedom—less than ninety to go.

APRIL 6 1967; EARLY MORNING

I am going out on a Death Patrol with a squad of just twelve men, the kind Charlie loves to strike. I am more tense than ever. I am "getting short," a term used for those getting close to discharge. By luck, I am with Willie Lane's squad, and in the middle of the pack. Willie is bringing up the rear—a position equally as dangerous as walking "point." His job is to lag behind as far as possible, stopping every now and then, waiting, looking, smelling, and covering our six— possibly foiling Charlie's attempt to ambush us from our rear flank.

Because my contact with Charlie has been so sporadic and quick, I really never had the opportunity to see him face to face in firefight. It is mid-afternoon, 3 or so, and we are headed back toward BSOP. I purposely picked a spot in the rear of the column to be near my homey, Willie. Directly behind me is the machine-gunner, Mark Spooner, a big guy; his ammo bearers; and then Willie. Directly in front of me is a buck sergeant, a hardcore lifer type. I don't particularly like him because he thinks he is tougher than we are. But I have to admit that he knows his shit, appearing very competent and gung ho.

The pace is excruciatingly slow. The sun's rays are burning our necks while the mosquitoes, despite the heat, continue to bite us. One step leads to another and yet another. I secretly wish never to make contact with Charlie, while the crazies among us look forward to contact. Before we realize what is happening, the world is filled with the sounds of automatic weapons fire. Bullets make smashing sounds as they hit trees, foliage falling like rain. The enemy machine-gunner doing the firing is not firing in short bursts. He doesn't stop firing. He simply holds the trigger, allowing in excess of 700 rounds of ammunition per minute to rip through us and the jungle.

At this moment Charlie is solely in charge. And he isn't very bashful about initiating contact and taking charge.

Everyone drops to the ground. Bullets buzz, pop, and smash into trees near me; some are moving the air near my face. Despite that, I am determined to spot Charlie. Everything appears to be in slow motion, as if I am in a drug-induced state.

I turn slowly to my left rear and spot them—three of them, one huddled behind the machine-gun doing the firing, the others on either side of him. One is holding the ammunition, feeding it into the hungry, cold metal monster reining destruction and terror on us, while the other one is catching the spent cartridges in a type of wicker basket. I feel no fear though, just a strange fascination, as if I were watching a war movie and I can't possibly get hurt.

The firing is nonstop. Maybe five seconds have gone by. Foliage continues to fall. As the bullets spew forth, I can see them more clearly. Upon realizing this scenario is real, I jerk, tripping, and falling backwards. Again, everything seems to be happening in slow motion, even my fall toward the earth. Simultaneously the squad leader directly in front of me screams, while in a fetal position, *"Jesus Christ, Doc, get down, you fucking asshole! Get down!"*

As I fall, I look the squad leader's way. He looks panicky, rolling side to side as if he were a kid having a bad dream. Something snags the lip on the front of my helmet, causing the back of it to violently dig in the nap of my neck. Ouch!

The equipment in my rucksack cushions my fall. Rolling onto my side, I see Mark kicking ass, firing back at Charlie with a vengeance. I grab for my helmet and notice a hole in it on the front lip. Turning my attention back to our machine gunner, I think, geez, he'd better slow down or he'll run out of ammo. He appears to be firing in the right direction. Foliage in front of him is disintegrating.

Lying here, I realize a portion of my wish has come to pass. I have actually witnessed my enemy trying to kill me. And they saw me looking at them, too. But I renege on the other wish to get a million dollar wound, permanently taking me off the line. I want to go home without a scratch. Screw those war stories I might tell with the tangible evidence that I was in the war. The buck sergeant is now on the radio attempting to call in our position, screaming over the sounds of the two machine guns locked in a deadly dual with one another. Charlie won't let up on the trigger and neither does Mark.

The "wild west" gunfight lasts all of two to five seconds. Here, the picture is much different. No one else has fired a single round yet, instead they're trying to learn where to fire. If we fire indiscriminately, we might shoot our brothers. Men on a squad patrol have a rough total of one hundred twenty feet of separation, from point man to tail man. It's therefore suicidal for the men up front to shoot our way.

I am in the thick of it when I hear the scream for medic. It is coming from where Willie Lane might be. Then it dawns on me. Christ, Willie's even closer to Charlie than I am! I'll have to crawl dangerously close, right in the direction of the firing. Shit! I can't! I let go a burst from my rifle, but it jams almost instantly. My weapon is so jammed I can't even pull the bolt back. *Shit.*

"Somebody help me! I'm hit! Medic! Harry! Help me!" Willie screams, calling me to help him.

Fuck it. I've got to try. So I yell to him, "Willie! Is that you?"

I can't hear him. The sounds of the two machine guns are deafening. I wait for a pause, but Mark, the machine-gunner, is returning Charlie's heat, fire meeting fire. He doesn't let up on the trigger either. My God! How long can he continue before he or Charlie warps the barrels of their weapons? I look around for cover, anyplace to shield my body from the bullets as they buzz by merely a foot or two off the ground—some smashing into trunks of trees, some continuing through the jungle, seeking their intended targets.

Realizing that there isn't cover, I frantically feel for that bullet that I always carry in my breast pocket. I feel better once I touch it, and then I scream at the squad leader to call for some air or artillery support. He has been yelling into the handset of the radio with the radio operator at his side. "Can't get any. They're engaged in another support mission. Estimate of availability is ten minutes."

"Ten minutes! Are you shitting me? We'll be dead in ten minutes."

The sergeant shouts commands. "Dig in, men! By the numbers! Dig in, goddamn it! We are not running!" We trained for this, but none of us ever believed we would actually be caught in a position to use that training. Just then Charlie opens up from another direction— this time, it is coming from my right rear. Jesus Christ, they're organized! How many are there? Are they NVA regulars? Are they filming this too?

Everyone but the machine-gunner digs in. Mark and his ammo bearers nearby are still firing nonstop. Digging frantically, I think I hear Willie again. "Medic! Medic! Harry, I'm hit in the head and legs—both of them! Help me!" I begin shaking so badly that I remind myself of my grandfather trying to eat soup. His hands shook so much that he'd spill half of it before it reached his mouth. I used to laugh then, but I am not laughing now. Forgive me, Grandpa, I'm sorry I laughed at you. Please forgive me. Grandpa, can you help? Help me if you can.

Despite the danger, I have to get to Willie. It's a miracle that no one else has been hit so far. Maybe our luck will hold out for ten minutes. Just maybe, I hope as I continue to crawl toward Willie.

I reach Mark. Five minutes has gone by and he continues firing nonstop, attempting to suppress those who would kill us. He appears to be in control of himself. That makes me feel a little better. I crawl next to him and notice the barrel of his machine gun is glowing orange. As I brush up against him, he looks at me with indifference. His eyes, however, are bulging. Boy, he's an ugly dude. I know he'll be nearly deaf from firing his weapon steadily for the last few minutes. I have to communicate with him, though, because I have to get a fix on Willie's position, and because Charlie's nonstop barrage of bullets is shredding still more of the jungle, exposing our position. Time is critical.

I finally get his attention, and Mark nods in recognition and stops. He calls for a new barrel to his ammo bearer. "You still out there, Willie?" No response. "Willie, talk to me, homey. Where are you, man? I'm coming. Just let me know you're still with me, brother. Because if you go down, we all go down with you! Talk to me, goddamn it!"

Willie responds in a weaker tone, as if he's succumbing to his injuries. He says he's all right and that he got lucky, finding refuge behind two boulders.

I respond, "Alright, homey, I'm coming."

Mark, the machine gunner, tries to stop me, saying, "You crazy fuck, stay put. You'll get yourself killed going out there."

"What if that was you out there, you piece of shit! Just keep me covered."

With a fresh barrel in his machine gun, he resumes firing, laying down a field of fire in hopes of pinning Charlie down and distracting him from possibly spotting me. I crawl just like I did at West Point, when I demonstrated the proper method of crawling for the pleebs over those killer stones! The only real difference between then and now is I see tracers flying out of the corner of my eye right over my head and to my right. Just when I think things are getting better for us, a great thunder erupts to my rear—where the bulk of the squad is. The earth shakes with such intensity it momentarily lifts my body. I am on a mission though—nothing can distract me from getting to my patient, my homey, my Willie Lane.

I want to yell for him, but if I do, it will give away my position. Just keep going, Spence, I think to myself. You'll find him. Kaboom! Kaboom! Kaboom! Something is raining hell fire on us. Jesus Christ. The jungle's canopy from high atop is falling around us; the branches are considerably larger than those that fell under the assault of Charlie's machine gun. The explosions command undivided attention, as if they're saying, "I'm here and I'm the baddest, the strongest, toughest motherfucker in the jungle!" I pray the explosions are from our side.

When I find Willie, he is laying on his side. His chin is resting on his chest, and his face is soaked with blood. He has propped himself up slightly, resting his upper torso on the boulder that provides cover for us both. I immediately pull him down to the ground. I figure he is unconscious from the hole in his windpipe, starving his brain of oxygen. Because of the amount of blood on his face, I run my hand through his hair, feeling for a wound and recoil when I feel something soft and warm.

I pull my hand from his head and pieces of bone and brain matter ooze between my fingers. I flick them aside, grabbing Willie, trying to shake him awake. Nothing! I rip open his fatigue shirt, pushing my ear hard onto his chest and detect a faint beat. I look over his legs, pulling at his trousers, which are tucked in his boots. He has taken numerous hits in the legs. I can't tell how many. They look bad enough that, should he live, he'll be without legs.

Blood is everywhere, the most I have seen from any injury. I put my ear next to his open mouth to determine if he is breathing . . . he isn't. His body then begins to dance to the tune of the Grim Reaper. Post mortem muscle spasms! I panic, grabbing him by the lapels, pulling him up to my face and scream, "No, Willie! No! Come back to me! Don't leave me! Please! Don't leave me." I wail in grief as if I am a kid again, playing on the school playground screaming. "Stop! Goddamn it, stop! Time fucking out! Stop! Please stop!" And then I curse God himself. "God, damn you for allowing this to happen!" I lay my head on Willie's chest, fighting the rush of blood that drains from my head. My brain wants to escape what my body cannot. And then it's all over. Silence. Nobody speaks. Nobody moves.

When we emerge from the jungle, back at BSOP, men stand up to greet us as we file past. Today another part of me has died along with Willie Lane.

The eleven of us returning are drained of energy and emotion and look ghostly as we emerge into the clearing of BSOP. Letting members of his squad carry his machine gun, Mark Spooner, the biggest among us, carries Willie's body back.

Mike Sand is waiting for me. Mike is a gentle soul and goes out of his way to help when others wouldn't even think of it. Seeing the dried blood covering both my face and fatigues, he reaches for my rucksack, slipping it off to relieve me of its burden. I don't object. There isn't anything left in me. I lost a homey, and I cursed God. I feel void of all feeling except one—I am condemned, judged. It's a matter of time. I'll be next, but I don't care. I stare the 1,000-yard stare. Part of me died out there, and I don't care.

Later that evening I am evacuated, diagnosed by my fellow medics as unfit for duty. The shock of Willie Lane dying on me tipped the scale. As I ride in the chopper back toward base camp, I remember meeting Beatrice just a short month ago. It feels like it took place in another lifetime. I was somebody else then, much different than who I am now. Thinking of Beatrice and her warm glow of life and energy sparks something that I said, "By sheer 'will' alone, I will return to you." As I sit here in silence on my way to base camp, thermos cause the chopper to bounce up and down violently. My eyes fill with tears at the thought of Beatrice. I'm trying, babe. I'm really trying. Then a song jumps to the fore. *"There must be a cloud in my head, a man ain't supposed to cry. It must be raindrops falling from the sky."*

I am reassigned to be in charge of the medical platoon's jeeps and three-quarter-ton ambulance vehicles. A couple of days later, Dr. Pierce calls a halt to Sergeant Flock's intentions of sending me back out to another firefight as a replacement for one of my fellow medics. I hear them arguing. Flock tries to pull rank based on his experience. "Look, Captain—Doctor Pierce, you're effective at what you do, but I'm a career soldier. I ain't here to pad my resume looking to impress a future employer. I'm telling you, Spencer is going back out there tomorrow. I need to rotate my men—my way. Do you understand me, Sir?"

Pierce, normally a soft-spoken, kind-hearted man, won't bend and responds, "Sergeant Flock, I've reviewed all the medics' records. I have them right here on a spreadsheet. I've correlated the factors of time in and time out of the boonies, taking into effect the types of exposure each man has sustained." His voice grows stern as he continues, "Now, I'm not suggesting anything, as you have implied my authority is limited to an advisory capacity, I'm telling you, and hereby putting you on notice. I'm aware of what you have been attempting to do to Spencer. I've given you a lot of latitude and haven't interfered with you running your platoon. But I just concluded my research last evening. The evidence is overwhelming, Sergeant. You've tried several times to have Spencer killed in the line of duty, and I cannot ignore the empirical data supporting that viewpoint. Are you getting my drift, Sergeant Flock?"

Flock is taken back at the unexpected information. Both men are the same age, about thirty-three. One is an altruistic professional who genuinely cares for those under his command. The other is only concerned with the power of managing a group of men in battle from behind a desk. He has the power to make or break a man. He knows that, but now Dr. Pierce knows that as well. Flock is checked in this tournament of human chess.

Shaken, Flock storms out of the doctor's office in the aid station. As he passes me, he gives me a look that scares the living shit out of me. His eyes seem to burn right through me as he says, "It's not over yet, Spencer."

Chapter 21

GOING HOME

I AM WORKING ON the jeep in the motor pool, tightening an alternator belt, concentrating on the task at hand, when Flock appears out of nowhere. His presence, just a couple of feet from me, startles me, and I hit my head on the jeep's raised roof. "What's up, Sarge?" I ask.

Then I notice the gentle giants, Ted Dziengelewski and Leon Dallas, standing alongside the jeep. They're the guys who tackled me, preventing me from killing Flock and living in prison for the remainder of my life. They both have shit-eating grins as they look at me.

Flock is rocking on his heels, hands behind his back, and breaks the silence, "Oh, nothing much." he hands me a few sheets of paper adding, "Here, I've got some news I think you might be interested in seeing."

My hands are pretty greasy so I gingerly take the papers from him and place them down on the jeep's radiator. The bold print on top of the cover sheet says it all: United States Department of Army, Compassionate Reassignment. I straighten up with such force I hit my head again on the hood of the jeep. Oh, my God! I'm going home! I'm really going home!

Flock steps back, getting out of my way as I jump up and down like a kid receiving the best Christmas present of his life. This present is a hundred times better to me because this is a gift of life, my life. "I'm coming home, Beatrice! I'm coming, baby! I'm homebound!"

Flock interrupts, snickering, "I wouldn't be wasting too much time, trooper." He turns his gaze, looking away to spit, and states, "Your plane leaves in under two hours." He looks at his watch saying, "You've got to clear post."

The process of discharge is lengthy. Under normal conditions it takes eight hours of standing in endless lines with others going back stateside. I run directly to Ted, grabbing him as if he is my personal secretary, and I yell, "We have no time. Let's go. We'll take this jeep. I have one hour and forty-five minutes to catch that freedom bird!"

I drive like a madman. There are rules of the road, but I don't care about breaking any of them. I am going home! I have to get to brigade headquarters fast. Once there, I have to clear post by first going to the administrative offices and showing them the authorization of a Compassionate Reassignment. When I reach the building, at least a dozen guys are in line. I run up to the guy who is at the tail end, asking if all the men in line are here to clear post for reassignment. "You got it buddy. Take a number."

Take a number? Shit! Then I ask when he is slated to ship out. He responds, "Next week. Why?" I ask a guy halfway in the line the same question. "Next week. Why?" I blurt, "My fucking plane leaves in one hour!"

While making my way to the front of the line, I shout, "Sorry, guys, I'm taking cuts. My plane is leaving today." And then I add, "Are any of you guys leaving in the next hour?" They all look at me like I am crazy. One shouts, "You'll never make it, man."

Bullshit. I'm outta here now! Today! I rip open the door and scan the administration offices, seeing dozens of desks with clerks busy doing whatever it is they are do, and shout to get someone's attention, "Excuse me, gentlemen! I need some help clearing post! My plane leaves in one hour! Please can somebody please help me?"

One of the clerks coldly responds to my plea, "Take a number, trooper. We'll get to you just like we get to everyone else."

He holds the rank of a specialist fourth class, just one paygrade over me. He, therefore, doesn't threaten me, and I immediately object to his offer to take a seat, saying, "Maybe you didn't understand. I've got to clear post now! I don't have any time to waste! I may miss my plane!"

A bean-counter-type officer approaches me and says, "Let me see your orders, trooper. Let's see what I can do to help you."

"Huh? Oh, thank you, Sir! Thank you very much," I respond. "I've never cleared post before. I don't know what to do or where to go."

"Slow down, Private. Let me read your orders. I cannot listen to you and read at the same time, OK?"

I suddenly have an uncontrollable urge to urinate. I ask for the nearest latrine. The officer points as he continues to read. I am fidgeting so much I wonder if he might think I am on speed or some other illegal drug. When I return, the officer remarks that I should enter myself in the Guinness Book of World Records as the world's most expeditious urination artist. I pay him no attention. All I want is his direction and assistance.

He looks up and states, as if he is troubled by what he read in my orders, "Trooper, are you aware that you are not going to be reassigned under the guidelines of a Compassionate Reassignment?"

I lose my breath as a surge of adrenaline shoots through me. I bend over, putting my hands on my knees, feeling as if I just got hit by lightning bolt, and gasp, "No! What are you talking about, Sir?"

"Well, it says right here, you are to be discharged. You're not being reassigned to another outfit. But, that doesn't make sense. Why would they do it this way?"

As he continues to read every single word, punctuation and exclamation mark, along with every prepositional phrase and adjective clause, I try very hard to control my emotions at hearing him say I am to be "discharged." Christ, I hadn't expected that one. Another dose of adrenaline is involuntarily injected, and I begin to shake and twitch. My mouth becomes so cotton dry that I can't swallow or talk in an acceptable manner, which might convince someone I really am buzzed.

"Well," he eventually gets around to saying, "I'm not quite sure what to do at this point."

I stop him asking, "OK, Sir, what is it you do know that I can do to help facilitate my clearing post? Let's not get caught up in things we can't do, it's not rocket science, Lieutenant. Simply put, according to you, that document authorizes the military to discharge me post haste—is that a fair assumption, Sir?"

He looks at my oily motor pool fatigues and the PFC stripes on the arms of my fatigue shirt and comments, "You're very articulate, Private; are you a . . . "

I interrupt again pleading, "Look, Sir, just tell me where to go, and what to do when I get there, will you?'

He is obviously amused by that comment, responding with a slight grin, "Oh, I can certainly tell you where to go with your condescending expressions, Private, but I don't know what to tell you to do when you get there!"

I look at my watch, shifting my weight. What can I say to this guy so that he won't take offense? I respond, "OK, while you check on the technicalities of my paper work, what can I do?"

He replies casually, looks over his glasses and states, "Oh, you can go back to your outfit and turn in all your gear. Personal items can be mailed. Have your quartermaster sign off to indicate you did same," and then with a long pause, he lowers his reading glasses, making direct eye contact, while smiling and says, "Report back here. I should have something definitive by then as to how to proceed. OK, Private?"

I turn and run right into one of the men who is scheduled to leave sometime next week, knocking him down. But I don't let that slow me down as I head for the door and yell, "Sorry 'bout that, guy!" and run out to where Ted is waiting for me in the jeep. I jump in the passenger seat, yelling for Ted to floor it, after which I inform him that I have to start the clearing post process by turning all my gear in to our own quartermaster.

Ted pops the clutch and the jeep stalls. My heart sinks. Is there something wrong under the hood? Did I take all my tools out before we started out to come here? Did the fan belt come off? "Sorry, Harry," Ted apologizes as I beat the metal dashboard with my open hands.

"Come on!" I yell, trying to contain the volcano erupting in me. "Move it, Ted, step on it."

"I'm going, I'm going, just be cool, chill, man," he responds.

"Yeah, sure, easy for you to say," I retort.

We smile when the jeep finally comes to life as he dumps the clutch at full throttle, laying a patch of rubber, spewing dust and rocks from the dirt road. The posted speed limit is fifteen mph. All I need now is for the military police to stop us. And, sure as shit, the goddamn wail of a siren beckons us to pull over. Jesus Christ, this can't be happening to me, not now, not here.

I jump out in defense of Ted's driving and think to myself, I'll simply explain the circumstances. As I walk up to the MP jeep, I notice the guy has an I-don't-really-give-a-shit-what-your-excuse-is look, along with an I'm-still-writing-you-up expression. As I approach him, he puts his hand up, shaking his head before we are even close enough to talk.

My heart sinks. "Officer," I start. Wait a minute, he isn't an officer. I look at his name tag and notice he is a Specialist Fourth Class. So I call him by the name on his fatigue shirt, "Thomas. Mr. Thomas." He cuts me off. The goatsucker is going to bust my balls.

"I've heard them all," he says, "don't even try it, Private."

That son of a bitch, calling me Private; I'll give him something private. But he gives me an out, saying, "But, if you can come up with an original story, one I haven't heard before, I'll let you go."

"Mr. Thomas," I respond, "I'm trying to clear post. I'm on my way out, out of the Army."

"I've heard that one before, pal, try again."

"My plane leaves in one hour," I plead.

He searches me for signs of truth or consequences. "Are you serious? Let me see your orders. If that's true, I'll turn you loose."

I gulp, knowing the lieutenant kept my records while I go back to my base camp and turn in all my gear.

Just then Ted walks up to the jeep, stating, "It's true. He's going home today. I'll vouch for him. I'll be in country another sixty days or so, until my rotation. If it's not true, you can take me to jail."

MP Thomas breaks out in a big smile, stating, "Jesus Christ, and I thought I heard 'em all. You guys are serious!"

Ted retorts, "As serious as beating the bush," and gives Thomas his most sincere poker face—although to me, Ted's expression looks more like the cat who ate the bird.

The MP's face is animated. He looks a little like a grown-up Howdy Doody. "OK, guys, I'll pave the way. Let's go. I like a good joke," states the MP. He activates his lights and siren as we speed off like cheetahs, tearing up the back roads in excess of fifty mph, hell bent on catching our prey at all costs. Ted, normally a very conservative driver, rises to the challenge, scaring even me by tailgating the MP to encourage him to go faster.

We come to a halt right in front of the medical tent. I jump out before Ted's even stopped, nearly falling face first. Once in the platoon tent, I grab everything I can think of that the Army would want back, making numerous trips back and forth, to and from the jeep. Some of the guys in the tent help me, separating personal items from military issued equipment.

"What about this, Harry?"

"Pitch it," I respond. "The only personal item I want is my diary."

"Oh, yeah, can't possibly forget that, Harry. How could you ever write your book without it?" says Mike Sand.

I stuff everything I have into my footlocker.

"When you think you'll write that book? I'd like to buy one."

"Not a fucking clue, Mike. My first priority is to get a life. You'll allow me that, won't you?'

"Sure, makes sense to me. It would be kind of tough to write one before you get a job, I guess. A man's gotta eat."

"You got that right, Mikey."

One of the others helping chimes in, "What you gonna do, Spence? Any ideas?'

"School," I respond. "What the hell is this? A quiz show? Come on, guys, I'm down to fifty minutes. Just put all the military shit in a pile. You can have everything else . . . but don't touch my diary."

For safekeeping I take it from my footlocker and stick it in my leg pocket.

In between running back and forth from my tent to the jeep, throwing everything the military has issued me into it, I tell the MP to stick around. I'll need an escort back to brigade headquarters shortly.

He simply smiles and states, "I think I know how you feel. My ETS is May third. I'll be behind you by just a few days."

"Where you from?" I ask.

"Detroit."

I stop momentarily, responding with surprise, "So am I. What's your name?"

"John, John Thomas. They call me JT."

"Nice to meet you, JT. Maybe we'll hook up sometime down the road."

At the quartermaster's intake desk, I throw all my military gear, clothes, socks, underwear, boots, everything, even my M-16 that Uncle Sam issued me, on top of the counter. I am returning every single thing ever issued to me. I don't want any of it. I want to forget I ever served in the military.

The specialist fifth class behind the counter responds with the speed of a fucking turtle, examining every piece of clothing as if he were a picky bargain shopper. He holds up my helmet, saying, "Would you look at that," and puts his finger through the bullet hole Charlie drilled for me on the front lip. "Looks like that was a pretty close call, fella."

"Yeah, it was," I allow. "Do you have to examine every single piece of equipment? Come on guy, give me a break." I glance at my watch, thirty minutes. Shit!

Although common sense dictates that I won't catch the plane, I defy it, thinking somehow I'll still make it. "Come on guy," I state, flipping him a twenty dollar bill. "Sign the fucking paper. It's all there. I'm down to thirty minutes." He smiles and signs off immediately. Ted and the MP are waiting, engines running, motors gunning. With lights flashing, the jeeps kick up a cloud of dust as we barrel down the road at break-neck speed. I stand up, waving my arms wildly, screaming to anyone and everyone, "So long, people! I'd like to say it's been nice!"

The road passes the end point of the air base's runway. As I look to my right, I see a civilian airliner lifting off the concrete runway, coming right at us, passing some 300 feet directly over us. I look at Ted when he says, "You don't think, Harry . . . naw, couldn't be. The military is never on time."

With my heart sinking I respond, "That's a civilian jet. Time is money to them."

Ted tries to console me, "Wait a minute. Before you turn lunatic on me, just hold your horses. It ain't over till it's over, Harry."

It was my plane. Back at brigade headquarters, the lieutenant points out where someone very carefully erased and then typed over my actual departure time of 1330 hours to 1400 hours. I immediately know it was Flock. But before I can confront him, I need more proof. Because Dr. Pierce knows what I know, about Flock trying to have me killed, I'll show him any evidence I uncover. My departure date is rescheduled for April 29th. I have one week to come up with any evidence that might implicate him. I am madder than a hornet. I'll start my investigation the minute I get back to base camp.

I know I don't want to initiate an investigation by filing a formal complaint to the officer's on duty at battalion headquarters. I have to be careful. Therefore, I'll only approach enlisted men below the rank of sergeant, my peers. And even then I have to exercise caution not to make a false accusation of a career soldier. Without proof, solid proof, I could be brought down on charges under the guidelines of the Uniform Code of Military Justice's rules and regulations. Slander and defamation of character charges would negate the possibility of an early release from the army.

That little voice addresses me as I walk up to the intake counter, saying, "Be careful, Harry. Don't do anything to delay your discharge. You may be playing right into Flock's hand." I get angry at that thought. Screw you, little guy. If there's proof I'm going to take him down. "Ah, Ah, that's foolish, Harry."

I recognize one of the enlisted men sitting at his desk. We have spoken from time to time. He was interested to know what it is really like out in the boonies and sought me out. I am known as a straight shooter.

"Hey, Al. Psst, Al. Can I speak to you a minute?"

He looks up and comes toward me. "Sure, Harry, but I thought you left already. What's the problem?"

"Al, is there any way for you to tell me when my orders came in for my Compassionate Reassignment?'

"Sure, everything is time stamped. Why do ask, Harry?"

"Please trust me on this—you do not want to know. The less you know, the better off you'll be in the long run, OK?"

I hand him my copy of the Compassionate Reassignment order. He studies it carefully and then says that he'll be right back. He's going to pull the master copy out of the file to compare them. I scan the others in the large room as I wait. Some of the guys look at me with suspicion, others don't even look my way. I stand there at the intake counter trying my best not to look upset, smiling and tapping the counter. My biggest concern is that an officer will check on Al and me to see what is going on. If that happens, the investigation will take on proportions I might regret later. Flock is no one's fool. If he is behind this, he'll have covered his tracks.

Al lays the two pieces of paper side by side, comparing the type line by line, as I strain to see myself. Within one minute he spots two discrepancies, stating, "Yep, here it is. The date received on the master copy is April 17th. We received it at 1000 hours. The copy you have indicates it was received April 22nd. See, it's right here. The time stamped on it is 0800 hours."

I look and compare the two sets of orders myself and, sure as shit, somebody has altered my copy. I then ask, "Who picks up paperwork such as this from each company?"

"The individual company clerks, why?"

"You've been a great help, Al, thanks. This conversation never took place—remember that if things get a little hot around here."

He waves me off as I am leaving, asking, "What took place? What are you talking about, Spence?" He winks at me and says, "Good luck and adds, "Hey, when are you scheduled to leave now, Harry?"

"Next week. Seven more fucking days and counting."

"Let's get together for a beer between now and then."

As I walk toward the door, I smile and state, "If everything goes smoothly, I'll buy."

"Sounds good to me," he replies.

I then march straight toward headquarters company, my company of record. I have known the company clerk for nearly eighteen months. Jim Hottle is a nice guy, small, fragile-looking, and wears glasses. I walk in to headquarter's tent. It is at least three times bigger than my platoon tent. Jim is stationed right by the door to greet those who enter. He looks up at me from his desk and states, "What the hell are you doing here?" A puzzled smile crosses his face.

"I missed my silver bullet, Jim, and I've a couple of questions I'd like to ask."

"Fire away, I'm all ears."

"Not here, Jim, can you take a walk?"

"Sure."

Once outside I ask him if he knows who picked up my orders for reassignment.

"That would be Sergeant Flock, comes by a couple of times a day. Why?"

I decide not to tell Jim what I am doing or why I missed the plane. We chat some. I am trying to minimize the info he gave me. Just as we are parting ways, I ask him if he knows of a unit within the brigade that has the capacity to perform printing for anyone's needs, officer or not.

"Yeah, of course," he states. "Brigade headquarters has a small print shop with state-of-the-art equipment. Why do you ask, Harry?"

I play it down. "Oh, nothing, Jim. I thought I'd like to get a couple of things copied that I wrote while being here—put to professional print. You know, my observations in poetic form, stuff like that."

"Yeah, yeah, I'm sure they can help you. Go for it, Harry." And then he adds as I start to walk away, "How'd you miss your flight?"

I shrug my shoulders, throw him a smile, and respond, "Because of my own stupidity, I guess."

"Man, that would have bummed me out. You seem to be taking it well. See you later."

I don't turn, just wave my hand in the air as I walk away. I look at my watch. It is 1600 hours. Administrative offices are closing for the day. I'll go see them tomorrow.

The next day I locate the printing shack, which is located on the periphery of the brigade's administrative compound. When I walk in, I know how best to couch the subject. An older-looking staff sergeant greets me, "What can I do for you, young man?"

"Hi. I was in the area and Sergeant Alvin Flock from the 4/503rd, our medical platoon sergeant, wanted me to stop by and tell somebody here—forgive me, he told me the guy's name, I just forgot, but he said to say hello."

He smiles, "That would be me, son. Al and I go way back. We served together in the 187th in Korea, back in the Korean War. Hell, I just saw him the other day, too. The man must be losing his mind. I'm going to see him later. I'll tell him myself he's losing it."

I mentally choke on that one. "So long, Sarge." I want to get out of there as quickly as possible. As I cross the door's threshold, I turn casually to ask his name.

"Booker T. Washington, what's yours?"

"That's not important, Sarge. I'm just a lowly messenger."

Booker T. Washington, I muse, and Sergeant Alvin Flock. Huh. Well I'll be damned. But, short of a confession by one of them, I'm just twisting in the breeze. All I have on Flock is delaying the delivery of my orders just enough to cause me to miss my plane. They won't do shit about that, but maybe give him an oral reprimand. He's a career soldier. The military protects its own. They'll throw a guy like me to the wolves before they turn on him. My best shot is gaining the confidence of Dr. Pierce, but there, too, I have to be careful.

I sit on the info for a couple of days, mulling over what I should or shouldn't do. How can I let Flock know I am onto him without pushing him over the edge? After three days, I finally decide I'll only use it as insurance, should he begin to mess with me. It's strange, I think, that he hasn't been around very much lately. Previously, it was nearly impossible not to bump into him sometime during the day. And for the most part, I am not given anything to do, which in itself is very unusual. Four days to go. I'll record this in my diary, all of it. Names, dates, times, who I spoke to and when. After which, I'll mail my diary to Beatrice.

I am paranoid. Flock might have a connection with the quartermaster as well. Flock knows the size of my diary and may have alerted them to the possibility of my mailing it. If he gets a hold of it, everything I have on him will disappear. I decide to walk over to a sister battalion and mail my diary. He couldn't possibly collaborate with everyone.

APRIL 28 1967; EVENING

The men are throwing me a going-away bash. Nothing elaborate or formal, just a round table talk in the EM Club, the "Friendly Fire Club." They are not only celebrating my obvious victory, surviving without a scratch, but also that I am the first medic to rotate back to the states and be discharged—unscathed. All those that I like are there: I make it a point to write all their names into my diary: Steve

Probst, Charles Huller, Thomas Cook, Choate, Walker, Goodwin, Guerello, Ethington, Price, Houston, Sutton, Darby, Mosley, Mike Sand, Ted Dziengelewski, Dan Renyolds, Glen Middler, Leon Houston, Chiefoot, Steve Best. Even J.T., the MP who tried to help me catch the plane last week, is there.

We toast each other. We toast those wounded in action, and we toast the dead. We all agree that they are the real heroes. Salute, comrades. The atmosphere is gay and light-hearted as we swap war stories that can only be shared among ourselves. Each man's story brings out the lighter side of life in the bush. We all carry the guilt of surviving, and, because of that, no one boasts.

Toward the end of the night, while the talk is still upbeat and festive, I begin to feel as if I am crying deep down inside. And, like a tidal wave coming straight toward me, I realize its origins. I am terribly sad and afraid for them. I'll miss them and worry about them. I am, in effect, abandoning them. I feel terrible and seek to hide my true feelings. I can hide my feelings from them, but not from myself. It is a devastating feeling.

With a sleepless night spent tossing and turning, I wake at the crack of dawn and for the last time in my military life, I slowly, very methodically, take my time as I shower, shave, and put on my class A uniform. I glance with pride into the mirror at the rows of ribbons I've earned in the nearly three years I have been in the army. I am not very proud of some of the things I have done; however, I am proud that I made it. I somehow beat the odds. I persevered. My day of reckoning is upon me.

If the stories we hear are true, in twenty-four hours I'll be back home. Home to see and be with Beatrice. Home where I can sleep as long as I want, and the food is great. Home where I'll find peace and security and never again have to worry about being shot at. And finally, home where fear and fatigue do not exist. My plane departs from Bien Hoa's Air Force Base at 1100 hours. I have nothing to worry about. I've cleared post, received my plane ticket, and verified everything for a fail-safe departure. My Freedom Bird is waiting. My silver bullet to another world and lifestyle is waiting, and to which I barely remember. I muse, I'm coming. I'm coming home, guys—I made it.

As I slowly walk to the aid station, which is approximately five tents away from the medical platoon's tent, catcalls and cheers echo throughout the compound. Everyone knows I am the first to leave, and wish me well. All the men are looking at me, some with envy, but most are genuinely happy for me. I compare the high I feel now with being in Hawaii, but really there is no comparison. I am walking on air, slapping five with the brothers, shaking hands with the white guys. I'm on my way. God, what a great feeling this is, thank you.

I report for the last time to the aid station medics-on-duty, which is an everyday ritual in base camp. I shake hands first with Dr. Pierce, thanking him for all he has done for me and that I'll never forget him. I also speak to Lieutenant Edmore and all my fellow medics who have gathered to see me off. I thank each of them, and acknowledge everyone, but Flock. I have nothing to say to him. Not a goddamn word, although I consider telling him off by letting him know that I had a conversation with Staff Sergeant Booker T. Washington, and that I learned he purposely delayed and altered my orders so I would miss my flight last week. But I decide, what the hell does it matter? I'm a civilian now. Screw him. He's not worth the breath it would take to tell him. I feel I have won the game, despite the odds.

As I turn to leave the aid station, Flock is standing in the doorway. He grabs my arm and whispers in a solemn tone, "Wait a minute, hold up. I want to talk to you privately." He then orders everyone out, even asking the doctor and lieutenant if they wouldn't mind stepping out for just a minute. He seems to be in deep thought, and I guess he is going apologize for how he has treated me. And my response will be to tell him to kiss my ass.

He follows the last man to the door, closes it, his back still to me and then locks it. As he slowly turns, he still has that puppy dog look, but, in a blink of an eye, a devilish sneer comes over his face. Oh, shit. An alarm bell goes off. His black skin glistens in the partial light. He looks like the devil incarnate—his eyes, coal black, burn through me. I meet his stare though. I know what it means. I even manage to smirk in response. I've had at least 200 fistfights in my life, plus my boxing experience. He has the look of a challenge, a dual to the death expression. He says nothing as he begins to unbutton his shirt, getting ready for a fight, still staring at me. He is taking off anything I can grab a hold of, pretty smart. But I am determined not to engage him. I reason that I'll let him get a few slaps in, it won't hurt that much, and in the end it'll show him who the better man is. That is the plan, but like all plans, it may require a few modifications. I am comfortable knowing I can handle myself if I have to. But shit, he outweighs me by forty pounds.

He slowly lays his fatigue shirt on a chair and stretches, loosening his shoulders and chest muscles. Pretty smart move. All athletes loosen up before they compete. Been there, done that. But I don't move. I won't provoke him. I'll take what he has to give for as long as I can take it, and just smile back at him. He knows I've won, but he can't bring himself to admit it.

He begins by circling me, dancing the Cassius Clay shuffle, jabbing the air, stopping dangerously close to my nose, forcing me to blink. Better get ready, Spencer. I think next time around he may not stop an inch from your nose. He continues circling me. I feel the wind of his punch rush by my ears from my rear. He nicks me on the right ear, causing it to bend violently forward. I jerk my neck in response, putting my hand over my ear, feeling it, touching it to see if there is any blood.

As he comes into my peripheral view on my left side, I see him jab with his left, and unload with his right. I know enough about boxing to know that if you hit a man just right on the jaw, you'll snap his head, pinching off the flow of blood just long enough to knock him out and possibly break his jaw. I rear back to see his fist graze my nose. "Smooth move, Spencer, I'm impressed," he snarls. When he is right in front of me again, he fakes a right and jabs with his left thinking, I'll go for the fake, giving him time to nail me with a straight left stick. That doesn't work either.

He stops dancing and starts talking. Oh yeah, I think, the old set 'em up sucker punch routine. Disarm your opponent with words, stay in striking distance and pick your move. Unfortunately, I am within his striking distance, but I won't give him the pleasure of seeing me backup. However and fortunately, he telegraphs his next move, coming at the left side of my head with a roundhouse right. More air. He doesn't like that one. His nostrils flare as if he is the bull and I am the matador without a cape. I know my luck won't hold out, and, sure as shit, he fakes a left hook, which I feign, and catches me square in the nose with an open palm straight right.

I feel the cartilage crackle and pop. I recoil in the shock, my vision blurs, and my nose fills with blood and mucus. But I let it drip onto my dress khaki shirt, trying not to pay attention, still not taking a defensive posture. He catches me again, before I can recover my eyesight to evade his punch, his fist lands right into my solar plexus. As I bend over in pain, he comes across with a hard right to my temple. I tumble to the ground, writhing in pain, but manage to hold up one hand, gasping for air.

"Hold it. One second. Let's get the rules of engagement out in the open. Give me a second," I say, still gasping for air.

The son of bitch knocked the fucking wind out of me. I roll in pain, trying to force myself to breathe, and continue, "Hold it—hold it for a second. Let's just pretend here for one moment, Flock. Let's just say for the sake of argument that I get up and kick the living shit out of you. What happens then?"

He stands directly over me, his legs spread on either side of my torso, when I think I might have a chance. He bends over menacingly at the waist, lips pulled taut displaying his teeth as an animal might just before devouring its prey, before penetrating its throat with a set of powerful killer jaws. He responds, "Then you go to jail, *boy.*"

Suddenly that little voice I have grown accustomed to hearing comes alive, screaming, *"Harry! This is the place! This is the time! Run, Run for your fucking life!"* I kick Flock in the groin, the toe of my boot penetrating the soft spot from back to front, and I jump up in one fluid motion. My life is on the line. I've got to get out of here.

Once out of the aid station, everyone who has been displaced at Flock's request stands frozen at the sight of blood spurting from my nose, but no one speaks up, no one asks what happened, and no one comes to my aid. I must have a terrified look because they sure do. As I begin to run, I feel as if this is a bad dream, a realistic nightmare. I can hear my own heartbeat in my ears. I feel it constrict and release again, while the blood pulsates and spurts from my nose.

My legs feel as if they have fifty-pound weights attached to my ankles. I can't run as fast as my mind is telling me to. I can lift my feet easily enough, but the forward thrust comes in laboriously slow strides. I hear men screaming, "Stop, Harry, don't run." Others scream, "Run, Harry, run. Get outta here now! Faster, man, faster."

Flock's booming gravel voice cries, "Stop! Freeze!"

I push even harder to reach the corner of battalion headquarters. Just another ten feet and I'll be out of his line of sight.

I hear the metal on metal clank that an M-16 makes as its bolt is released, slamming a bullet into the chamber.

Again he calls for me to stop. Only this time he screams, "Stop! Or I will shoot!"

Oh, God, please, no, not this way . . . .

CHECKMATE

Back at Fort Benning, Georgia another young, wannabe paratrooper is being pushed mentally and physically to his limits by a drill instructor. The drill instructor leans closer to the young kid, who thinks he's got the right stuff, and screams. "Son, did I hear you just state you want out, that you're not tough enough, and not strong enough to put up with this shit? Did I hear you say that soldier?" Without waiting for an answer the sergeant then proclaims to all within earshot, "Ah-huh, that's it; he said it. . ." The young, tough, cocky kid responds with a defiant scream.

"No Sergeant. I ain't quitting. Nothing you do is going to make me quit Sergeant, nothing!"

The two lock eyes as if they're going to get it on any second. The sergeant rears back, smiles subtly, and states, "You're going to do just fine young man; keep it up." He then screams into the kids face, "Airborne!"

The young man, responding to his training, retorts with equal force, "All The Way, Sergeant."

Off in the distance the beat and the tempo play out. The sound appears to be coming from all directions; the chant, the beat, the tempo, and the words can be heard off in the distance: "Airborne. . . All The Way. . .Everyday. . .All The Way. . .Airborne."

EPILOGUE

CCORDING TO VIETNAM Casualty Statistics and Documents found on the Internet, 47,322 individuals were killed by *Hostile action* in the Vietnam War. In this same report under the heading of *Non-Hostile action*, 10,700 more either died or were killed. Within this latter category homicides claimed a total of 1,173 lives in Vietnam, or 2.02 percent of all who paid the supreme sacrifice for their country, which totaled 58,022.

Scripture states: "—man has dominated man to his own injury." Ecclesiastes 8:9. "—and so there is nothing new under the sun." Ecclesiastes 1:9. Therefore, in any war . . . we become the raptor and the prey.

This book is written in tribute to: Gerald Bartram, Dennis Hammond, John James, Daryl Korfman, Carlos Moore, Louis Soward, and Freddie Torrence. These seven young men were my platoon mates, friends, and comrades in arms. Rest in peace guys. . . I've told it, albeit a writing of fiction; after all, in the final analysis it was just a dream—right?

Finally, I would be remiss of my patriotic duty if I did not say something regarding the national tragedy, which occurred while this book was in its final stages of production.

As a combat veteran, I know all too well exactly what many Americans sustained as a result of an unprecedented attack on the World Trade Towers in New York City, and the Pentagon on September 11, 2001, by terrorists hell bent on destroying our way of life in the name of their God. Like many others I wept; I was shocked and dismayed at terror reaching into our united hearts. It is one thing to be terrorized in combat on foreign land, but it is an all together different feeling when terror strikes at the heart of the land all veterans fought to protect.

Also, as a former Detroit Fire Fighter, I watched the television just as millions of others did, and I knew, based upon my life's experiences, that my brother firefighters were fighting a foe to certain death. I not only grieve for America, but for all our first line of defense civil servants who fought so gallantly to save our fellow citizens. Love is manifested in many different ways. To paraphrase scripture found in the book of John, Chapter 15 verse 13:

Greater love has no man than he who would lay his life down for a stranger.

As I wrote in this book's first few pages, real heroes, like those aboard United Airlines Flight number 93, always die. Real heroes die because that is the *ultimate* act of heroism—to give your life so that others may live. Those few heroes aboard that ill-fated flight chose to save the lives of thousands on the ground. Those men and women ultimately demonstrated real love for their fellow man, just as our fire fighters, police officers, and emergency medical technicians did in the World Trade Towers. Our way of life may not be the best system in God's eyes to govern man, but it is undoubtedly the best man can do without direct divine intervention. Perhaps that is why we use the phrase, "In God We Trust," for man, in all his wisdom, falls short of perfection.

God Bless America.

G. K. Stesiak

ORDERING INFORMATION

Additional copies of *Raptor's Prey* can be ordered at

www.raptorsprey.com

or by calling toll free:

1-800-247-6553

The author can also be reached via the *Raptor's Prey* website.

The suggested retail price of *Raptor's Prey* is $26.54 plus applicable taxes and shipping charges. The retail price of this book was established because there were 2,654 men and one woman from Michigan who never returned to their loved ones from the Vietnam War. G.K. Stesiak will also be donating twenty-five percent of the book's net profits to the Michigan Vietnam Monument in Lansing, Michigan.

THANK YOU FOR YOUR SUPPORT.

25% OF THIS BOOK'S NET PROFITS WILL BE DONATED TO THE
MICHIGAN VIETNAM MONUMENTS MAINTENANCE FUND